FIRST MODELS IN CARDBOARD

Cover: Cardboard models coloured with 'Finart' wax crayons; reproduced by kind permission of The Cosmic Crayon Co. Ltd. Crayons are most suitable for textured effects and for waterproofing model boats.

Below: A windmill taking shape. The model revolves on a post set in a clay base. Part of a project on wind power.

FIRST MODELS IN CARDBOARD

G. Roland Smith

LSIA, ACP, Head of the Art and Craft Department,
Cannock School, Chelsfield, Kent

The Dryad Press

Published by the Dryad Press, Northgates, Leicester
Printed by Soho Printers (Birmingham) Limited, Birmingham B18 5BL

Contents

Acknowledgements

The author wishes to pay tribute to Mrs Margarett Schofield for her invaluable secretarial assistance in connection with the manuscript, and to his 'guinea pigs' – the pupils of Cannock School and Crockenhill Primary School for their candid advice.

Thanks are also due to Mr J. A. Graham, former editor of *Art and Craft in Education*, for permission to include drawings of the Harbour on pages 98-103; and to the Cosmic Crayon Co. Ltd. for permission to use the cover photograph and the model village on page 36.

Note on author

G. Roland Smith, LSIA, ACP, studied first as a commercial artist, and then, some time later, as a teacher (not, he says, as an 'art teacher'). During the interval he exhibited widely as a painter.

His active concern with education began some eighteen years ago when he first became a teacher of general subjects. Since then, except for two years as a full-time industrial designer, he has been consistently at work with children, and has been involved in primary, secondary, and further education.

He now divides his time between teaching, and the demands of a private practice, working mainly as a consultant designer in the field of educational materials. He is also known as a lecturer and frequent contributor to educational journals.

Introduction

Model making, as an art form, deserves no more respect than spelling, or counting, or navigation, or any other useful skill. It is true that geometry is a living thing: artists have discovered that graphs and mathematical models are infinitely more wonderful than their practical usage alone might suggest. Children in schools find increasing scope for personal discovery and expression in the most unlikely subjects. Indeed, in many schools, the subject barriers have almost disappeared. One interest now evolves logically from another: an artistic approach often provides the individual links in the educational chain, and learning becomes an active, creative pursuit.

But this is not a book about aesthetics, or art. It is not even a particularly 'creative' book. The practical discovery approach to learning requires plenty of material if the process is not to be unduly slow. This volume seeks to provide such material. It will probably not be of any great use to the specialist teacher of Art, because in the field of pure self-expression only *raw* material will really do.

The models are intended for general practitioners – teachers and children, who like making things, and who must spend at least part of their time in pursuit of factual information as well as of personal ideas. The examples cover a very wide range of topics: some could be labelled 'geographical', some 'historical', some 'mechanical', and so on. They all, of course, involve some simple mathematics.

Not all children are equally capable of inventing their own models. There are some who do so almost intuitively, and when things go wrong they have the patience and the intelligence to work out for themselves what needs to be done. Such children learn quickly: they profit most by being left to get on with it. Others, however, have ideas which are way ahead of their own practical ability. While they are wrestling with minor problems of construction they miss the opportunity to put wider schemes into effect. There are others, surprisingly, who seem to see no great value in originality anyway – who simply delight in the skill of their own hands, and prefer to be given precise instructions. It would be presumptuous to suppose they were learning nothing of value, even though not actually inventing anything. Childhood is a time for discovery. In the early stages it is a time for direction also.

My book is offered to children of a 'constructive' rather than a 'creative' genius. The aim has been to provide models for use in a variety of learning situations. The creative handling of cardboard is a separate study with its own fascination. The great educational value of an experimental approach to the material should never be under-estimated. My own pupils often display the richness of their imagination in forms of sculptural cardboard which certainly originate in no text book. But this is an aspect of the work which falls beyond the scope of the present volume.

The construction of purpose-made models is sometimes said to inhibit personal expression, but I have never observed, among children, any reluctance to accept limitations when the model is intended for a specific use which they can understand. When children work together in groups, or when the model embodies historical information, then some measure of conformity is inevitable.

It is also claimed that where children are encouraged in the creative use of cardboard, or any other material, they gain such insight into its propensities that detailed instruction becomes superfluous. I do not find that this always works. I do find, however, that when children have been shown how to make specific things according to certain basic information *in which they are interested*, they frequently acquire an understanding of the material. The creative and the constructive aspects of craft work are *both* valid in schools. They are not exclusive of each other, and it is an unfortunate dichotomy which has arisen in the minds of some educators concerning them. It is one of the functions of education to stimulate initiative and an awareness of what is implied in the processes we use in everyday living; but teaching can not always be purely creative. When they grow up, not all children will be architects and innovators. Some will be simply builders and decorators. In this far from perfect world they will have to contend with limitations which are not always inherent in the materials they have to use. In spite of the blessings of automation, and the abolition of repetitive donkey work, there will still be various technical pursuits for those who enjoy them, and who take a pride in doing them well.

In the primary school it is not too soon to learn how to read a simple technical diagram, or to work out how things fit together. Quite young children find it entertaining to translate a flat drawing into a three-dimensional model. This is mathematics in action. Some will employ more daring and originality than others. Some will learn by taking things apart, as much as by building things up. Cardboard cartons not only make useful building units: they can also be dismembered, and children will benefit from the opportunity to pry into the geometrical secrets of packaging designers. A book of cardboard models is best used in conjunction with discovery methods of this kind.

This, then, is a work of reference – not a 'course'; though, as it happens, the basic shapes are near the beginning and, once these have been mastered, there is no limit to the number of different models which can be made. Generally speaking, the models can be selected from any section as the occasion demands. The sections are arranged according to subject matter; their sequence does not demand any increasing skill. The processes involved are simple throughout, and the only ability which might be expected to develop is a social skill rather than a technical one – namely, the children's capacity to collaborate with each other in the production of composite models, as suggested in the final part of the book. An over-insistence on technique for its own sake tends to defeat the purpose of the activity. Craftsmanship, as an end in itself, is too subtle a motive for most children. Provided that the young model maker is not dissatisfied with his own efforts, and provided that his work does not fall to pieces prematurely, then, however makeshift, it can usually be turned to educational advantage.

Although, as I have explained, this is not, strictly speaking, a creative book because the basic structures have been prescribed in some detail; nevertheless it is not just a collection of stereotyped examples either. It would be rather tragic if children were obliged to turn out dozens of duplicate models, all exactly to the same pattern, for no better reason than that they had been told to do so.

I am convinced that teachers, these days, are responsible people who know enough about children to realise that it is not the ability to follow set rules that counts, so much as the ability to apply the rules intelligently. It is the personal *use* of the models which is important. Most children are well able to build on the skeleton shapes which have been provided, to an extent which would not be possible if they were left entirely to their own devices at the outset. The reasons for making models are as colourful as the children themselves, and the final results as varied. Somewhat like a composer, I have prepared some simple scores. I would not presume to say how or when they should be performed.

It is for this reason that the diagrams have not been drawn to any special scale, and no dimensions are given. The diagrams are designed to show the relationship between the various parts of a model, and the process of assembling them. Each model is composed of only a few component parts, so it does not require too much reasoning to see how one thing follows from another. It is valuable, from an educational standpoint, that the children themselves should have the opportunity to work out in practice the simple geometrical principles involved. The layout of the diagrams is planned to bring such principles within the children's grasp. As a general rule, they should look for the main shape and then relate the other parts to it, referring back to the main shape in order to work out subsequent dimensions. Otherwise, there is a danger that the whole business becomes just a matter of blind repetition – the pupils slavishly copying the drawings, without really understanding how they work. The children will find, however, that they not only have to decide on an appropriate scale for a particular job – they will also need to apply it consistently. Herein lies the value of the work as an exercise in applied mathematics. Another reason for omitting specific dimensions is that the size of a finished model will vary from one teaching situation to another according to the purpose for which a particular piece has been chosen, and according to the material available. If ready-made cartons are to be incorporated they will obviously dictate the scale.

Cardboard or stout paper marked out in squares is very helpful when it comes to measuring. There is no infallible reason why children should adopt the inch or the centimetre as a standard unit of measurement. Rulers are clearly intended to make life easier, but where children find their markings confusing there are plenty of other things, such as match-sticks, or plain number rods which can be used for determining the length of one piece of cardboard compared with another.

It often happens that the clumsiest child is the most ambitious and chooses to attempt the most intricate work. In view of this, model making is an activity which seems to work best when the children are organised in small groups. At the same time (especially when composite models are under construction) it is often convenient for individuals to have some easy repetitive task to fill in the odd moments while fellow builders are catching up with their part in the main scheme. Most large models need plenty of small items, such as trees, lengths of fencing, flags, or lamp standards; and provided it is not overdone mass-production has a certain appeal. Some of the basic material can, with advantage, be prepared in advance. This is the case when small children need initially some pieces of thick cardboard which they would themselves find difficult to cut. These are nearly always straight-sided and can easily be prepared in advance, using a guillotine.

Broadly speaking, model making may be said to comprise four main steps: 1. Measuring and drawing; 2. Folding and cutting; 3. Assembling and fixing; 4. Decorating and finishing. There is nothing specialised about the craft at the level covered by these pages, although it can later be developed into an architectural study requiring expert knowledge.

Model making enables children to take a bird's eye view (or even an astronaut's eye view) of the world. When different aspects of the environment are reconstructed in miniature, in the classroom, by the children themselves, then the educational possibilities are extremely varied.

Equipment and materials

Tools for the teacher. Cardboard model making is not a craft requiring elaborate equipment. Cardboard itself is not expensive. Being widely used for packaging and so on, there is usually a plentiful supply of raw material available for experiment. The beginner can afford to make a few mistakes. Like any other craft, however, the correct materials are essential if unnecessary difficulties are to be avoided. The same applies to the choice of tools.

Very few of the items mentioned in this chapter are absolutely essential, but most will be found useful sooner or later. In addition to the general equipment shown overleaf, the tools listed on this page are recommended for the teacher, even though they may not normally be required by the children themselves. They may be needed when preparing material for the class, for running repairs, and for occasional use in special cases.

Guillotine or *Card Cutter.* This is the most expensive item, but it will relieve the teacher of most of the donkey work. There is no other way of cutting quantities of cardboard to size quickly and accurately. For thick card it is almost indispensable.

Shears for trimming details when the card is too tough for small fingers and ordinary school scissors. Pinking shears are sometimes useful for cutting decorative edging to roofs and awnings, etc. (If there is a needlework department, they will not take kindly to theirs being borrowed for the purpose.)

Steel ruler—the non-slipping sort, for use as a straight edge.

Knives. There is a very wide variety and the final choice must rest with the individual craftsman. Some are fitted with replaceable blades and others require sharpening from time to time, in which case an oil stone is also indicated. Two knives are recommended – one which can be easily manipulated for detailed work, and a more robust instrument for larger pieces.

For elementary work these last two items are scarcely needed except to assist with occasional slots and details. However, a knife and a straight edge are standard equipment for every child expected to make models in thick card unaided.

Fretsaw. This is a useful aid when cutting templates for curved sections, especially when several thicknesses are required to be cut together.

Saw. A small tenon or bookbinder's saw is useful for cutting bases from hardboard, or slices from cardboard postal tubes, etc.

Leather punches. The adaptable six-way punch is best for holes to be made near the edge of the sheet. Otherwise use a single-hole punch and a hammer.

Stapler. A long arm stapler is a convenient instrument for making rapid fixtures, or to reinforce glued areas.

Pliers for use in connection with wire details. (It is also an effective means of applying pressure to any small parts which will not stick.)

Varnish brushes. If several brushes are reserved for varnish, they can be more easily cleaned and preserved.

Tweezers for manipulating any small details.

Pencil sharpener. If there is a good pencil sharpener in the room it will obviate a lot of annoying interruption.

Drawing instruments. The teacher need not be an accomplished draughtsman, but a few simple instruments are always useful.

Tools for the children. Some of these implements will already be in everyday use. It will probably save time, however, if the handwork equipment can be kept separately so that it is always ready when needed. This is especially true when the work is done away from the normal classroom. There is something to be said for the idea that each child might make for himself a strong cardboard 'toolbox' right at the beginning. This could be made from heavy-grade strawboard fixed with gummed bookbinding cloth, using method A on page 27.

Cutting boards. Pieces of hardboard faced with Formica provide a good working surface which will protect the desk or table. Plywood or strawboard will also serve the purpose and simplify the business of clearing up afterwards.

Drawing board clips. Attached to the boards mentioned above, these clips serve to prevent loose pieces of card from falling to the floor. They can sometimes also be used to hold freshly glued sections together while setting, or to hold a piece steady when two hands are needed for something else.

Scissors for general cutting. $4\frac{1}{2}$ in. scissors (preferably pointed) are quite adequate to complete much of the work outlined here.

Rulers for marking out. In the early stages a wooden ruler is sufficient for all work in thin card where the cutting is with scissors only. For thick card a *metal ruler* and a *knife* will be required.

Pencils and *erasers.* A fairly hard pencil (2H) will give a more precise line. If the model is made from thin card (3-sheet) or strong paper, then a decisive pencil line will automatically score the surface to produce a sharp fold in the right place. On coloured paper a darker pencil may be needed if the line is to show up.

Stencil cutters and *holders.* These cutting nibs will not stand up to very heavy usage, but they are easier than knives for young children to manage. They are quite adequate for card which would normally be cut with scissors, and they will negotiate slots and interior shapes more easily. Lino cutters may sometimes be useful in this connection.

Compasses and *set-squares.* These will *not* be needed for much of the earlier work.

Clips, etc. Bulldog clips, paper clips, and elastic bands of various sizes are all useful for holding parts together while setting, although modern adhesives frequently render this unnecessary.

Thimbles. Parts of certain models are fixed with pins which can be pushed home more easily with a thimble.

Brushes for painting. The size of brush will depend upon the scale of the model. Short-handled brushes are usually preferable to long one. Stencil brushes are useful for textured effects.

Brushes for paste. Models or parts of models are sometimes improved by covering with wallpaper or similar surfacing material applied with paste. Brushes should *not* normally be used for actually gluing the model together in the first place, as there are more convenient ways of doing it which are discussed later.

Materials for the teacher. The handwork cupboard should contain small supplies in addition to those for distribution to the children. These will include substances which may only be needed for special jobs, or for preparatory work. The assembly and display of composite models may often be simplified by the use of materials not generally handled by the whole class. They will enable the teacher to deal quickly with any little emergency which may arise.

Graph paper. This may be used for working out the scale of the proposed model and for plotting shapes in advance.

Hardboard. Offcuts make convenient base boards whenever the models require some rigid support, as, for example, when composite models need to be moved for storage. If cupboard space is limited, large 'shelves' may be improvised by tacking hardboard sheets to wooden battens. These can then be supported above one another with paint tins or boxes of uniform height placed at the corners.

Cellulose tape. 'Sellotape' is the obvious remedy in all manner of circumstances. It is extremely useful for patching and fixing, and for holding parts temporarily in position for gluing. Coloured Sellotape lends itself to decorative effects. Its glossy surface is easily kept clean. It should be remembered that fixtures in this material are not entirely permanent, nor can they be easily painted over.

Varnish. A final coat of varnish serves to harden and preserve the model. It will also enrich the colours, and impart some degree of waterproofing for boats. Paper varnish or spirit varnish is quick drying and more convenient to use, but copal varnish produces a harder glossy finish. This latter tends to discolour slightly any pale tints. Both types are best used over poster colours and not over wax crayon.

Methylated spirit for cleaning varnish brushes, etc.

Bookbinding cloth. Gummed strips are useful for strengthening any weak joints and for generally repairing work in thick card. Bookbinder's thread also has occasional uses for rigging, etc.

'Cellophane' and *'Celluloid'*. There are many different varieties of clear and coloured foil available, some of them self-adhesive. They are particularly useful for stained glass windows.

Wire. Several grades of soft wire will be found useful for certain details ('tubular' furniture, television masts, etc.). A very serviceable material is made by sandwiching a length of florists' wire between two thicknesses of gumstrip.

Sand paper. This is for trimming the edges of models in thick cardboard. It may also be used to rub down the edges when preparing several congruent sections. Sandpaper blocks as supplied for pointing pencil leads are convenient to use. Coarse sandpaper as a covering material also has its uses for imparting a textured effect to walls, etc. (When painting on sandpaper use a spray rather than ruin a brush.)

Plaster filler. One or two packets of filler or some self-hardening clay might eventually be of some advantage in preparing landscape effects for group models. Bandage, impregnated with plaster of Paris, as supplied for hospital use, is also recommended for this purpose.

Materials for the children. Apart from the cardboard itself, there is very little which could be regarded as necessary. There are, however, various accessories which will widen the scope of the craft.

Paper. It may be decided to introduce cardboard gradually, approaching the work by way of simpler exercises in stout paper. Oxford paper is such a material. Certain of the smaller sizes (20 in. x 15 in. and 10 in. x 7½ in.) can be supplied appropriately marked in ½ in. squares, and in four of the thirteen colours normally available. Brown Kraft paper can also be employed for actual model making.

The first attempts at real cardboard models are often rather grimy by the time they are finished. Inexpert joints are apt to be rather unsightly. These shortcomings can usually be obscured by a fresh outer covering of paper pasted onto the cardboard. A wallpaper pattern book provides quite a good selection. Patterned papers can be used to simulate upholstery. Wood-grained papers are useful, and ceiling papers (the knobbly sort) can be used for pebble-dash effects. Special bookcraft papers are helpful, also leatherette paper and dolls' house paper ready printed to represent stone or brickwork.

Carbon paper and *tracing paper.* These will assist the children in doing much of their own marking out, especially where several identical shapes are required. Carbon paper is available in several colours and this fact may sometimes be helpful in differentiating between the various parts of a model.

Gummed paper. This is usually supplied in squares and is available in many different colours. It is used mainly for decorative work but also serves for fixtures between pieces of thin card. Gumstrip is discussed on page 13.

Paints. Some form of opaque water colour is best. Poster colours or tempera blocks are suitable for class use. For more permanent work emulsion paints may be used.

Wax crayons. Younger children usually find these easier to manage than paints. When used with firm pressure they produce a remarkable strength of colour. Obviously, they are only really suitable when the model can be coloured while flat before assembling. If the crayon is applied in two layers—dark over light — then details such as brickwork, tiles, and windows can simply be scraped on the surface. 'Finart' crayons are recommended.

Foam plastic. Sheets of this material may be cut with scissors into various shapes to upholster cardboard furniture. It is also useful for trees.

Paper fasteners. The brass pierce-through type make door handles, centres for flowers, fixtures for wheels, and other details.

Pins and *Tacks.* Dressmakers' pins, drawing pins, berry pins, hat pins, map pins are useful for a variety of fixtures and as decorative features.

Boards and adhesives. The following general observations may be useful:

The choice of cardboard depends largely upon the scale of the model, and the scale of the model is partly governed by the ability of the children.

Small models need more precise measurement and allow less scope for detailed treatment. Being small, however, they need less support. Thin card is therefore adequate and there is no need for cutting knives – only scissors.

Large models are easier to handle, but other problems arise. Sagging and curling tend to occur unless the board is stout enough. Extra supports may be necessary and thick card is essential. Thick card cannot be folded so readily, nor can it be conveniently cut with scissors.

In order, therefore, to adapt the material to the work, or the work to the material the teacher must, as it were, pick a course between the cardboard swings and roundabouts. (The pupils are perhaps the least adaptable factor.)

If the model involves the use of ready-made components (washers, postal tubes, etc.) then these will automatically dictate the scale.

Throughout the book most examples have been designed as small-scale models to be built in thin card for the most part, but with occasional thicker supporting sections. These thicker sections, however, have been kept as simple as possible. If necessary they may be easily prepared for the children before they start work.

As a general rule thin card begins to become unmanageable when it exceeds the size of a post card (i.e. when unintercepted sections exceed 6 in. or so).

This list is offered as a brief guide:

Sugar paper. Available in various neutral shades, this inexpensive stout paper is a good substitute for thin card. (Also Oxford paper – see page 11).

Water Colour paper. This very substantial white paper is useful for occasional detail but is otherwise an extravagance.

Bristol board. Available in various thicknesses, this hard-surfaced white board is remarkably rigid. It is ideal for model making but rather too expensive for general use.

Coloured cardboard. Thin 3-sheet card is available in a variety of colours – also in black and white. The model making class will probably need more of this than any other sort. Thicker grades are sometimes an advantage.

Grey cardboard. Thick 10-sheet. This is a useful board, not too difficult to cut.

Strawboard. This general purpose box-making

material is the basic raw material for larger models. It is inexpensive and available in different weights. The 16 oz. variety, as prepared for bookbinding, can be supplied in convenient pre-cut sizes.

Mounting boards or *showcard boards.* These are pulp boards faced with poster paper. They are usually quite thick but easier to cut than strawboard. They provide a good painting surface and are consequently more expensive.

Corrugated cardboard. This is a most essential material. It gives reasonably good support but remains fairly easy to cut (even with scissors). It enables thicknesses to be built up quickly, presents a good edge for gluing, and the actual corrugations are a constructional feature in themselves. Packing cases are a good source of supply, especially for the more useful sort where the corrugations are sandwiched between two flat layers.

The art of squeezing a tube from the bottom is an accomplishment which few children seem able to acquire. Although this is obviously a most convenient way of using glue, in schools it is apt to be a messy and far from economical business. The use of brushes for glue is not to be recommended.

Dryad Vegetable Glue is an adhesive eminently adapted to school use. One 24 oz. jar will last the whole class for several models. In consistency and appearance it is very much like honey. Before the class begins transfer small quantities with an old ruler on to individual scraps of cardboard. Wooden spills or strips of strawboard cut on the guillotine make quite serviceable spreaders. Afterwards any left-overs can be returned to the 'honeypot' and all the dregs thrown away.

Paste or *Polycell* will be needed when models are to be covered with paper.

Impact adhesives. There are several makes. Such glues are not for general class use but the teacher may be glad of a tube for making extra strong joints for group models, especially if there are any wooden sections to be fixed.

Quick-setting glues. There are many from which to choose. A tube of effective, quick-setting adhesive is a sort of 'first-aid' kit for any models that may get into difficulties.

Gumstrip. This is another *essential.* Many of the models outlined in the following pages depend upon it as their main means of fixing. Rather than allowing for fixing 'tabs' when marking out, it is often simpler to add gumstrip at a later stage. It also obviates the need for careful butt joints in thick card. Although gumstrip will produce strong joints, the children should be told that it needs to be *rubbed* down and not just laid down.

Things worth collecting. It is not suggested that model making should degenerate into a scavenging after bits and pieces. The craft of the 'trash-can' does not fall within the scope of the present work.

However, the judicious use of scrap materials and accessories can sometimes simplify the work or add a touch of decoration.

The following list is only a sample:

Balsa wood
Beads
Boxes
Buckram
Buttons
Cane (basketry)
Cans
Canvas
Cartons
Centres (from coils of Sellotape, etc.)
Cocktail sticks
Cork mats
Corks
Cotton reels
Curtain runners (and rails)
Dowelling
Felt
Garden sticks
Ice Cream Tubs (and 'spoons')
Knitting needles
Leather
Matchboxes
Pipe-cleaners
Plastics
Postal tubes
Raffia
Sandpaper
Spills
Sponge
Straws (drinking)
Tins (and lids)
Toilet roll tubes
Tube tops (toothpaste)
Veneers
Washers
Wire netting

Preliminary pictures in relief

This is a transitional chapter intended to narrow the gap between flat paper work and three-dimensional model making. The main material is *thin card*. A packet of post cards may be useful, but with the younger age groups, particularly, model making should have a decorative appeal. Tinted cardboard is therefore recommended. The background cards on which the relief models are mounted should be thicker. These need not be plain. In fact there is ample scope for taking some pictures from the painting class and bringing them to life as it were. At this stage the colouring of the constructional part is best done with crayons while the card is flat. Relief models are best displayed against the wall, either along a shelf or at the back of a table. They may be regarded as complete in themselves, or used as backgrounds for larger panoramas. In this latter connection, the method applies also to more advanced models later on. The children need never really grow out of the technique.

Viking ship. Cut out the hull. Colour it, but leave the tab uncoloured. Draw several coloured shields and cut them out. Fix the shields to the hull with paper fasteners. Fold the tab under and glue the bottom edge of the hull to the base card. Glue the ends of the hull down on to the base card, but first bring them in slightly from their flat position so that the hull bulges. Cut out the sail. Colour it. Punch holes for the mast. Prepare the mast from cane and attach a coloured flag. Thread the mast through holes in the sail. Fold under the tab along the top edge of sail. Glue to the base card. (This is the only fixture required for mast and sail.) Tuck the bottom of the mast and one corner of the sail inside the hull. Glue a row of paper waves to the base card overlapping the bottom of the hull. This model will not stand by itself but can be pinned to the wall like an ordinary picture.

Flowers in a pot. Cut out the pot. Colour it but leave the tabs uncoloured. Bend it round. Fold the tabs inside and glue them to the base card so that the bottom of the pot rests on the ground. For the flowers, cut several circular petal shapes of different sizes (use tinted paper or colour with crayons). Arrange the shapes with the smaller sizes above the larger ones. Push a paper fastener through the centre and twist the prongs round a length of cane behind. (The fixture may be strengthened with wire if necessary.) Paper leaves may also be attached with wire.

Wishing well. Note the relative sizes of well and roof.

Cut out the well. Colour it except for the ends. Bend it round and attach it to the base card in the same way as the flower pot above. Cut out the roof section. (Card marked out in squares is recommended to ensure that the end triangles are identical.) Colour it but leave the tabs uncoloured. Fold the roof section into shape with the tabs bent inwards. Glue it on to the base card. (If fingers cannot reach to press down the tabs, use the end of a ruler). Glue wooden spills or strips of thick card at each side. (Alternatively, draw posts directly on the base card.) The bucket is simply a smaller version of the flower pot. Its handle is drawn on the base card.

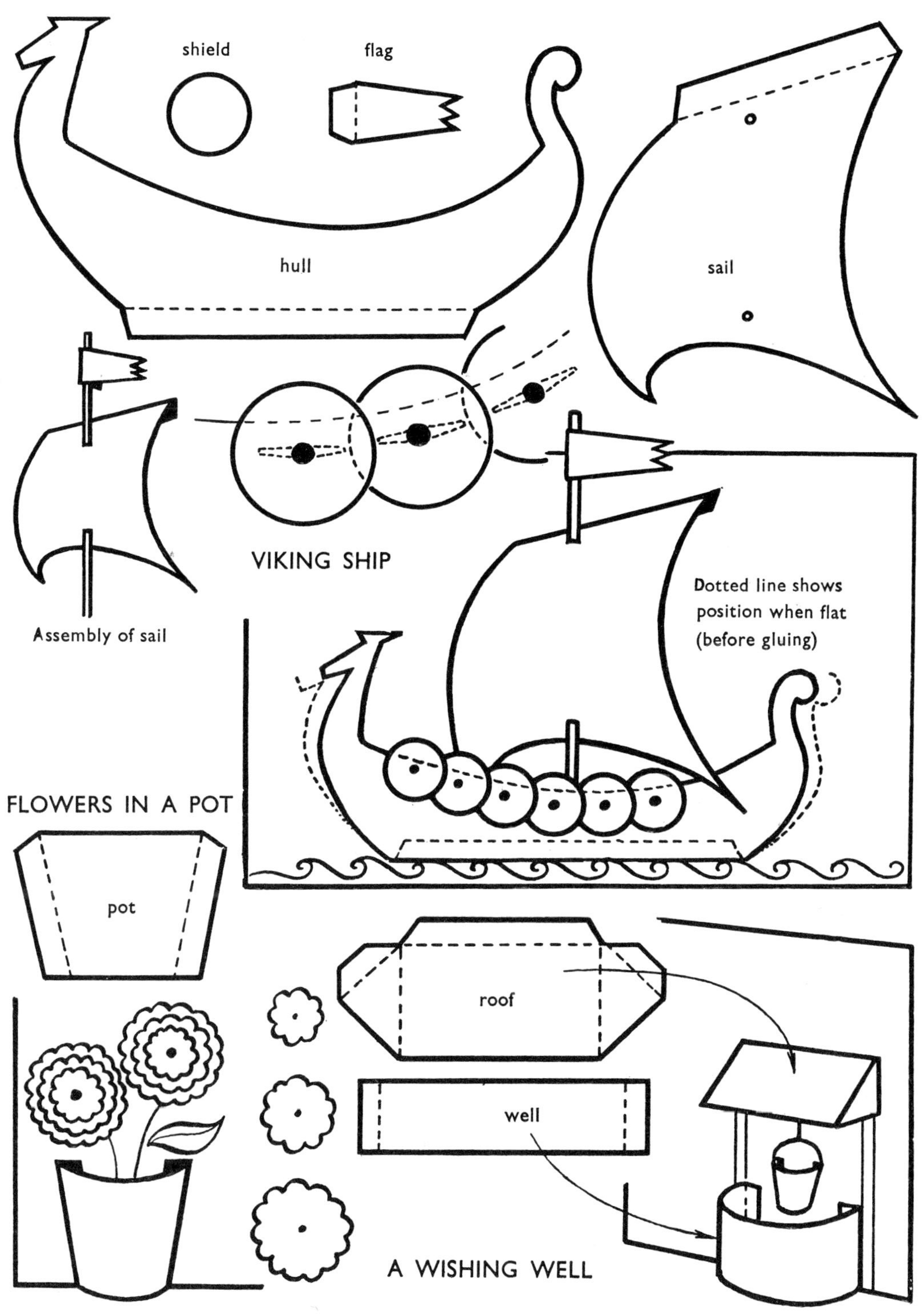
shield
flag
hull
sail
Assembly of sail
VIKING SHIP
Dotted line shows
position when flat
(before gluing)
FLOWERS IN A POT
pot
roof
well
A WISHING WELL

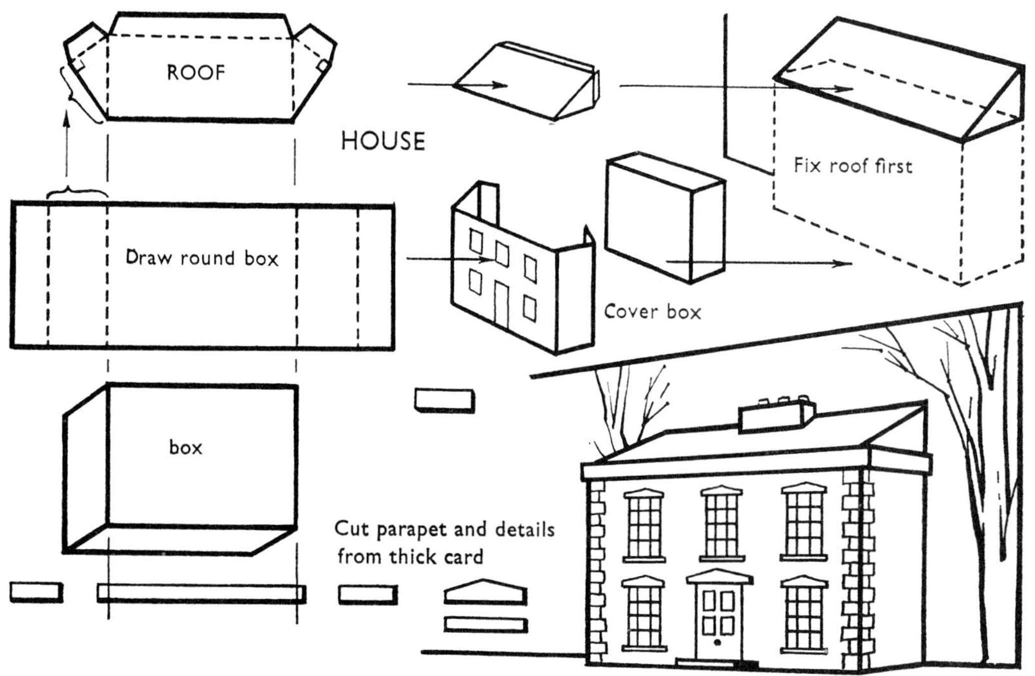

Houses and landscapes. The house above is a useful exercise in drawing out. All the measurements are based upon the actual dimensions of a box which itself forms the walls. A matchbox is a good foundation. Draw roof and wall sections using the box as a template. Cut out and colour them. Mark the eventual position of the box on the base card. Fix the roof; then the covered box.

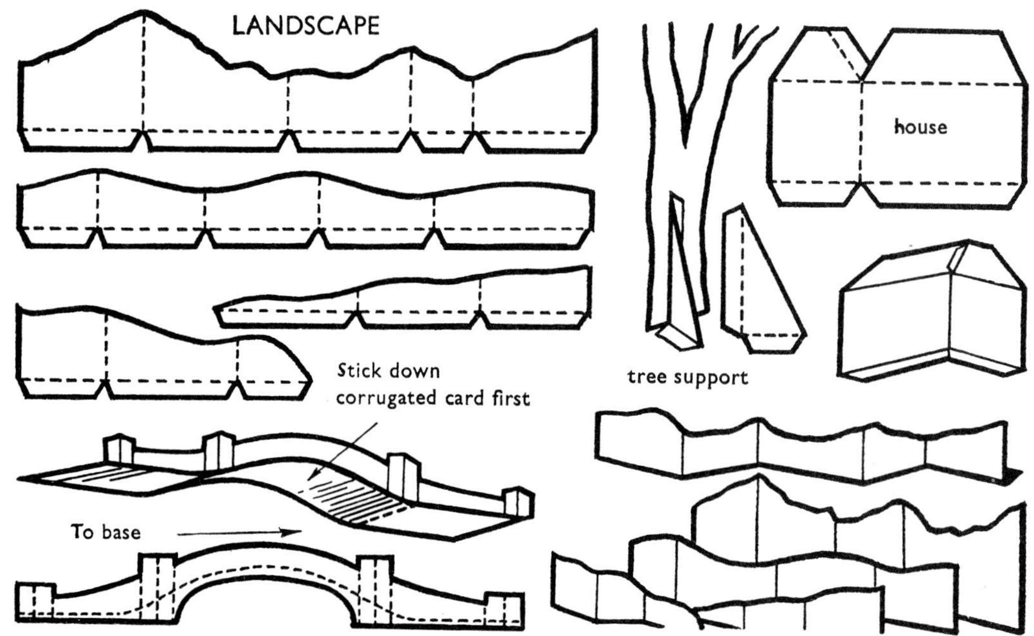

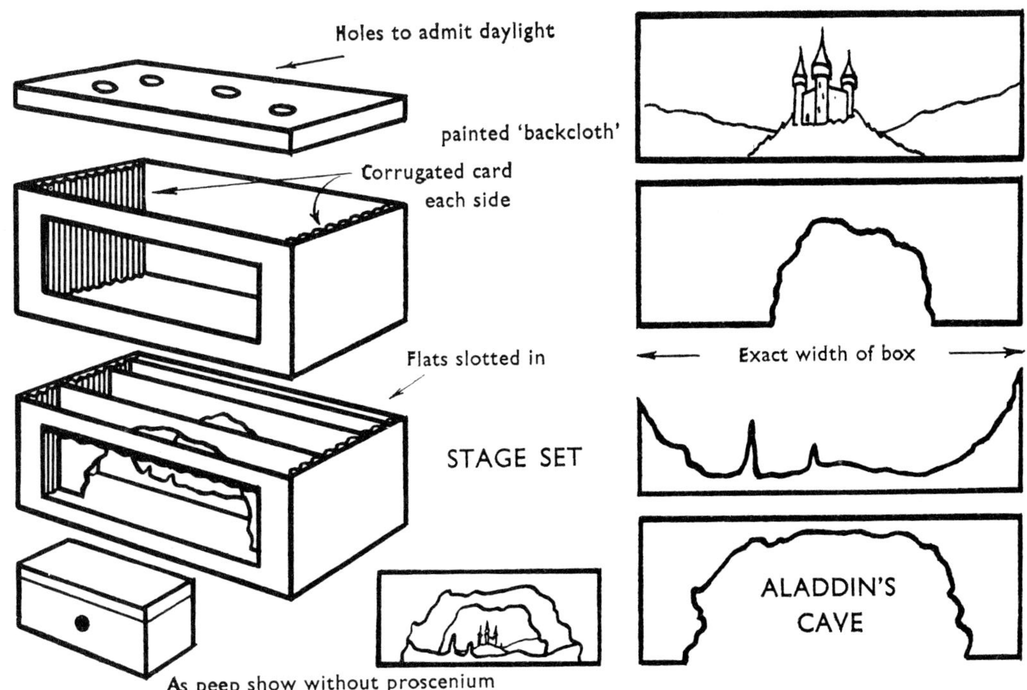

These examples represent the beginnings of composite model making, though they can only be viewed from the front. A stage or display box conceals some of the limitations of the method and is a modification which children often find intriguing.

The model below is composed of elements shown in the diagrams opposite. The use of zig-zag 'floor runs' helps to establish simple principles of recession. Torch bulbs may be easily concealed behind the flats.

Most of these early relief pictures can be interpreted quite freely by adapting the drawing of the backgrounds or by altering details. For example, the Viking ship on page 15 need not be a Viking ship. It could just as easily be some other simple sailing vessel. More than one sail can be threaded on a single mast, and more than one mast can be mounted on one hull. Similarly, the flower pot on the same page need not stand alone. If the background were to represent a greenhouse, then several such pots could be mounted on 'shelves' within the same picture, and a variety of exotic blooms displayed in them.

The imaginative possibilities only really become apparent when the models are grouped together. As three-dimensional pictures they will no doubt be used primarily to 'set the scene' and it is sometimes difficult not to allow a miscellaneous assortment of toys and plasticine animals to trespass upon the foreground. These could well be augmented with details which the children have made themselves. Such details make a useful occupation for the child who always finishes before the others.

Free standing details. Animals: Cut a template from fairly thick card (preferably soft enough to be cut with scissors). Coat one side with glue and press down on to a scrap of foam plastic. Trim the foam to the contour of the template. Coat the other side of the template with glue and repeat the process. Snip away any unwanted foam still remaining. Legs, tails, ears, horns, etc. may be made from a variety of materials and pushed into the foam.

Trees. Two methods are shown: 1. Roll a length of green paper several times round a pencil. Except for half an inch at the bottom, bind the lower half of the tube with brown gumstrip. Remove the pencil. Slit the tube at intervals down from the top as far as the gumstrip binding. Open out the resulting fronds and trim to shape. Do likewise at the bottom and cut off all but a few of the tabs thus formed. Those which remain are splayed out to be glued on to the floor of the model.

2. Bind several pipe cleaners along half their length with gumstrip. Bend the free ends to resemble branches. Paint them brown. Apply glue and add scraps of green plastic foam.

Fencing. The diagrams opposite should make this clear. The palings are made from scraps of basketry cane held in position either with wire or with lengths of corrugated cardboard. Make sure the grade of cane will fit between the actual corrugations of the board being used. Matchsticks or cocktail sticks may also be used for some types.

Another treatment. This shaggy creature was coated with glue and smothered with cut sisal string.

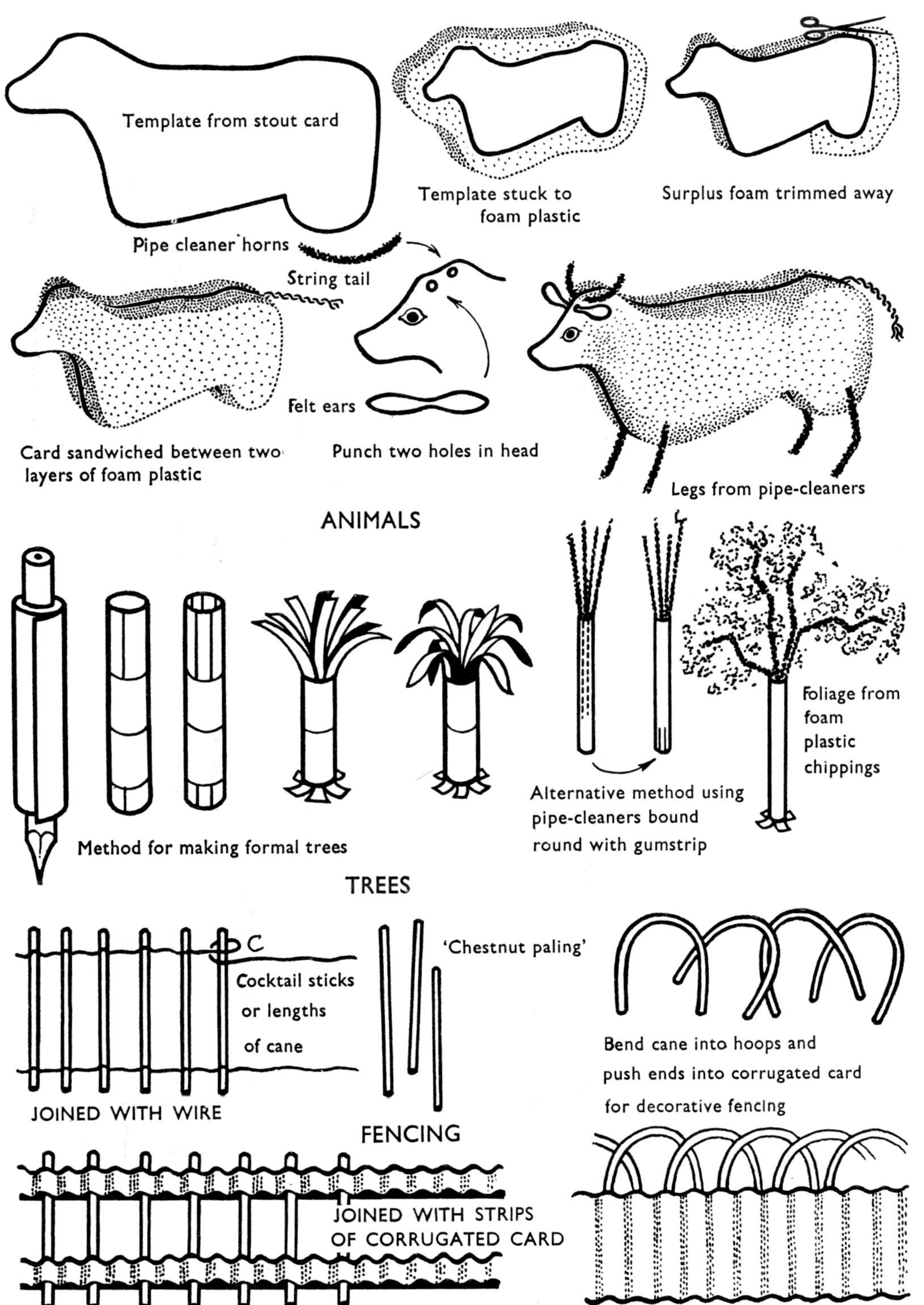

Template from stout card
Template stuck to foam plastic
Surplus foam trimmed away
Pipe cleaner horns
String tail
Felt ears
Card sandwiched between two layers of foam plastic
Punch two holes in head
Legs from pipe-cleaners
ANIMALS
Method for making formal trees
Alternative method using pipe-cleaners bound round with gumstrip
Foliage from foam plastic chippings
TREES
C
Cocktail sticks or lengths of cane
'Chestnut paling'
JOINED WITH WIRE
Bend cane into hoops and push ends into corrugated card for decorative fencing
FENCING
JOINED WITH STRIPS OF CORRUGATED CARD

Basic archway unit. Draw out the shape on a rectangular piece of card marked out in squares, five squares by eleven squares. Cut out the arches and the four slots at the top. Fold round like a box and glue section b over section a. Fold in the square top flaps on either side. Fold down the longer top flaps, one over the other. Paint on the stonework and paint the inside black.

The finished arch is a building unit capable of many combined variations. It may be formed into arcades to produce viaducts and arenas, or glued together to make tunnels.

For circular structures, note that all the units must first be connected along the inner wall. The joints are made with gumstrip. Lay down the required number of units side by side flat on the table. Rub down the gumstrip fastening them all together. Stand the line of arches up again and it will be found that the resulting arcade will only curve one way. Join the remaining end units and arrange in a true circle. The gaps on the outside will be more or less noticeable according to the number of units in the circle. They should also be covered with pieces of gumstrip long enough to fold over on top.

Industrial scene. Here, a viaduct is used to add a note of realism to a painted industrial backcloth. Until page 60 of the book is reached, even the passing train may be simply painted in.

Trellis arch. This is the same arch but with a rectangular opening. Actual twigs are glued on to produce a rustic appearance for use with model gardens. For the attached flower pots see page 15.

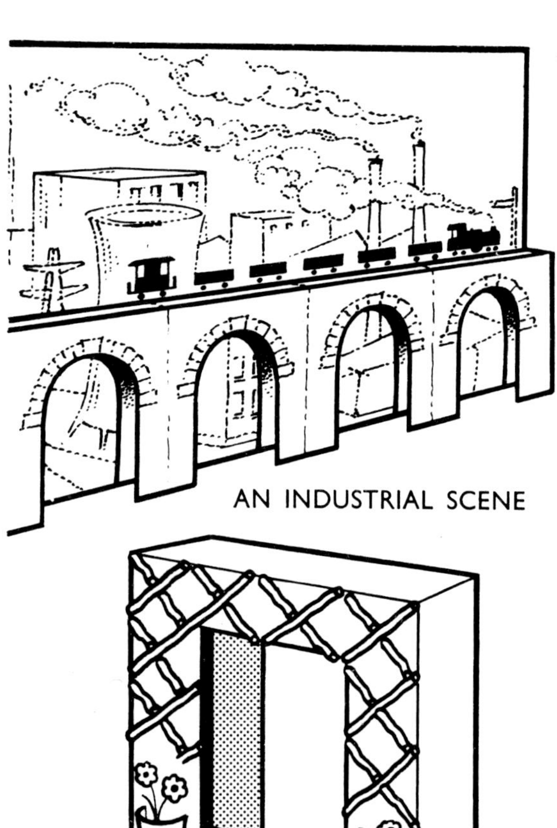

Viaduct. Individual archway units glued together forming continuous arcade. Each unit constructed from a single piece of thin card marked out in squares. Coloured separately with poster paints in various shades of grey. Height 4in.

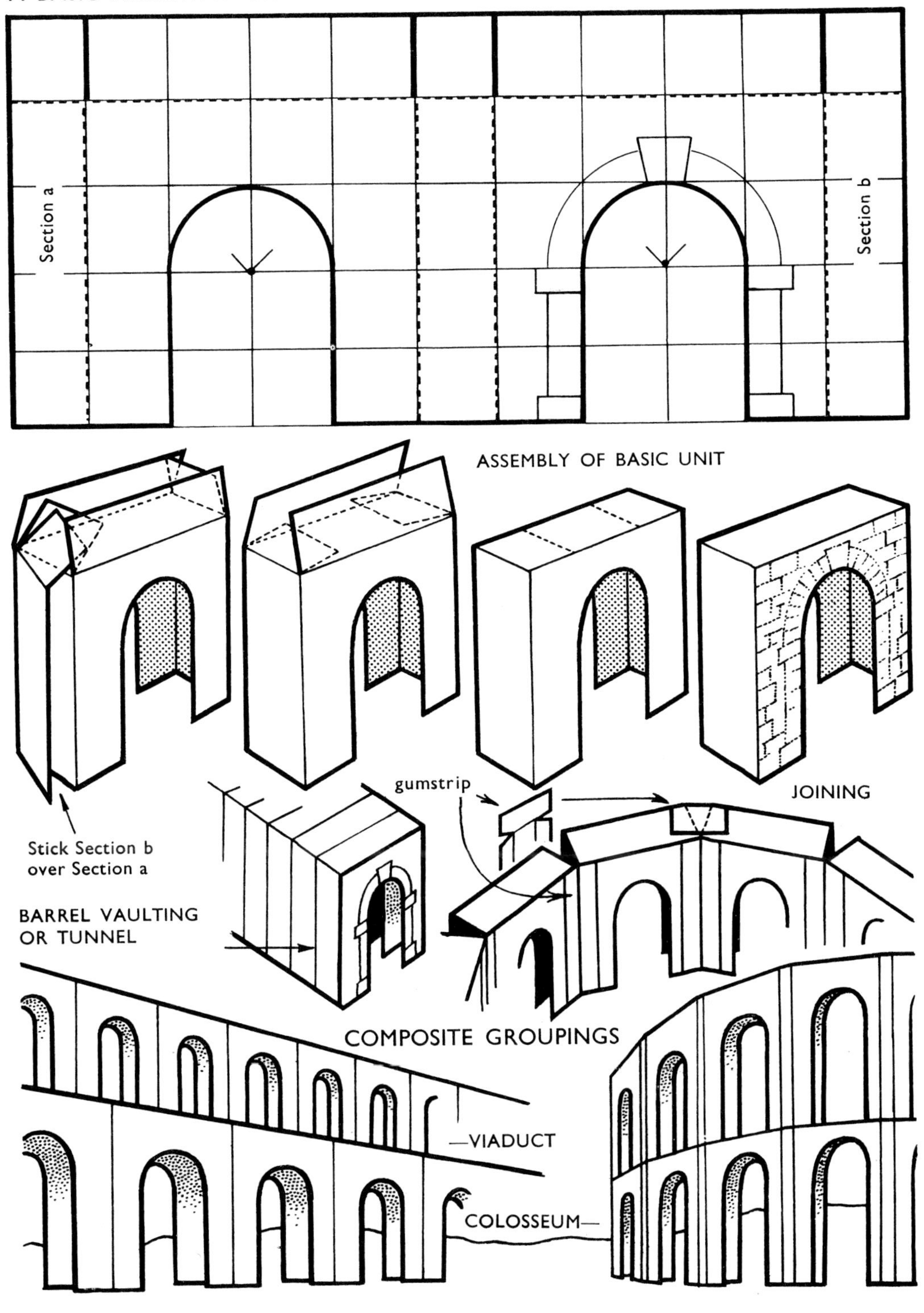
A BASIC ARCHWAY UNIT
Section a
Section b
ASSEMBLY OF BASIC UNIT
Stick Section b
over Section a
gumstrip
JOINING
BARREL VAULTING
OR TUNNEL
COMPOSITE GROUPINGS
—VIADUCT
COLOSSEUM—

Two three-dimensional friezes. (From material already described.) Instructions for the ships and houses will be found on pages 15 and 16. On this page the purpose is to show how they may be arranged as continuous friezes. A long shelf will need to be erected along one wall at about eye level. This need only be 6 in. deep and is also a useful classroom fixture for other forms of display. Quite apart from any other function it provides a convenient ledge for the paint pots during the initial painting of the background. Unlike ordinary frieze painting, the paper must be fairly stout. Continuous cartridge paper is most suitable but if this is too expensive, sheets of sugar paper or thick brown paper may be overlapped.

Pied Piper. Existing painted or cut-out friezes will frequently suggest schemes of development. The teacher in search of subject ideas may have no further to look than the pictorial efforts of a term before. Pin them up behind a table and consider which parts might be built out into the room. They will need to be interpreted quite freely of course. These diagrams demonstrate some possible additions to a flat frieze originally designed only in cut-out paper, and illustrating scenes from the Pied Piper.

The arch and the bridge are described earlier in this chapter.

Steps are often useful. Start with a box or carton. On opposite sides mark out a system of rectangles. (The grid must be identical on both sides). Cut out the step pattern on both sides. At each step cut horizontal slots. Cut treads from thick card and push them into position – (a little glue may first be applied to the slots).

The mountain shows a useful method for building up irregular land shapes. Build the shape roughly from matchboxes and various small cartons glued together, see 1. Cover these with strips of gauze bandage (or similar fabric) glued down where possible, see 2. Finally stick down scraps of torn sugar paper all over, until a fairly rigid undulating surface is achieved. At least four layers will be required, see 3.

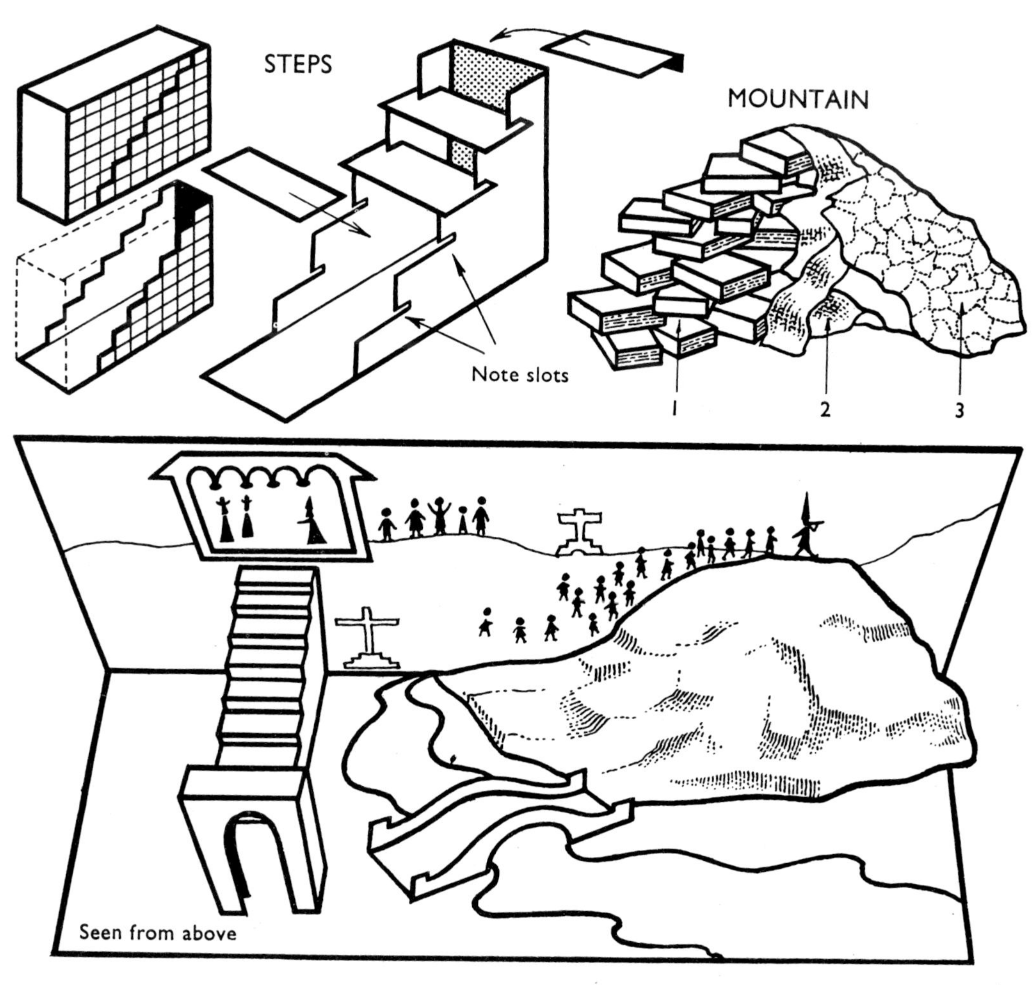

Venetian gondolas. Three models in thin card arranged in front of a scene by Canaletto. Demonstrates the use of large coloured reproductions as background material for simple models. Foreground models each about 8in. long. Unpainted.

The Pied Piper. A flat frieze about 7ft. long assembled from cut-out figures in white and coloured paper glued to a black ground. Made originally by 8-9-year-old children simply as a wall decoration. Later used as a basis for development in three dimensions.

Viking ship. Approximately 8in. long. Bulging sail and flag mounted on flat background drawn with crayons on blue card. Shields in various colours cut from paper. Sail red and orange on white cartridge paper. Flag red cut-out shape on white. Ship brown and orange on green and blue sea with waves scraped through.

Mill by a river. Made by a group of four children. A relief model 12in. long with free standing bridge, boats, and trees. Fully coloured with Finart wax crayons on thin tinted card against a blue sky. Trees are of Sugar paper coloured green. The roadway over grey bridge is corrugated cardboard. Boats blue and yellow against green and purple hills.

Basic shapes

This chapter consists mainly of geometry in disguise. The forms represented constitute the very ABC of model making. More complicated shapes are only variations of them, so it is obviously important to have understood the basic methods involved. There is no need to bore the class with a lot of unadorned mathematics. The principles are embodied in a few simple objects which, it is hoped, may have a more imaginative appeal. Simple though they are, they will quickly demonstrate the limitations of different grades of card. Some experiment at this stage would not be wasted.

The diagrams opposite show three distinct methods for making a cube. They are of prime importance because they exemplify the main methods of construction which will be needed again and again. They also apply to any rectangular shape.

Method A. This procedure combines strength and simplicity, but as the joining strips are sometimes visible on the outside the model will usually need a good coat of paint. Cut six identical squares from thick card, see (i). Lay down four of these pieces and cover the joints with gumstrip. One of these strips is first folded along its length and only half its width stuck down along the side of the first square, see (ii). The remaining half is ready to be stuck down on the inside of the fourth square when the four walls are set up to form a box. Note that the strips are on the inside. For the top and bottom take squares 5 and 6 and apply gumstrip round all four sides of each. This should overhang the edges in the same way as the strip just described. It is simpler to make these strips longer than actually necessary and trim off the unwanted corners afterwards, see (iii). Place the top and bottom in position and stick down the overhanging gumstrip. Note that this time the strips are on the outside.

Method B. This procedure is suitable for models in thinner card when the entire shape can be drawn out in one flat piece. The position of the original six faces can easily be seen from the diagram, but notice that the shape has been extended along certain edges to provide tabs for gluing – (i). If the card is thin enough then the pencil lines will themselves predispose it to fold cleanly in the right places. Otherwise the folds must first be 'scored', i.e. partly cut through. The fold is always *away* from the cut so that the scoring is visible on the outside. The order of folding and gluing is shown in the diagrams (ii) (iii) (iv) (v). The gluing of the final tabs may require gentle handling, but in practice completely enclosed solids are seldom necessary. There is usually room to exert pressure from inside.

Method C. This procedure uses both thick and thin card. All tabs and joining strips are eliminated. The surface to be glued is the actual thickness at the edge of the thick card. The four thin walls are made in one piece, folded, and fitted to the end sections, see diagram (i) (ii) (iii). This is known as butt jointing. It is probably the most professional way of doing it but by no means the easiest. There is no reason why the thickness could not be increased by sandwiching several layers together.

These methods are often used in conjunction with one another.

Actual models are given on page 28.

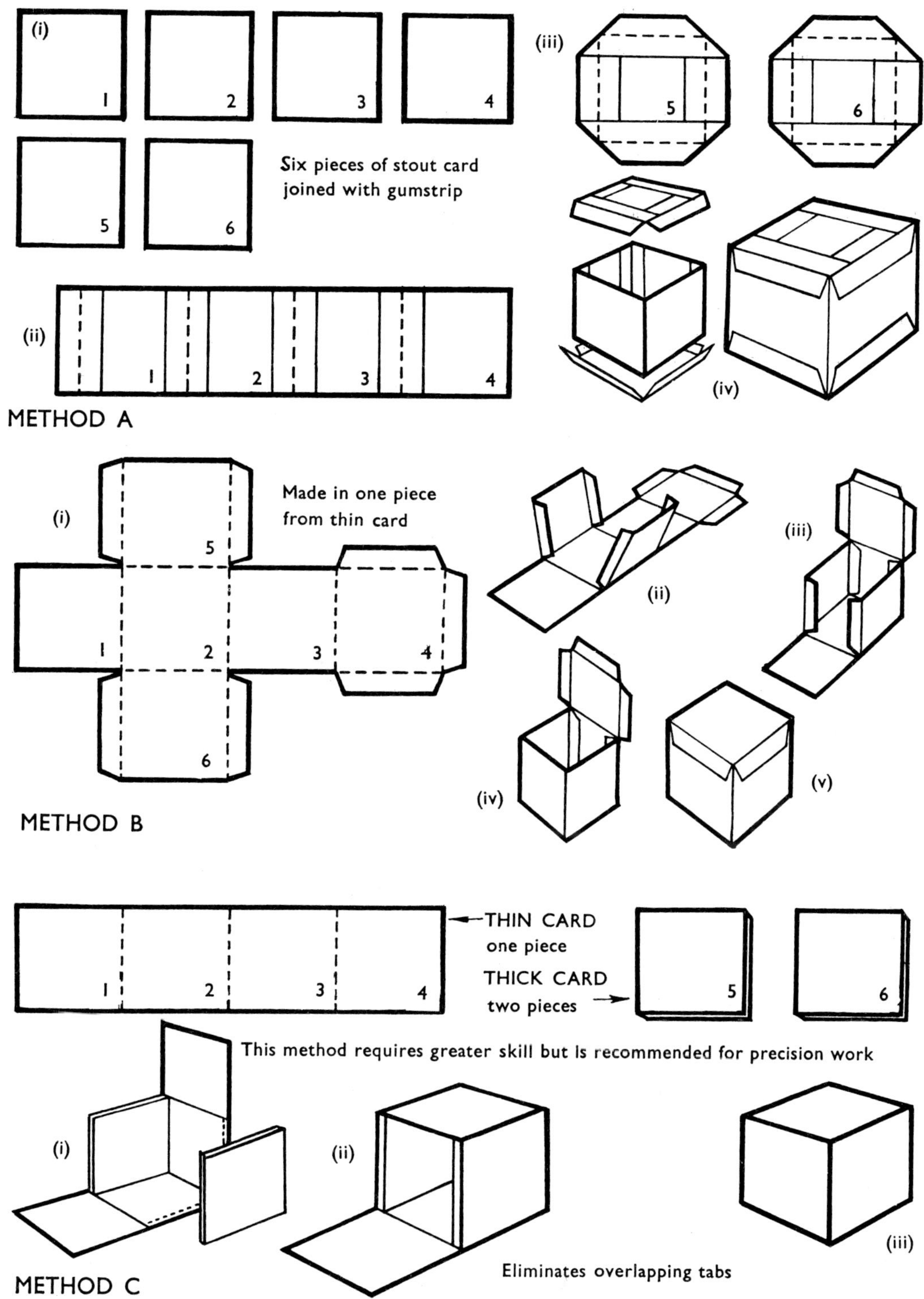
(i)
1
2
3
4
5
6
Six pieces of stout card joined with gumstrip
(iii)
5
6
(ii)
1
2
3
4
(iv)
METHOD A
(i)
5
1
2
3
4
6
Made in one piece from thin card
(ii)
(iii)
(iv)
(v)
METHOD B
1
2
3
4
THIN CARD one piece
THICK CARD two pieces
5
6
This method requires greater skill but is recommended for precision work
(i)
(ii)
(iii)
Eliminates overlapping tabs
METHOD C

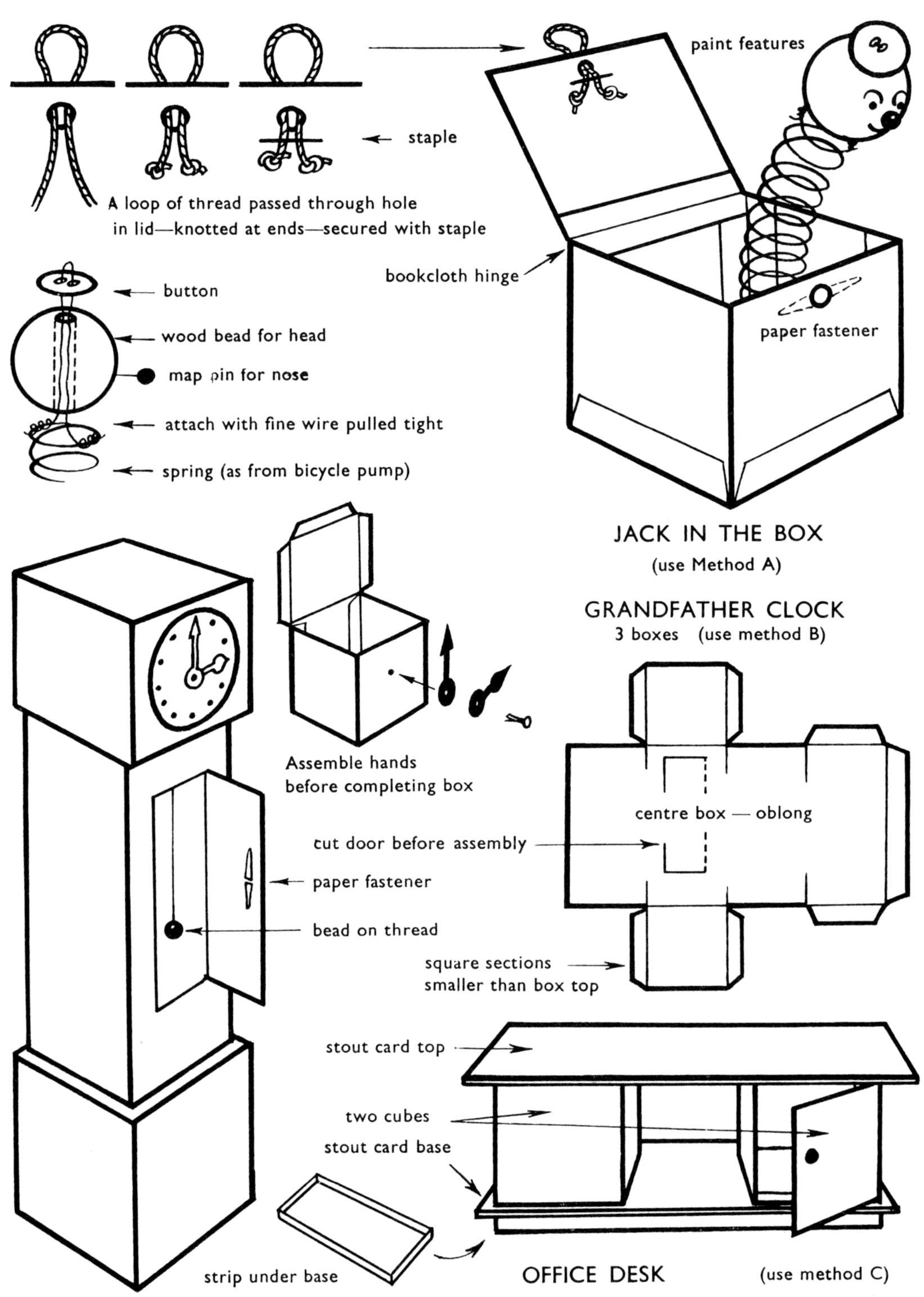

JACK IN THE BOX
(use Method A)

GRANDFATHER CLOCK
3 boxes (use method B)

OFFICE DESK (use method C)

Cones and cotton reels. Cones are made from discs of card. The card must be sufficiently pliable to be curled round upon itself without cracking. For small cones, therefore, use thin card or strong paper. There will almost certainly be a tendency for the card to uncurl while setting unless it is held with a large bulldog clip. Alternatively, it may be temporarily fixed with staples or immediately bound with an ample length of gumstrip.

The diagrams below are intended to show in a general way what shape of cone may be expected from various proportions of the circle. As it is difficult to estimate in advance the exact *size* at the base of a cone, it is often wise, once having decided upon the *shape*, to construct a cone larger than necessary. The base may then be carefully trimmed until it conforms to the plan on which it is required to fit.

It is sometimes required to fit a conical section on to a cylinder, or to a cone of a different shape. To do this, fit the cone into the end of the cylinder as far as it will go and draw round the cone at this point – a. Withdraw the cone. Cut off the point. Cut down at intervals as far as the pencil mark and open out the resulting tabs – b and c. Apply glue to the tabs and refit the cone pressing the tabs down inside the cylinder.

Diagram – e shows the effect of assembling cones of different pitch into one unit. Such a shape may be useful for fountains, lampshades, and certain sorts of roof, etc.

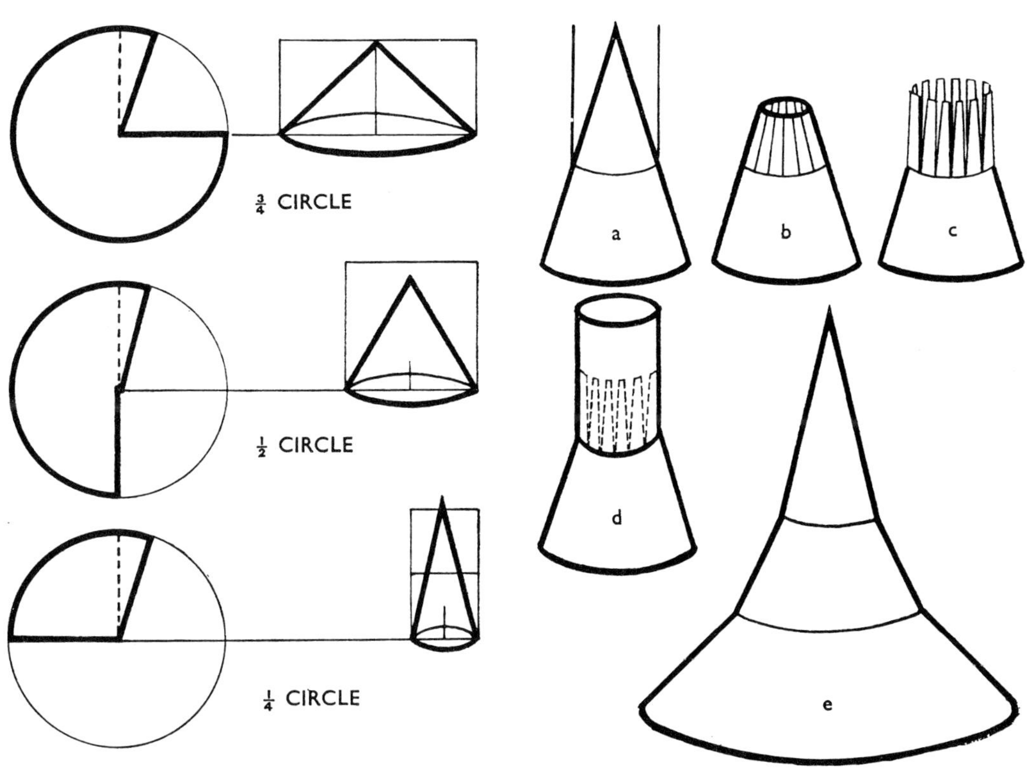

Rocket. Construct a cylinder from thin card rolled upon itself, glued securely, and tightly bound with a soft bandage until set (see pages 32-33). This should be made first. Alternatively use a postal tube or ready-made canister.

Then make a suitable cone (see previous page). Insert the point as far as possible into the top of the cylinder and draw round where it fits, see (i) and (ii). Turn the cone the right way up and cut off the unwanted lower portion. Stick a length of gumstrip round the top of the cylinder so that half its width extends beyond the edge. Cut this free portion into a number of V-shaped tabs. Bend these outwards to allow the cone to be lowered into position. Moisten these tabs and press them down on to the cone, thus holding it securely. For each fin fold a piece of medium thick card in half (it will need to be scored) and cut the shape from double thickness. Draw round this to ensure identical shapes for the other two fins. Fold back the tabs for fixing and mount on the cylinder. Each fin should be slightly open at its base.

One group of young enthusiasts, confronted with this model, conceived the idea of stuffing it full of fireworks and despatching it into outer space. There is, however, no guarantee that this would have any but disastrous effects.

Tower. This is a simple cone mounted on a column of cotton reels. Apply glue liberally to the perimeter of the topmost reel. Turrets using only one cotton reel may be effectively mounted on pencil stubs fixed at the corners of buildings. Towers may be fixed to walls with gumstrip wrapped round each reel and anchored on either side of the cardboard section. (a.b.c.d.).

Huts. For this settlement, actual twigs are used to support a stout card platform on which the dwellings are arranged. Each hut is made like one of the turrets above. Raffia covers the roof. (For trees and landscape effects – see chapter two).

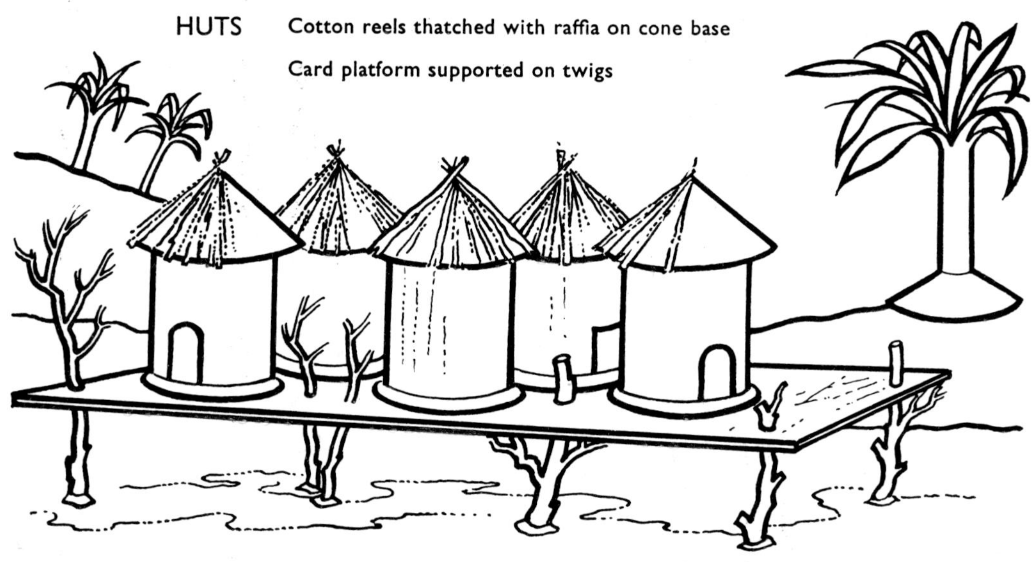

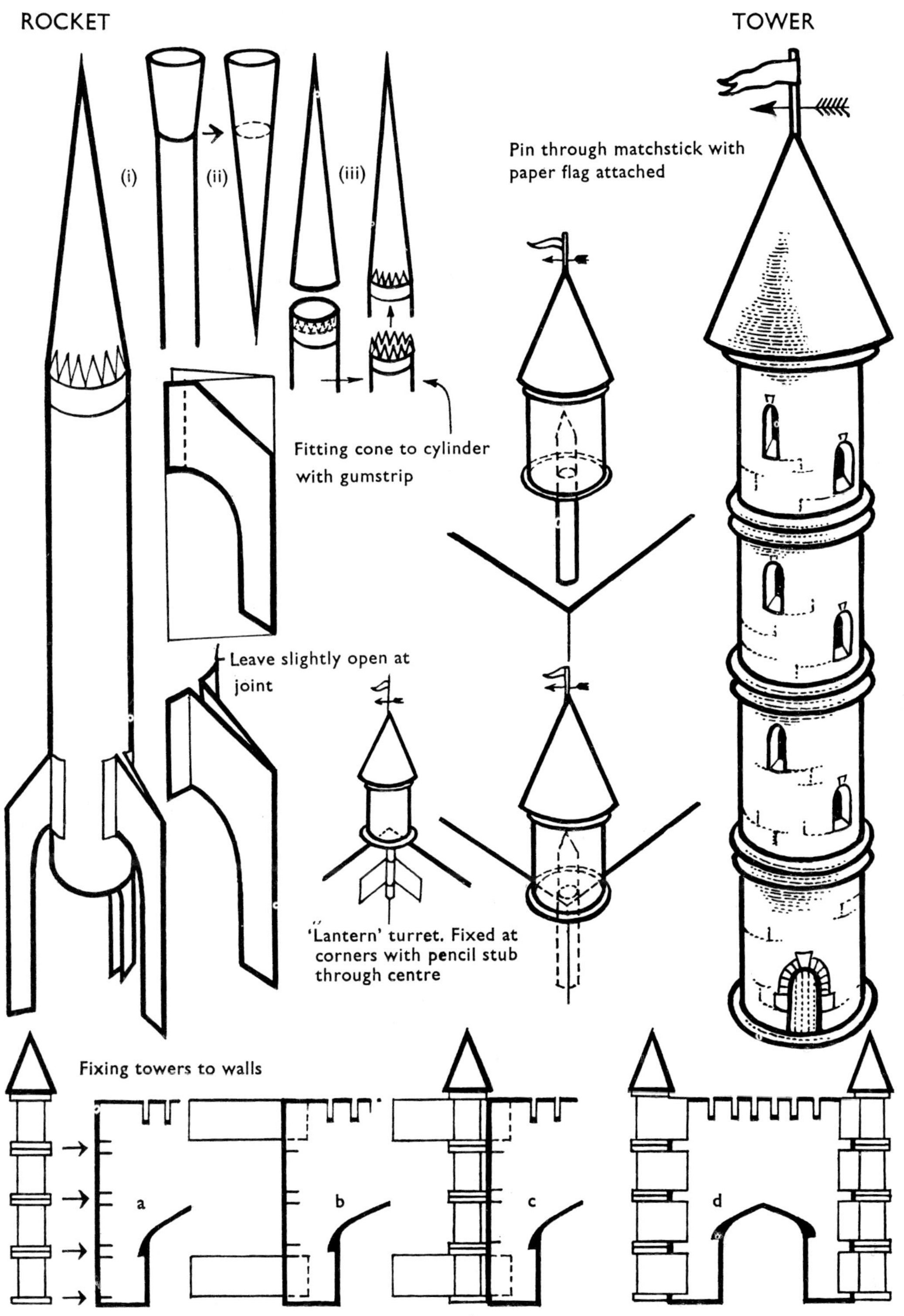
ROCKET
TOWER
(i)
(ii)
(iii)
Pin through matchstick with paper flag attached
Fitting cone to cylinder with gumstrip
Leave slightly open at joint
'Lantern' turret. Fixed at corners with pencil stub through centre
Fixing towers to walls
a
b
c
d

Cylinders and saucepans. Cylinders may be constructed round any suitable former – pencil, broom handle, coffee tin, etc. Paper or thin card is used and the whole shape bound round with gumstrip. For larger cylinders, and in the absence of any former, the circumference (and consequent length of card required) may be determined by rolling one of the end pieces along a straight line ruled on the card. A point should be marked on the end piece and its position noted after one complete revolution. Alternatively make the tube first and draw round it to determine the ends. To support the overlap when gluing, pass a ruler through the tube, see a.

Another tidier method, see b, is to make the ends as thick as possible and stick the surrounding thin card to their edges, but this is not very easy, and in any case the ends should first be connected by some rigid support such as a length of wood inside.

If an existing stout tube is used, see c, or if the cylinder has been lined with corrugated cardboard to provide a good bearing surface at the ends, then the end discs may be stuck directly to this thickness. The safest method is to use gumstrip tabs and fold them down on the outside of the cylinder, see d.

Saucepan and **Roller** are fully explained in the diagrams. For the drawbar of the roller use a strip of thick cardboard folded as shown.

The Temple is built round a simple box. Fluted columns are made by covering cylinders with corrugated card painted white.

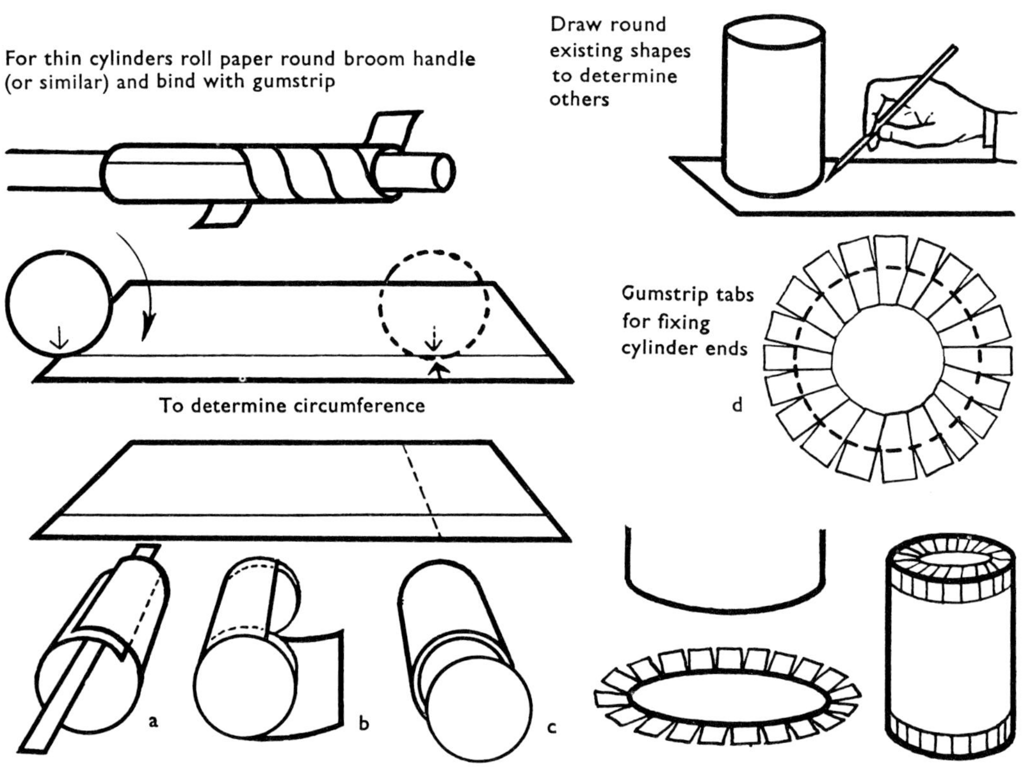

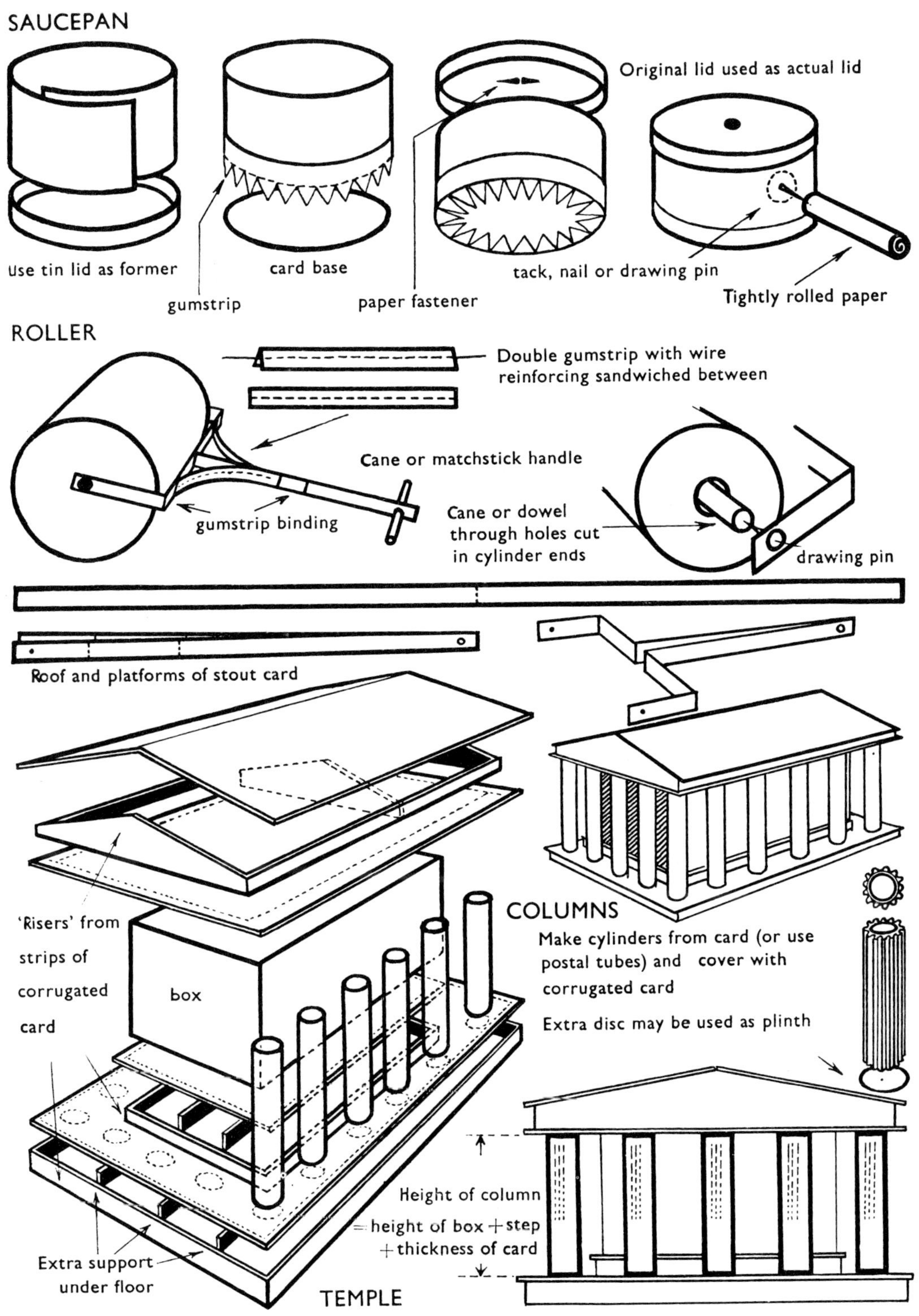
SAUCEPAN
Original lid used as actual lid
Use tin lid as former
card base
tack, nail or drawing pin
gumstrip
paper fastener
Tightly rolled paper
ROLLER
Double gumstrip with wire
reinforcing sandwiched between
Cane or matchstick handle
Cane or dowel
through holes cut
in cylinder ends
gumstrip binding
drawing pin
Roof and platforms of stout card
'Risers' from
strips of
corrugated
card
box
COLUMNS
Make cylinders from card (or use
postal tubes) and cover with
corrugated card
Extra disc may be used as plinth
Height of column
= height of box + step
+ thickness of card
Extra support
under floor
TEMPLE

Pyramids and spires. Pyramids are composed of congruent isosceles triangles. Their shape may be varied by the pitch of the triangle and the number of triangles used. The base may always be exactly contained within a circle. As a general guide to proportion it may be useful to refer to the shapes given for cones on page 29.

Method A (below) shows a simple four-sided pyramid on a square base. Thick card is used and the joints are made with gumstrip. The base is fixed last.

Method B. The walls of the pyramid are all made in one piece using thin card. First draw a circle. Then mark off equal distances round the circumference with compasses or dividers (as many as there may be walls required). Join these points, connect to the centre, and add a fixing tab before cutting out. Fold and assemble. Hold this shape down firmly on a piece of thick card and draw round it for the base. To fix the base apply glue liberally to the edges and hold the main section down on to it until set.

To use this method without a pair of compasses, use one triangle as a template and draw round it repeatedly for the others. Ensure that the sides are in alignment each time.

Method C. This employs thin card throughout and is made in one piece entirely. It is a rather more advanced geometrical exercise.

N.B. It is useful to know that when a pyramid has six sides, then the base of one side is equal to the radius for the base of the whole pyramid.

The examples opposite are self-explanatory.

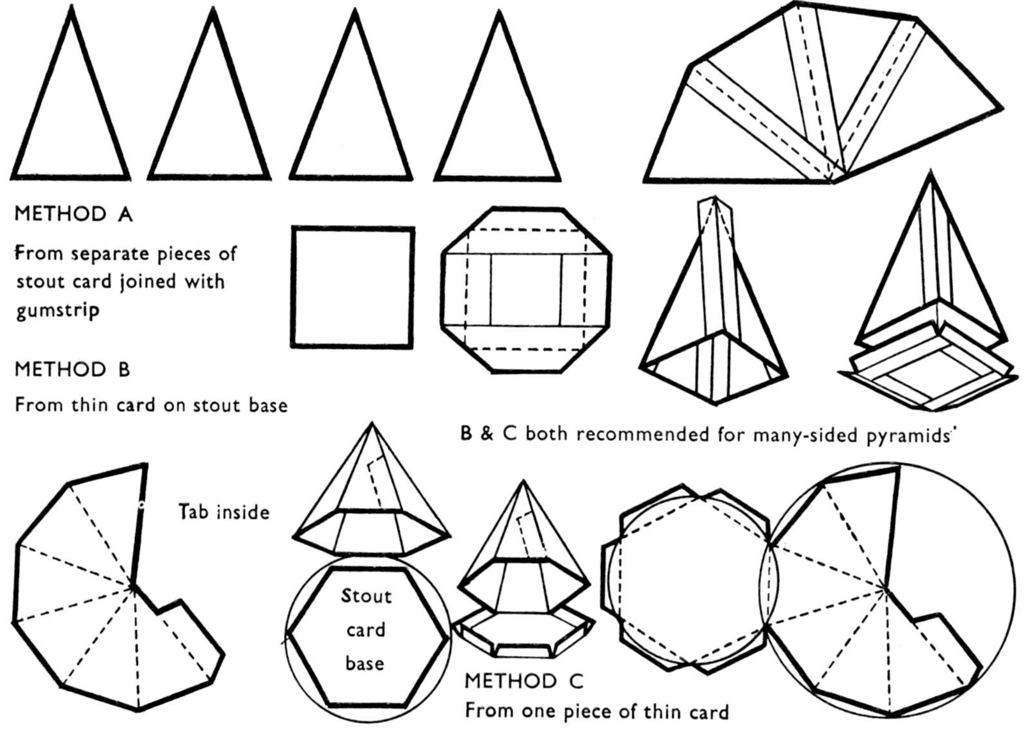

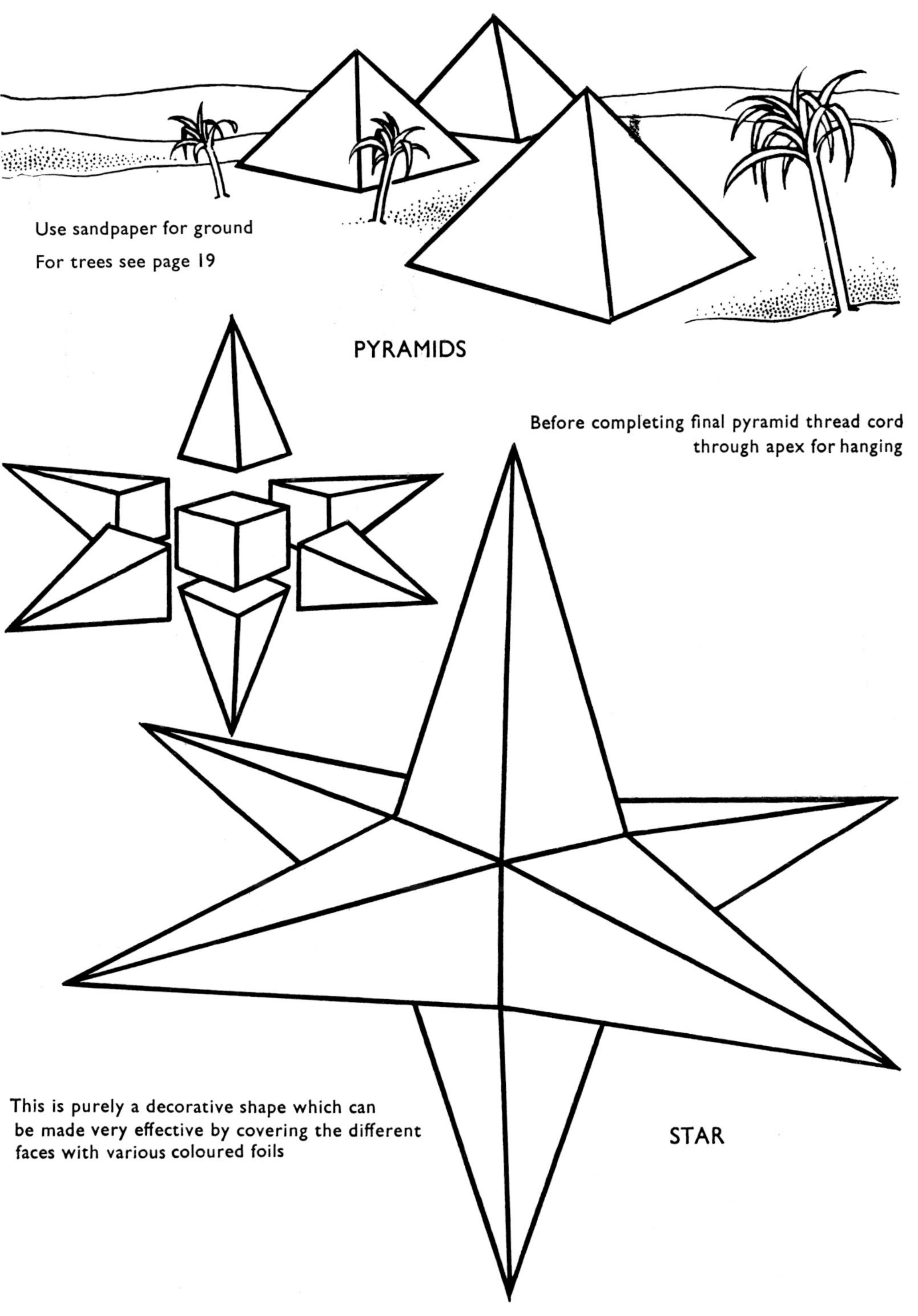
Use sandpaper for ground
For trees see page 19
PYRAMIDS
Before completing final pyramid thread cord through apex for hanging
This is purely a decorative shape which can be made very effective by covering the different faces with various coloured foils
STAR

The Church opposite will provide the opportunity to combine in practice several of the features outlined in the previous pages. It is best constructed by a group of six children working in pairs. One pair may be made responsible for the main boxes and roofs. Another pair may be entrusted with the spire and the corner pinnacles. The third pair may make the buttresses, parapets, and windows. Windows are more easily painted separately on white paper, cut out, and finally pasted on to the wall surface. Brilliant coloured effects can be achieved with transparent, self-adhesive foils pressed over designs in black outline. This allocation of the work enables each pair to work independently of the others until the final stages of assembly. Adequate planning by the teacher is, of course, necessary to co-ordinate the structure.

The boxes should be made from thick card. They may be left open at the base. If there is any tendency for the top to sag, then extra walls should be fixed inside for support. The chancel and the porch will need extra end walls extending up into the gable to support the roof. Additional roof supports are mounted as required on top of the boxes. Make sure that they are identical in shape and mounted in alignment. Each roof is simply two rectangles of thick card hinged together. The nave roof meets the main box. The chancel and porch roofs overhang their boxes.

The tower and nave should be glued together first: the chancel and porch should then be added; then the end walls and roof supports, then the roofs.

The main spire and corner pinnacles may all be constructed separately. As they will probably be made from thinner card they should be fitted with their own bases to facilitate gluing to the tower. Buttresses are made from congruent shapes of corrugated card sandwiched together (a template is indicated here as the shapes will be required in quantity). Any thick card would serve but corrugated is easier to cut. Small roofing pieces of thin card are glued to the buttress as shown. The more buttresses there are, the less chance is there of the walls tending to curl in at the base, as sometimes happens with large models. For the exact shape of the parapet it will be necessary to refer to the completed nave.

As far as possible, it is better (but not essential) to paint the various components as they are finished rather than wait until the whole model is assembled.

Mass production of stereotyped buildings limits self-expression, but allows practical use of models at short notice for simple survey work. Coloured with 'Finart' wax crayons.

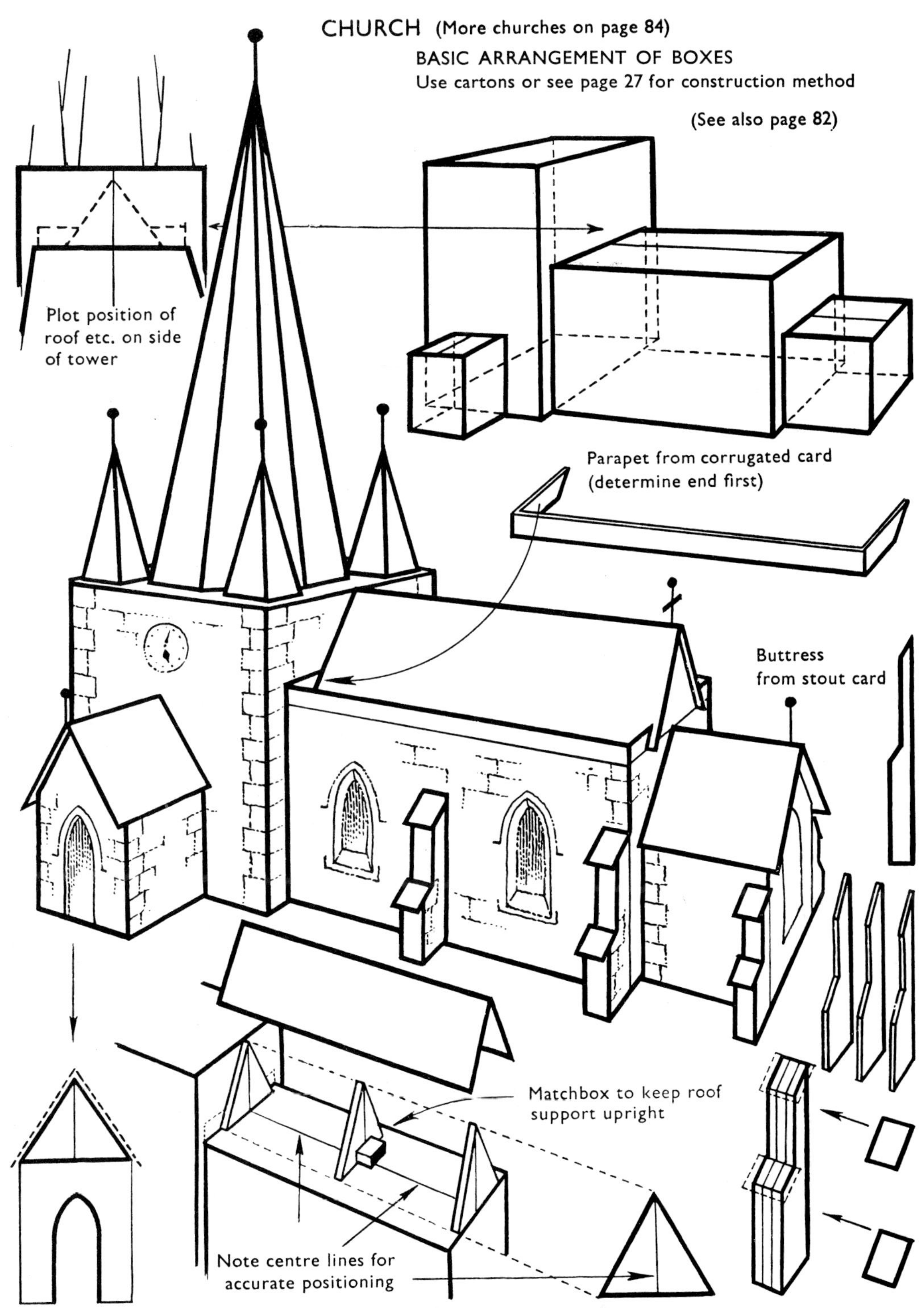
CHURCH (More churches on page 84)
BASIC ARRANGEMENT OF BOXES
Use cartons or see page 27 for construction method
(See also page 82)
Plot position of roof etc. on side of tower
Parapet from corrugated card (determine end first)
Buttress from stout card
Matchbox to keep roof support upright
Note centre lines for accurate positioning

R1
IA

Space rocket and launching pad. Made by a group of twelve boys. Height of rocket alone about 3ft. 6in. Thick cardboard canister painted grey with black and white markings. Fins of strawboard fixed with gumstrip and painted grey. Nose cone of Sugar paper bound with gumstrip and painted red. Tower sections of corrugated cardboard painted black on white and supported on paint brush handles. Steps of corrugated cardboard. Main box papered with grey Sugar paper. Block houses of strawboard painted grey and black with white paper windows marked black and glued on. Roofs cut from insulation board.

Right: An imaginative treatment of a simple cylinder.

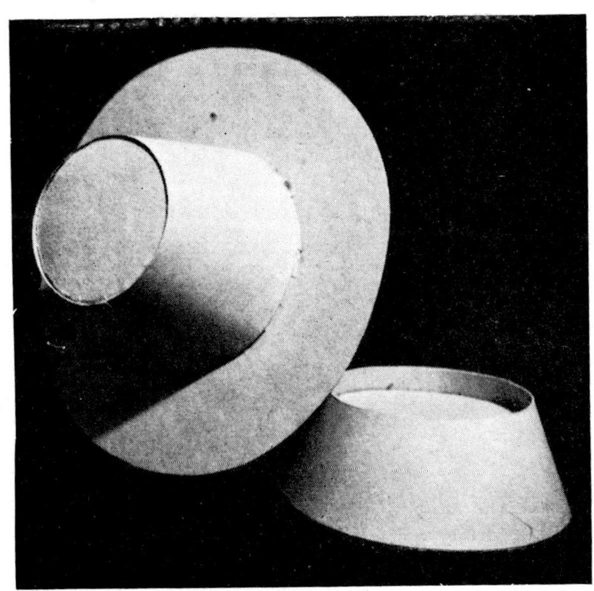

Two hats or tubs. An exercise in making cones. Thin card used throughout. Conical shape made first and drawn round for crown and brim to fit. Outside diameter of brim 6in. Inside of brim has tabs extending and glued inside cone. Unpainted.

Simple railway engine. Boiler and cab of thin card on thicker cardboard base about 4in. long. Funnel rolled paper. Wheels thick cardboard pierced by cane axles attached beneath with gumstrip. Front and funnel attached by means of tabs reinforced with gumstrip. Unpainted.

Individual models

'Can we take it home?' is a plea often heard from the younger ones. The next fifty pages are devoted to a varied selection of models, most of which *can.*

It would be a pity, however, to overlook the many possibilities for effective grouping and classroom display. The models lend themselves quite naturally to composite arrangement without any elaborate setting-up. All that is necessary to begin with is a large sheet of strong paper and several imaginative children to paint a ground plan. This might take the form of runways on which to arrange model aircraft and a few hangars; or a boating lake on which to arrange yachts; or a road junction on which to arrange some vehicles and buildings. There are innumerable other versions.

There is perhaps a temptation to select only the better examples to incorporate in the assembled scheme. The result would certainly be more impressive, but there is a danger that the outcasts might take umbrage. A 'competitive' spirit sometimes raises the technical standard. It also tends to split a class into the duds versus the experts, and this is an unfortunate state of affairs if group work is ever to achieve any educational purpose. Variety is every bit as important as excellence.

The following models are not normally detailed to quite the same extent as in the earlier chapters. It is presumed that many of the simpler fixing techniques will have been already learned. In some cases, where the models are only variations upon a theme, the diagrams have been left to speak for themselves.

The chapter begins with a short section on **Aircraft**, the simplest of which are shown opposite. Type 1 is very easy. The beginners should have no difficulty with it provided they have some means of cutting the wing slots. The wings and tail plane may be inclined at a slight angle as will be seen from the diagram of the back view. Run a little glue along the joints after assembly.

Type 2 is also very easy and can be made on a slightly larger scale than Type 1. First make the box and build the other parts around it. Note that each of the fuselage sections, see B should be scored in two places. If the wings should begin to flap (as might happen if the scale is too large for the grade of cardboard used), take a length of wire from a point half way along one wing over the fuselage and down to the other wing. Paper fasteners or staples fixed at these points will provide anchorage for the wire.

Type 3 is a more ambitious model fully explained in the diagrams on pages 42 and 43. For a more detailed account of the cone and fuselage assembly see also Rocket (pages 30-31). The most important feature of this model is the rigid support piercing the fuselage in order to carry the wings.

When using gumstrip for joints, fold the strip along its length, gummed side outside, to enable half the width to be moistened and attached before the other half. Gumstrip needs to be rubbed down firmly.

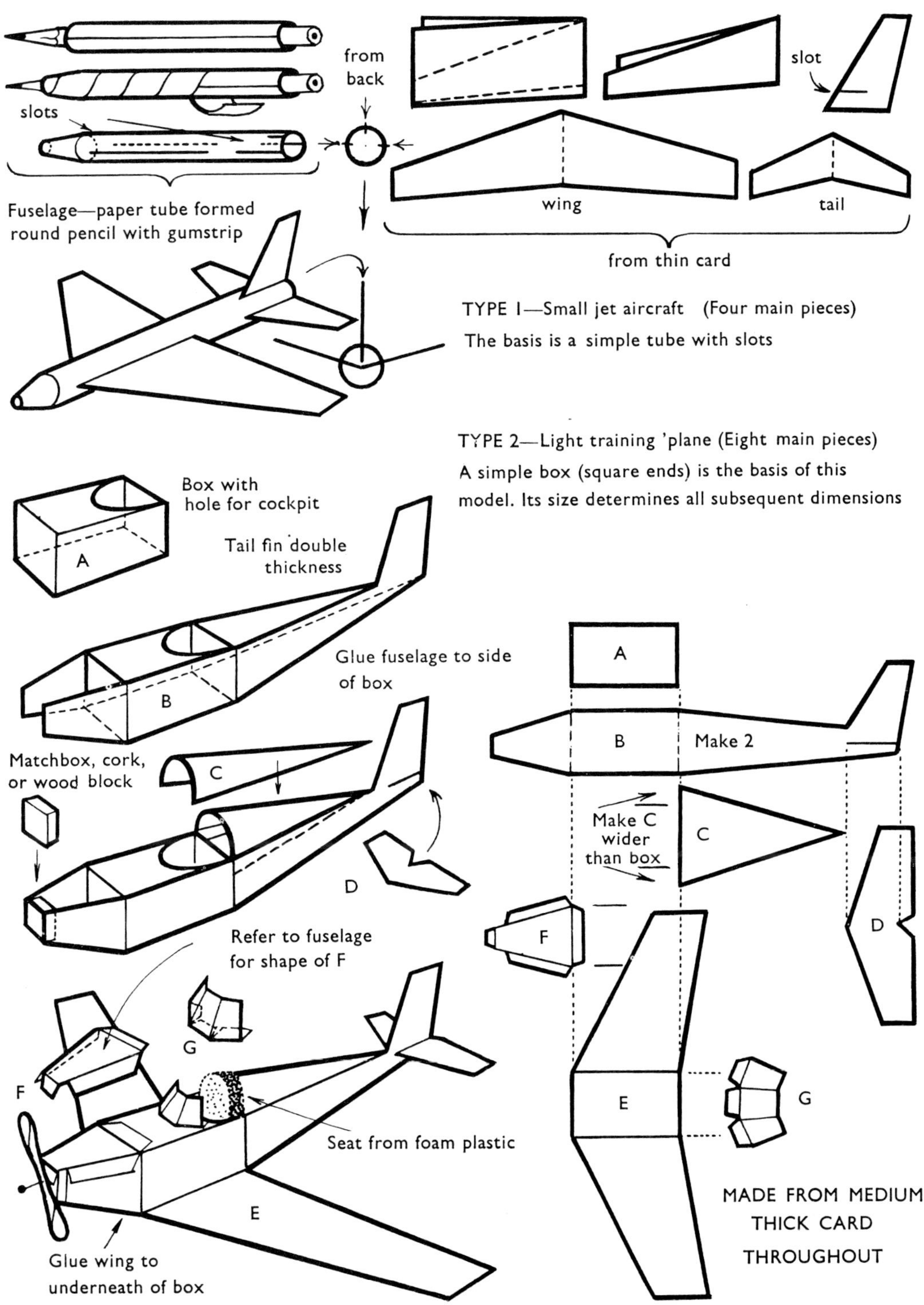

from back
slots
slot
Fuselage—paper tube formed round pencil with gumstrip
wing
tail
from thin card
TYPE 1—Small jet aircraft (Four main pieces)
The basis is a simple tube with slots
TYPE 2—Light training 'plane (Eight main pieces)
A simple box (square ends) is the basis of this model. Its size determines all subsequent dimensions
Box with hole for cockpit
A
Tail fin double thickness
B
Glue fuselage to side of box
Matchbox, cork, or wood block
C
D
A
B
Make 2
Make C wider than box
C
D
F
Refer to fuselage for shape of F
G
F
Seat from foam plastic
E
Glue wing to underneath of box
E
G
MADE FROM MEDIUM THICK CARD THROUGHOUT

Make cone larger than actually necessary—thin
Mark here
FUSELAGE
To make cylinder roll paper round broom handle or similar object and bind well with gumstrip (or use postal tube)

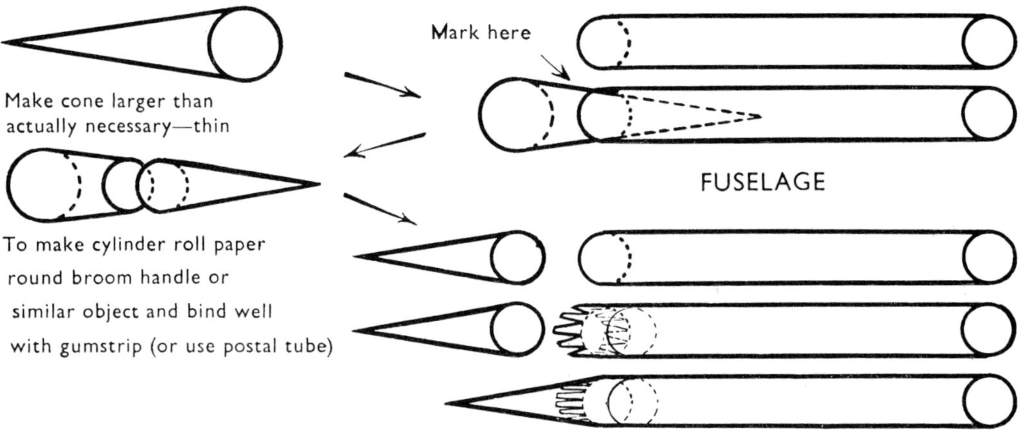

Insert point of cone fully into cylinder to determine length required—mark and cut away surplus cone. Turn the trimmed cone and fix to cylinder with gumstrip

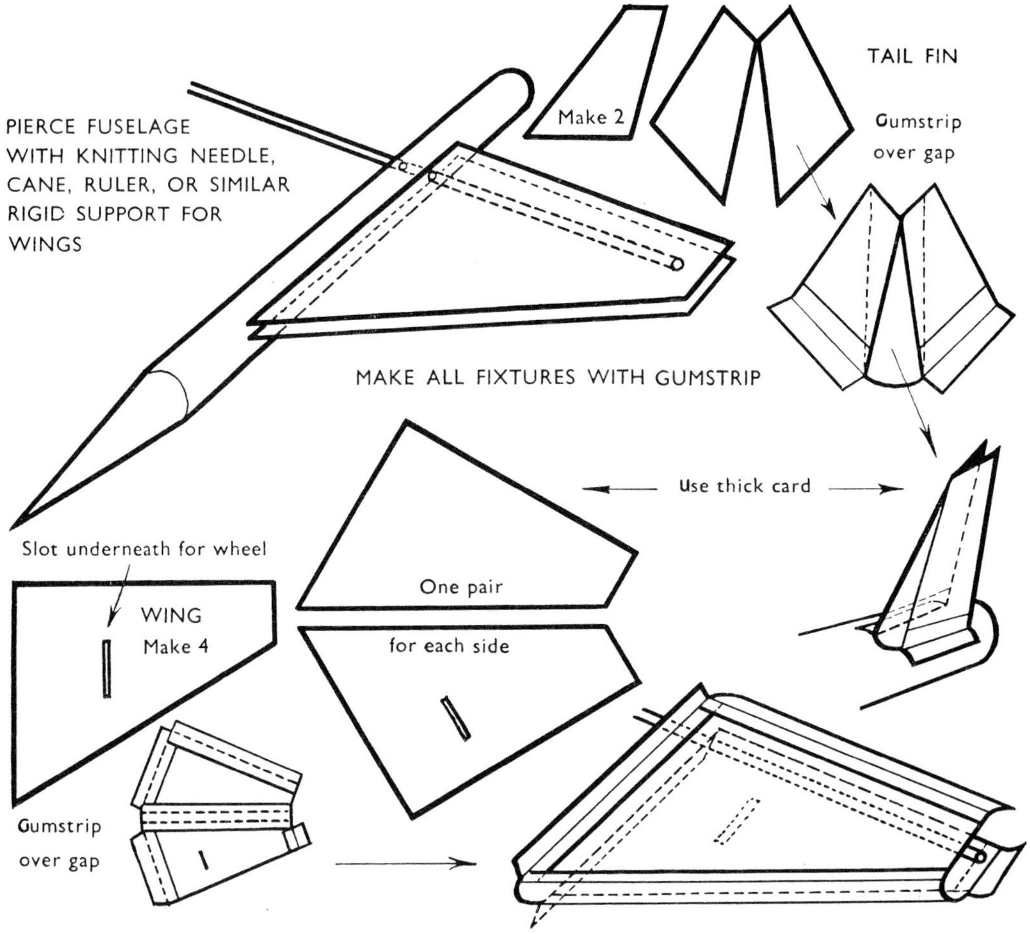

Make 2
TAIL FIN
Gumstrip over gap
PIERCE FUSELAGE WITH KNITTING NEEDLE, CANE, RULER, OR SIMILAR RIGID SUPPORT FOR WINGS
MAKE ALL FIXTURES WITH GUMSTRIP
Use thick card
Slot underneath for wheel
WING
Make 4
One pair
for each side
Gumstrip over gap

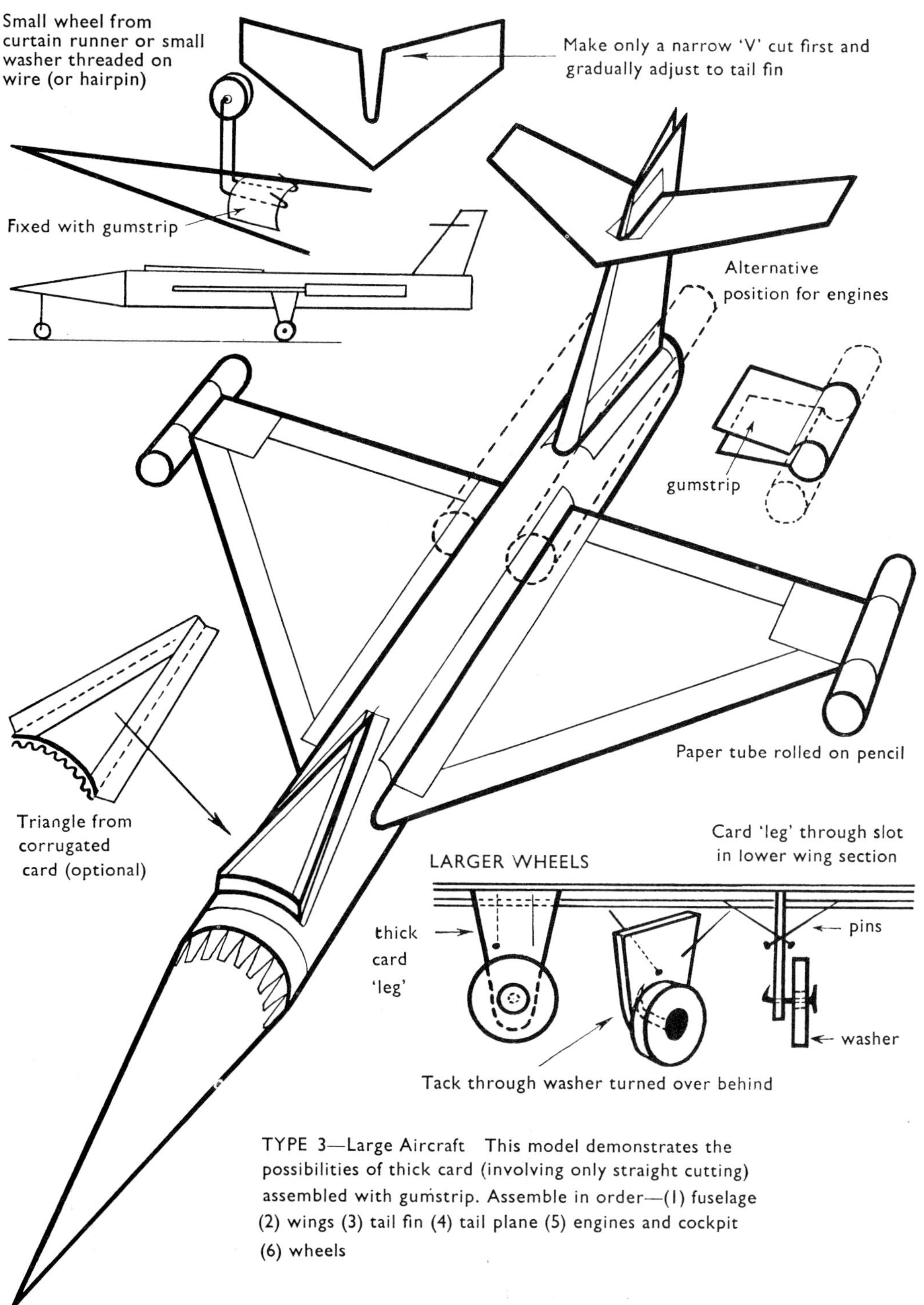

TYPE 3—Large Aircraft This model demonstrates the possibilities of thick card (involving only straight cutting) assembled with gumstrip. Assemble in order—(1) fuselage (2) wings (3) tail fin (4) tail plane (5) engines and cockpit (6) wheels

Furniture. Except for special modern and traditional types (see pages 50-51) most items of furniture are of simple box-like structure and therefore require little detailed instruction.

More than a dozen such examples are illustrated on page 48. These are random suggestions intended simply to show the range of styles which may be achieved with only a few basic methods. The three methods of fixing divisions (also on page 48) should be studied, and reference made if necessary to 'Cubes and Cupboards' (page 27).

Furniture provides ample opportunity for the use of decorative scraps for upholstery, cushions, etc. Foam plastic is particularly useful, also self-adhesive plastic surfacing material, actual fabrics, 'leatherette' papers, and veneers. Minor faults in construction can often be disguised by the careful use of these materials.

As a simple geometrical exercise in cutting and fitting thick card, the 'refectory' type furniture at the foot of page 48 is particularly recommended.

Settee and **Table** opposite combine the use of thick and thin cardboard. Pieces A and D should be thin because they require bending or folding. Pieces B and C should be as thick as possible. Attach a gumstrip tab to the bottom of piece A. Fix this tab under the back edge of piece B. Bend round the ends of piece A and secure them to piece B by means of ordinary dressmakers' pins driven into the edge of the thick card. Glue may be added to strengthen the fixture or as an alternative method. Mount piece C under the seat. Make sure that piece D when folded will fit exactly round piece C. Apply glue to the edge of C and fix D. Colour the model and add fitted cushions.

The top of the table should be as thick as possible. The legs should be fairly thick but not so thick that they will not fold cleanly when scored. Work with the table upturned. Fix all four legs a little distance in from the edge of the table top. They will not be firm until supported. Cut four strips of thick card to fit between the legs. Apply glue to one long edge of each strip and to the outside top of each leg. Mount the strips in position as shown.

The **Desk** is a simple variation of the method just described. It is best to make the box first.

Two important accessory materials are introduced in this section – Wire (on page 50) and Basket-work Cane (on page 51). Their use is explained in the appropriate diagrams, but it should be stated that in both cases corrugated cardboard is also a feature of the method. The actual thickness of wire or cane will depend upon the size of the corrugations in the cardboard into which these materials are required to fit. In the case of the cane, grade 4 or 5 is usually about right.

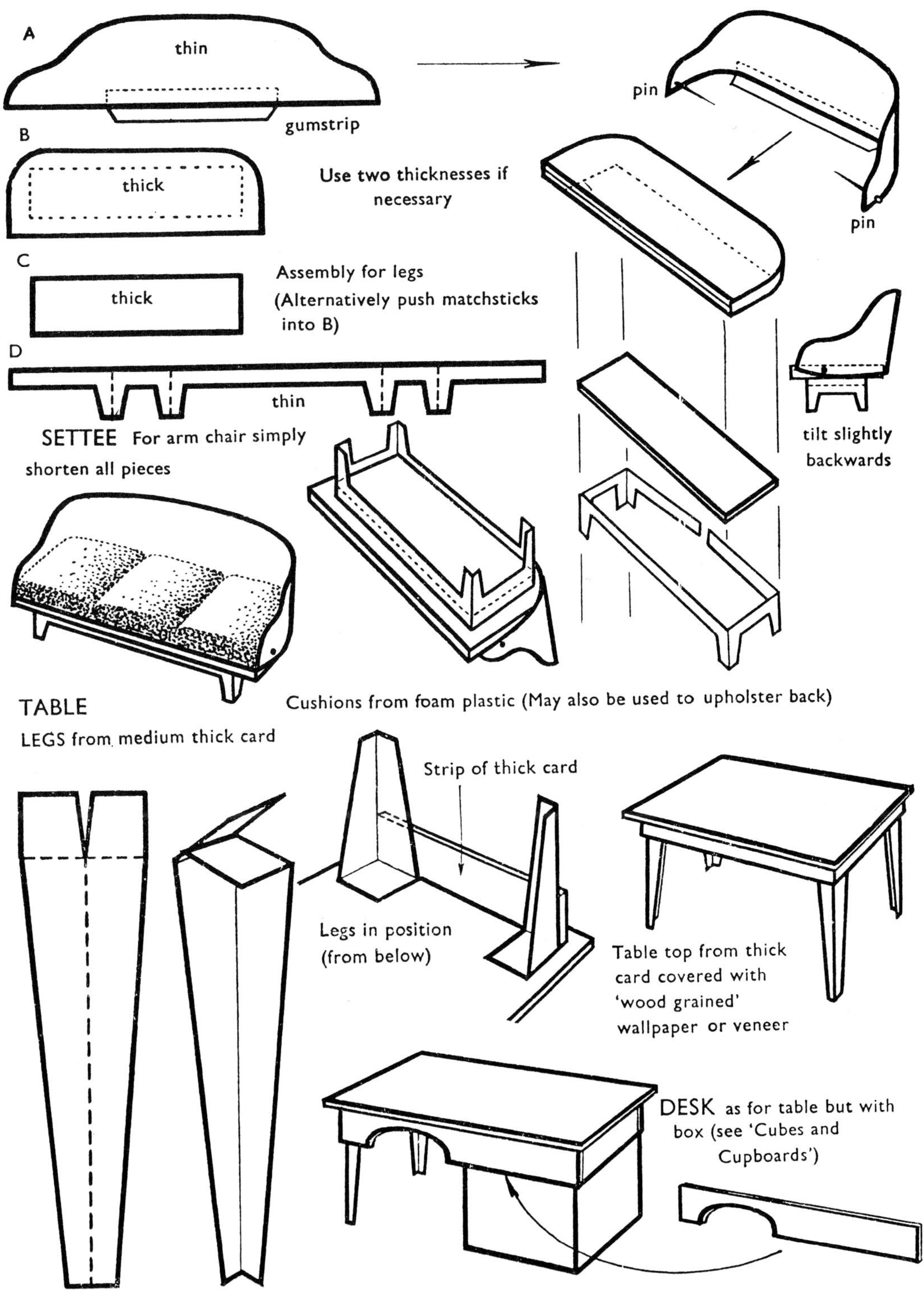
A
thin
gumstrip
pin
pin
B
thick
Use two thicknesses if necessary
C
thick
Assembly for legs (Alternatively push matchsticks into B)
D
thin
tilt slightly backwards
SETTEE For arm chair simply shorten all pieces
Cushions from foam plastic (May also be used to upholster back)
TABLE
LEGS from medium thick card
Strip of thick card
Legs in position (from below)
Table top from thick card covered with 'wood grained' wallpaper or veneer
DESK as for table but with box (see 'Cubes and Cupboards')

This **Easy Chair** is shown in considerable detail because it clearly demonstrates four convenient steps in the evolution of a simple model. It therefore provides a useful analysis for teachers intending to design small models themselves.

Marking out. Make a diagram of the intended model on graph paper. The squares make it easier to visualise the scale. They also help in checking dimensions against each other, and in comparing the size and shape of different views of the object. The dimensions must then be transferred to the cardboard. This is best done with a pair of dividers, or with tracing paper. Note that some measurements may be taken from the front elevation, and some from the side elevation. It is essential to discern which is giving the true dimension and which is giving only an appearance of it. In this case all the dimensions on the side elevation are true, but on the front elevation only the horizontal dimensions are true.

Cutting out. There are three different 'solid' shapes – two arms–A, the back–B, and the seat–C. Each arm is composed of three pieces – A (1) (double) and A (2), so four of A (1) and two of A (2) will be required. Likewise the back is composed of three pieces – B (1) (double) and B (2). The seat is composed of one piece only – C.

Construction. A, B, and C are all made up independently into their solid forms. As C is only a single piece it can, of course, only be folded into an approximation of its final shape.

Assembly. Counting both arms, there are four shapes altogether. Now these have only to be fixed to each other in order. Start with a single shape – one of the arms (i). Fix the back to it (ii). Fix to these two the seat (iii). Finally fix to these three the other arm (iv).

This sequence of events may seem unduly long-winded for what is, after all, a very simple model. It is given in order to clarify the approach when inventing models in the absence of any existing diagram.

For anyone simply requiring a chair in a hurry an empirical approach is probably quicker.

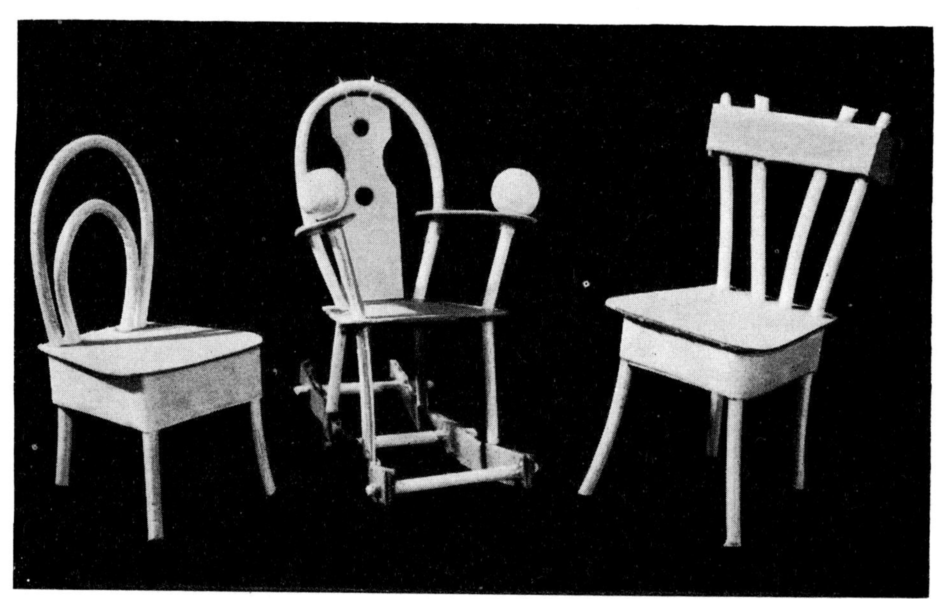

Traditional chairs. Height about 3in. Frame and supports of unpainted cane topped with white wooden beads. Seats, back-rests and arm-rests of grey cardboard punched to admit cane. Rockers corrugated cardboard. Seats glued to supporting boxes of corrugated card with legs passing through corrugations. Page 51.

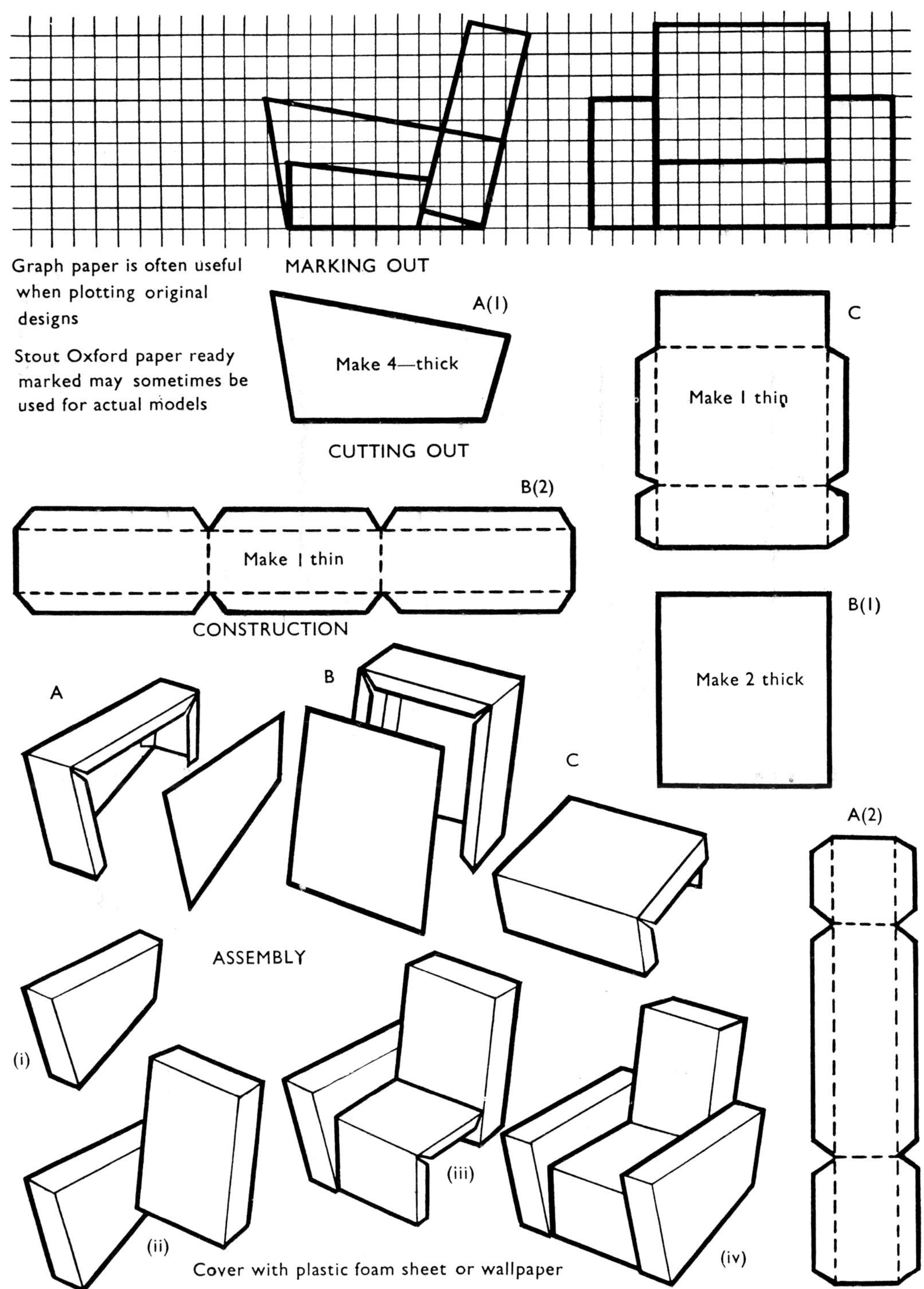
Graph paper is often useful when plotting original designs
Stout Oxford paper ready marked may sometimes be used for actual models
MARKING OUT
A(1)
Make 4—thick
CUTTING OUT
C
Make 1 thin
B(2)
Make 1 thin
CONSTRUCTION
B(1)
Make 2 thick
A
B
C
A(2)
ASSEMBLY
(i)
(ii)
(iii)
(iv)
Cover with plastic foam sheet or wallpaper

SOME VARIATIONS AND DETAILS OF CONSTRUCTION

see previous pages for basic 'box and table' methods (See also 'Cubes and Cupboards')

No step by step instructions are given here but only broad principles for individual development

Ready-made boxes and cartons often provide suitable raw material

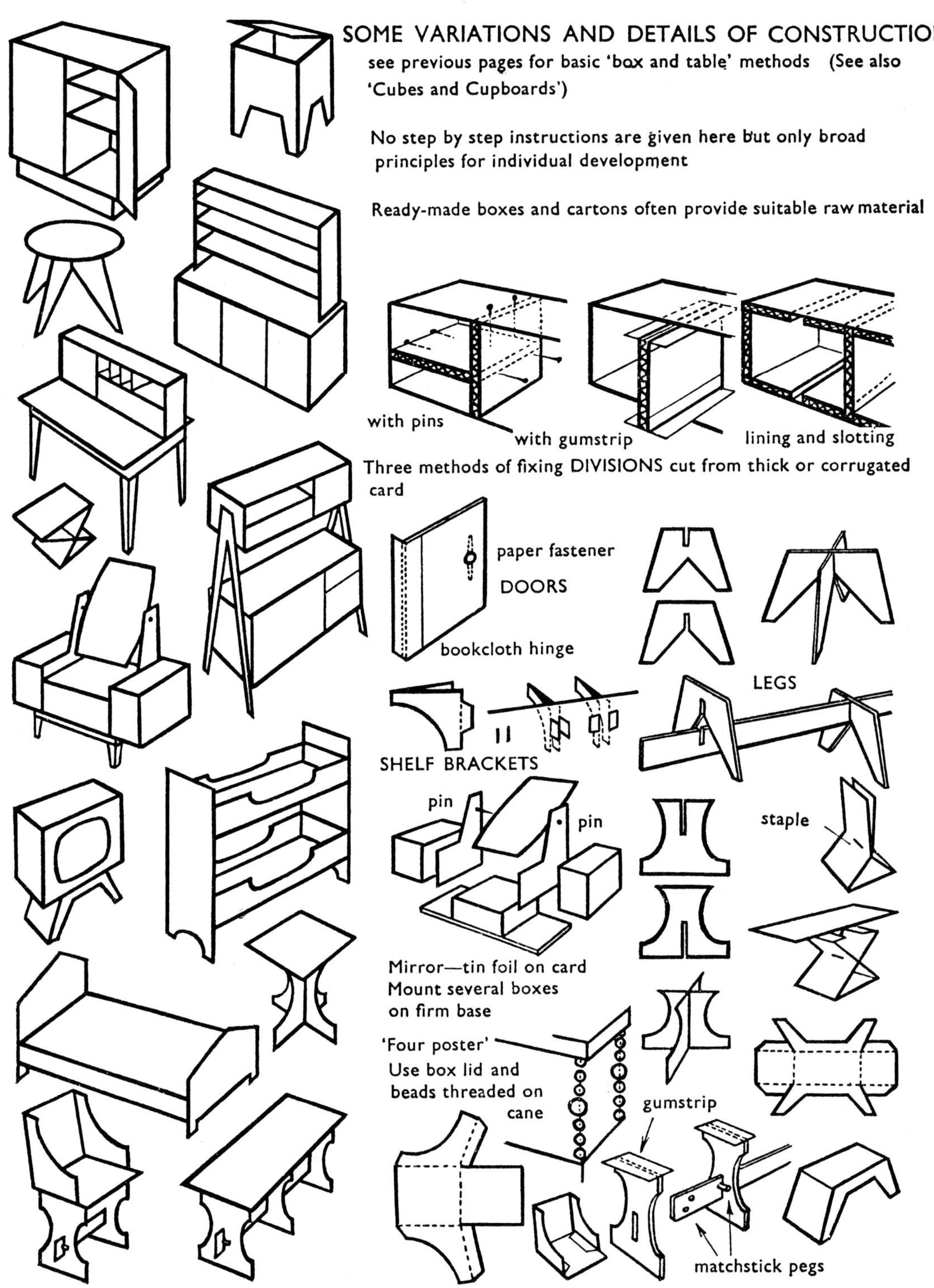

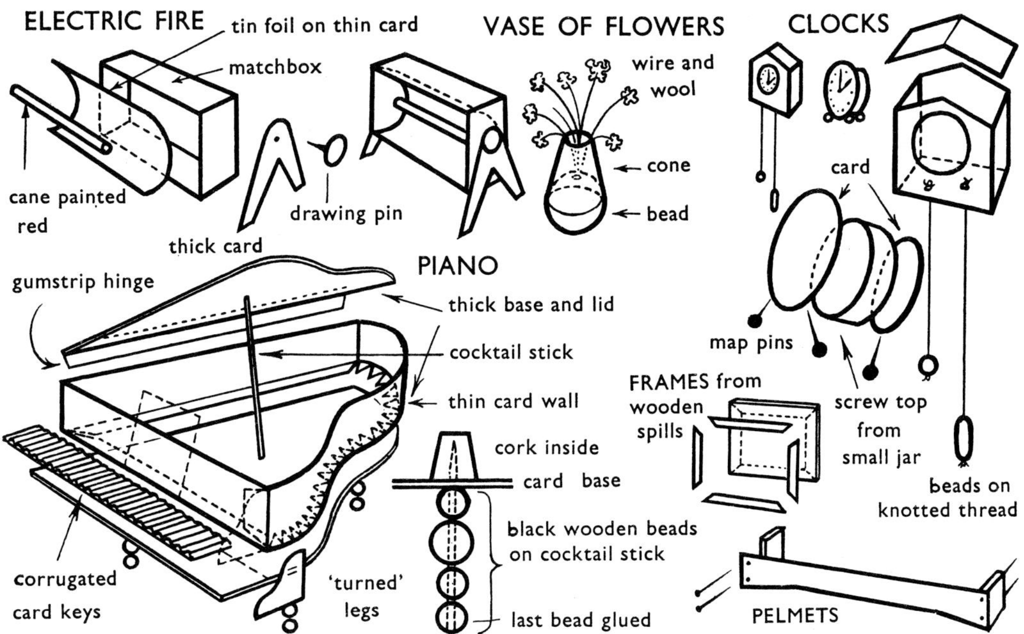

Furnishing Accessories. In a composite model the details often contribute very largely to the general effect. These are sometimes so small that ready-made components, such as beads and corks, must be brought into play. It is difficult to avoid slight inconsistencies of scale between details, but such problems need not become a burden. The children seldom worry. (See also page 29).

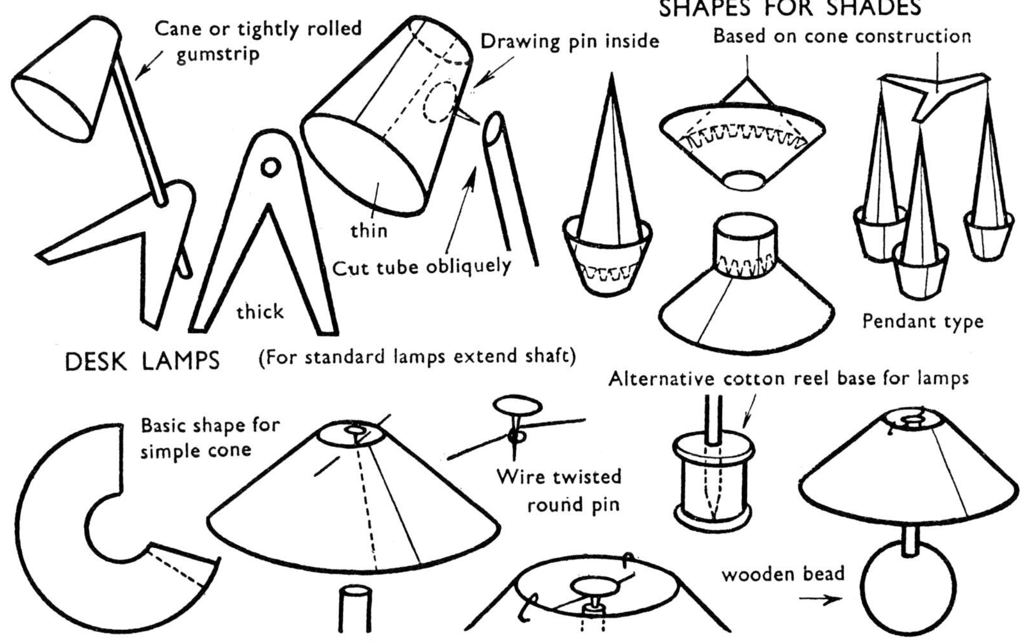

CARD AND WIRE

Plastic covered electrical wire in bright colours is suitable. Also copper wire

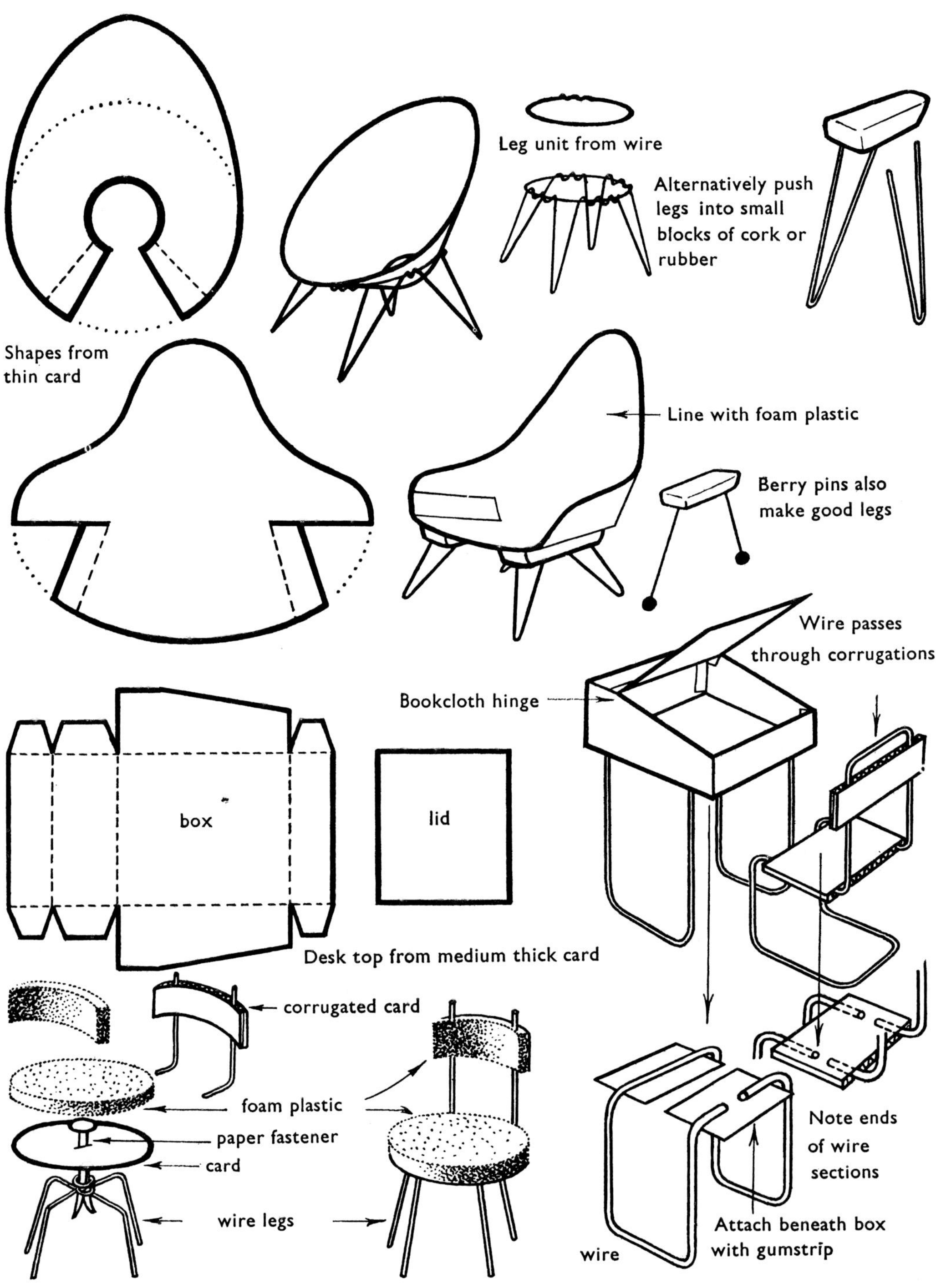

THICK CARD AND CORRUGATED CARD WITH BASKET CANE
Actual basketwork cane (unsoaked) is passed through holes punched in thick cardboard shapes
Cut this shape last
ROCKING CHAIR
Beads glued on
TYPE A
Use leather punch for holes
Ensure cane fits tightly
glue
(i) First assemble the rocker
Legs held in corrugations
Secure joints with glue when finally assembled
pins
Gumstrip under seat
(ii)
(iii)
(iv)
(v) Finally cut and fit shape for back
Other types of 'Windsor' furniture which may also be fitted to rockers
TYPE B
From behind
corrugated
TYPE C
corrugated
corrugated

An Interior. If the whole class participates, then models of interiors tend to look rather more like furniture showrooms than living rooms. Several smaller groups are usually a better proposition. It may even be possible to study an entire house, allocating each room to a different group of children.

Each model room should be set up inside a large box or carton from which the front and most of the top have been removed. A window opening, glazed with a sheet of clear Perspex provides another viewing angle. First consider the general decor – colour of walls, fabrics for curtains and floor covering, etc. Curwen papers and other bookcraft papers are very suitable for certain walls. Then assemble the furniture inside.

Ships. Shipping provides a wealth of material which is at once both decorative and functional. Small pleasure craft, particularly, give scope for bright colours and look cheerful bedecked with gaily patterned sails or flags. Some children are rather apt to overdo this aspect of the craft, but teachers who are familiar with their pupils will already know the realists from the romantics.

Some of the simpler vessels may be made reasonably watertight with a thick coat of wax crayon, or better still, varnish. Even so, the floating of cardboard models should not be undertaken lightly. There must be no gaps in the waterproof covering, and if the glue is not impervious to water the launching may soon end in disaster. Only flat-bottomed craft float properly. Other types usually capsize.

It is quite a simple matter to construct a model beach as a setting. Push a table up against the wall and seal the angle with a length of gumstrip. (No doubt it is already apparent that the author regards this material as a sovereign remedy for most of the ills which the model maker is likely to encounter). Spread upon the table some fine sand heaped up towards the wall. Cut breakwaters from thick cardboard and push these into the sand. A simple jetty or landing stage may be devised (see page 30 and the bottom of page 73). Such a setting will enable round-bottomed boats to be set up which would otherwise topple over on any hard surface.

The diagrams on pages 58 and 59 are self-explanatory. It may be useful to point out, however, that miniature vessels attached to a large-scale wall map help to pinpoint shipping routes, and may be helpful in illustrating the Geography lesson.

For **Dinghy** 1, opposite, the main material is corrugated cardboard – the sort which is flat on one side and corrugated on the other. This material is fairly strong, yet reasonably pliable. Lay down the piece to be used – corrugations upwards – and rub firmly with a ruler in one direction only. This will flatten the ridges and the card will more closely resemble 'shiplap' boarding. Fold it in half and cut the shape of the boat through both thicknesses. Apply glue to the inside ends and clamp between bulldog clips until set. Cut the seat from thick card. Carefully ease the sides of the vessel apart and insert the seat which will then act as a prop. Finally cut strips of card or pieces from coloured wooden spills. Use these for the mast and to trim the ends as shown.

For **Dinghy** 2, the sides of the vessel are cut from a folded length of thin card. The base and stern are of thick card hinged together. This should have glue run along the edges and be laid flat on the desk. The sides can then be attached, fixing at the bows first.

For the **Gondola,** take two pieces of thin card and glue together at each end (see shaded portion on diagram). The characteristic shape for the sides may then be cut. Ease the two sides open in the middle and lower them round the glued edges of the thick base. Again it is essential to work with the base flat on the desk.

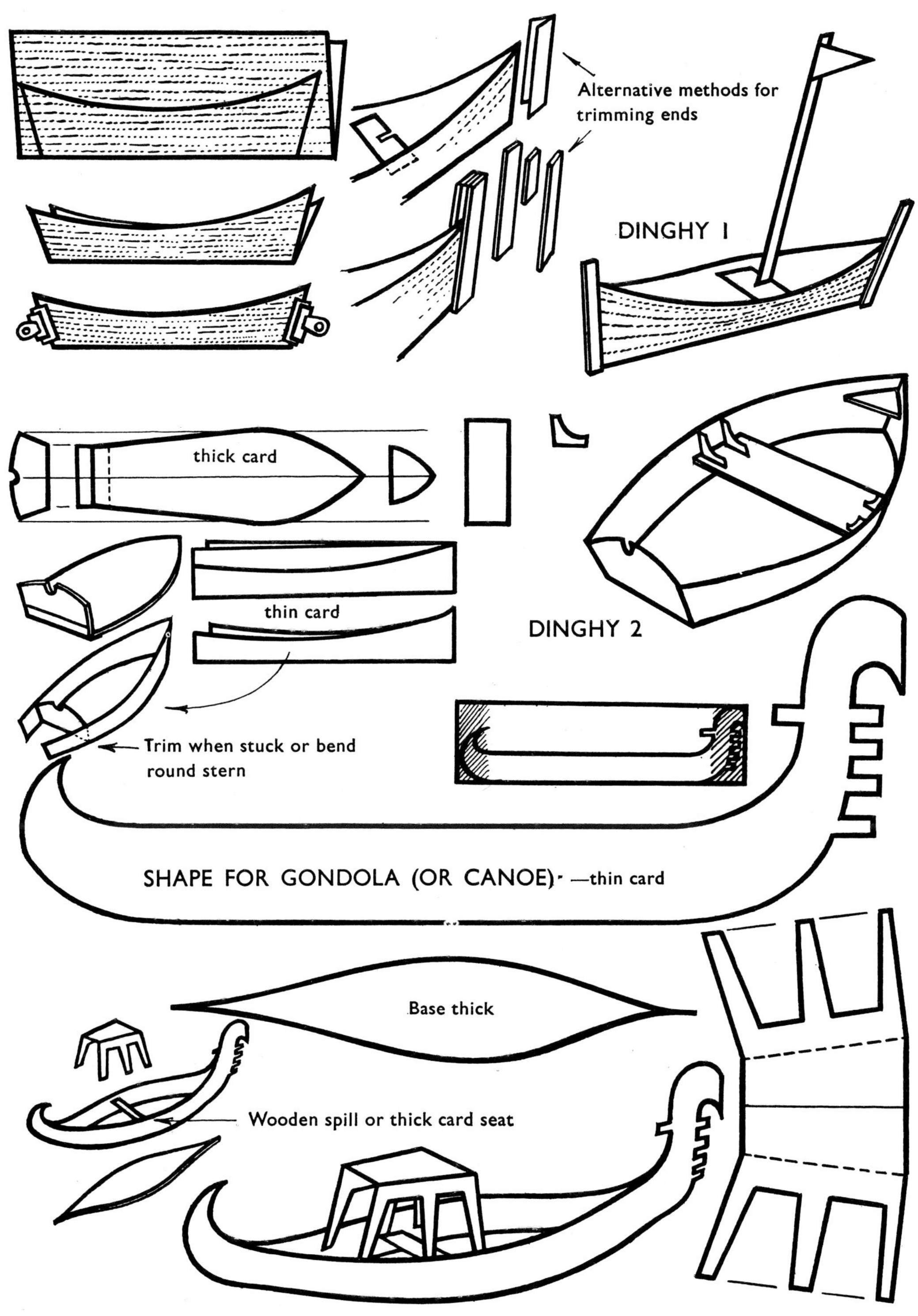
Alternative methods for trimming ends
DINGHY I
thick card
thin card
DINGHY 2
Trim when stuck or bend round stern
SHAPE FOR GONDOLA (OR CANOE) —thin card
Base thick
Wooden spill or thick card seat

The **Punt** offers quite a straightforward piece of marking out. It should be quicker to draw and assemble this in one piece as illustrated. The important thing is to ensure that the open plan is symmetrical, and that the sloping line at each end of each side is exactly the same length as the section to which it must fit. Assemble the main shape, but punch holes for the uprights before gluing the final tabs. The uprights are lengths of cane or knitting needles. They support the canopy which is shaped like a box lid with a decorative edge.

The **Barge** employs the same basic construction as just described. To make pointed bows, adapt the model as indicated. Fold in the sloping part at each side until both meet in the centre. Glue these down to the sloping floor of the bows and trim off the surplus card. Obviously the vessel must not be too broad in the beam compared with the length of the sloping part. A stout deck is mounted above and secured to the sides with gumstrip tabs. The superstructure (if any) is mounted on top of this.

The **Tug** needs two thick identical deck shapes. These are fixed, one directly above the other, with matchboxes or layers of thick card between to give the vessel depth. The sides are made from one continuous length of thin card, rising at the bows, and overlapping at one side. Apply glue to the edges of the deck shapes and wrap the thin card firmly round. At the bows and at the stern, snip the thin card down to the level of the deck. Overlap the resulting edges and pinch to a sharp fold, thus inclining the sides inward over the deck. Attach a length of string round the vessel as a fender. The superstructure is adequately shown in the diagram.

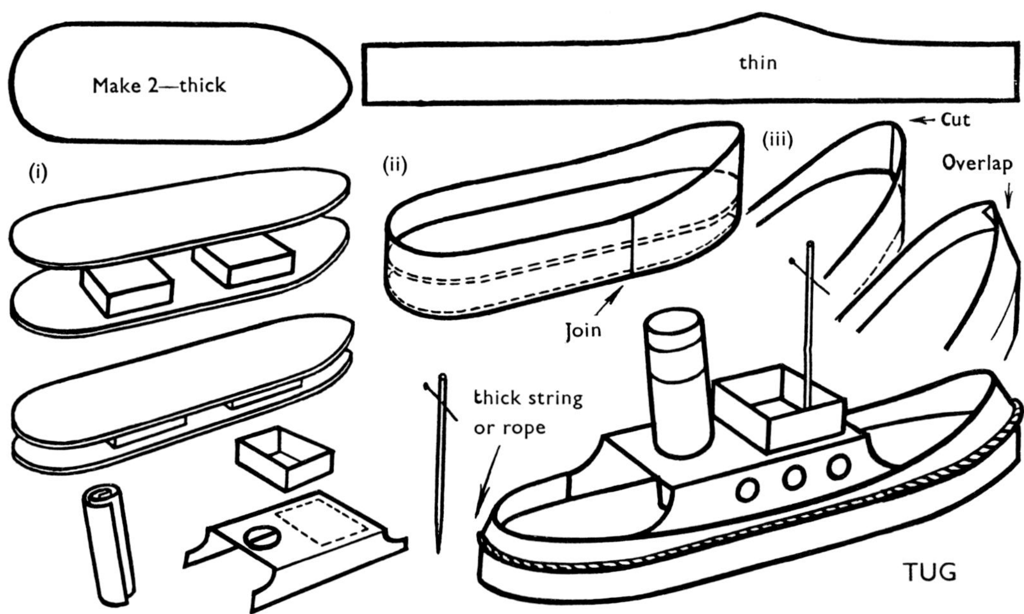

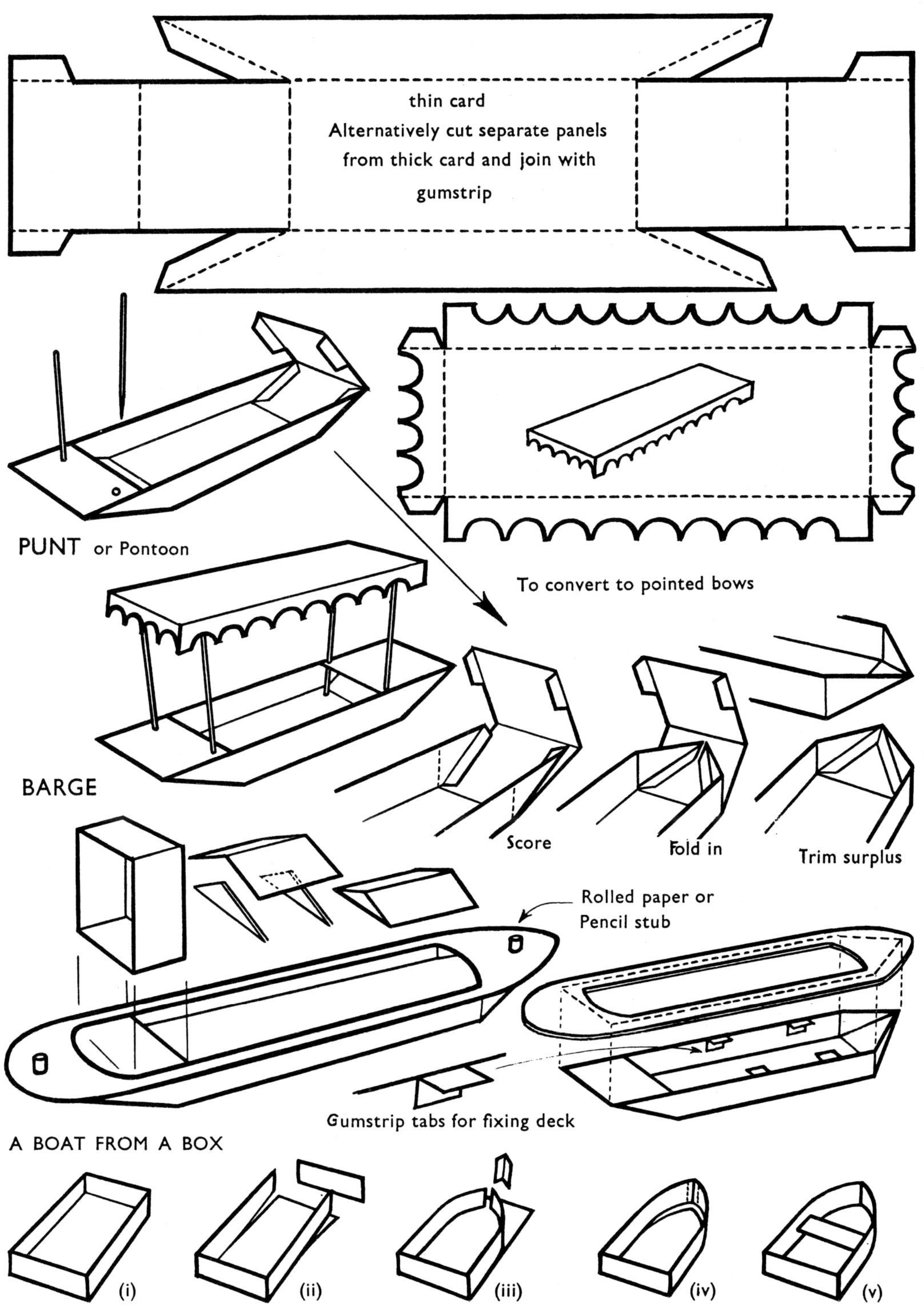
thin card
Alternatively cut separate panels
from thick card and join with
gumstrip
PUNT or Pontoon
To convert to pointed bows
BARGE
Score
Fold in
Trim surplus
Rolled paper or
Pencil stub
Gumstrip tabs for fixing deck
A BOAT FROM A BOX
(i)
(ii)
(iii)
(iv)
(v)

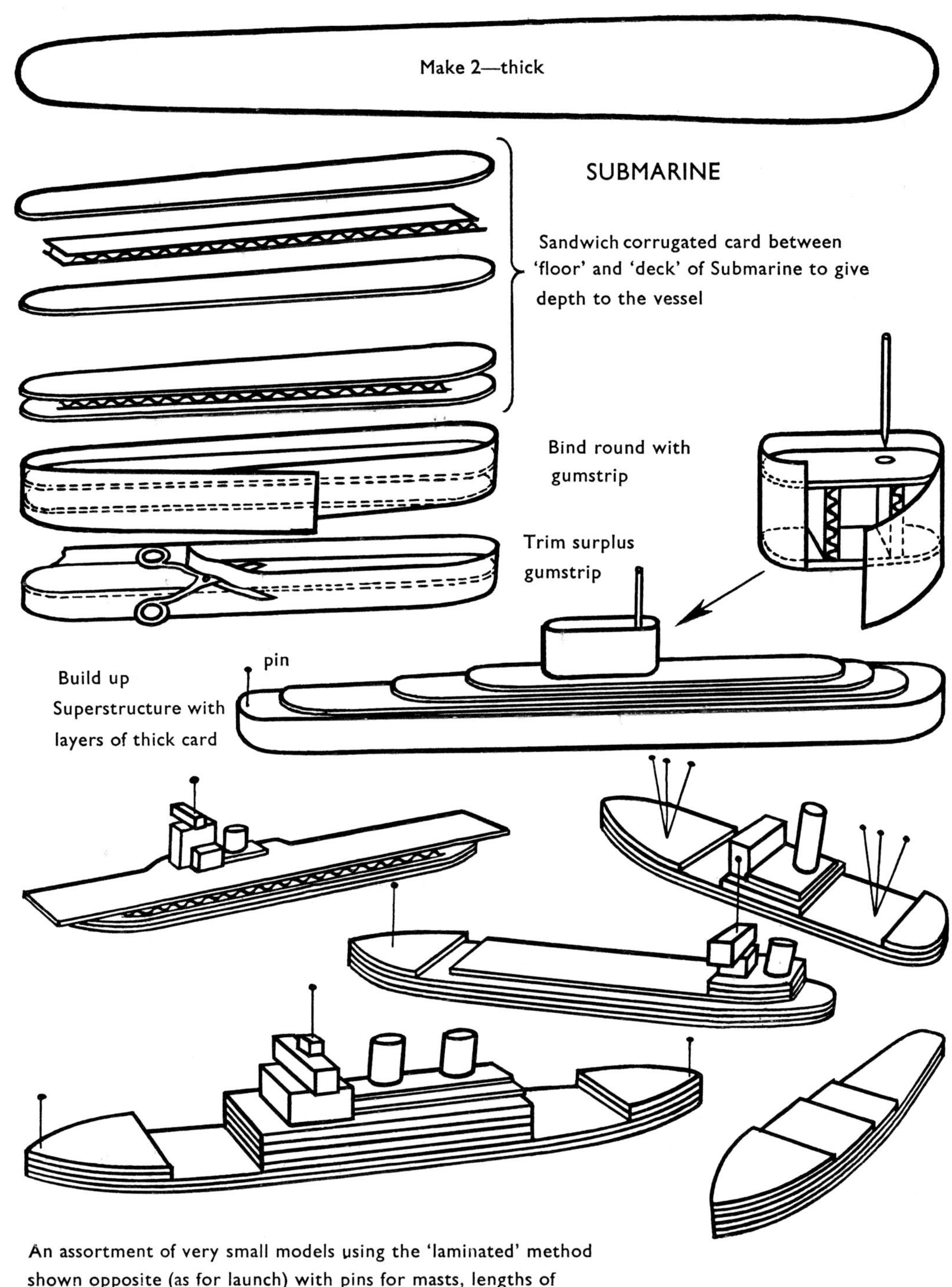

An assortment of very small models using the 'laminated' method shown opposite (as for launch) with pins for masts, lengths of dowel or cane for funnels, and other details from cork or rubber

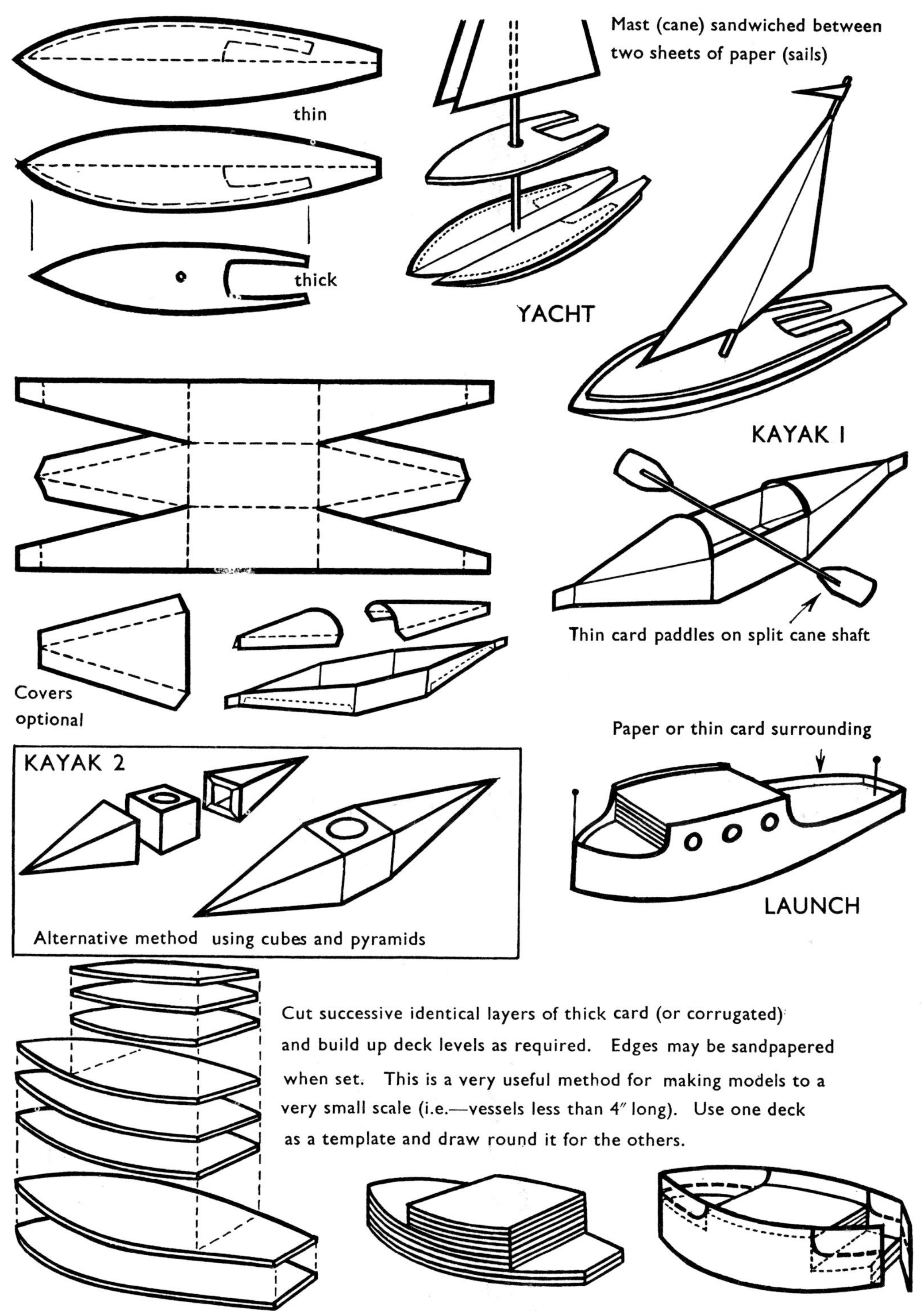

Cut successive identical layers of thick card (or corrugated) and build up deck levels as required. Edges may be sandpapered when set. This is a very useful method for making models to a very small scale (i.e.—vessels less than 4″ long). Use one deck as a template and draw round it for the others.

Things on wheels. For children, wheels are not the easiest of shapes to handle, especially if they are intended to revolve. They must invariably be cut from thick card, and this in itself presents a difficulty for the younger ones. Although they may draw round a penny quite successfully, the wheel sometimes assumes a very peculiar shape by the time it has been chopped out. In any case, although coins make convenient templates, it is still difficult to know where the middle is, except for certain foreign coins with holes in the centre which might almost have been made for the purpose. It is always possible to draw a square round the circle and mark in the diagonals, but the only reasonable method is to use a pair of compasses. School compasses are seldom adapted to the drawing of small circles, and for precision work the class will probably be wise to resort to some ready-made expedient.

Washers of various sorts will be found useful. Otherwise cut slices from corks with a sharp knife or a fine saw. A bread knife with a serrated edge is a handy instrument, and a small table vice to hold the cork will preserve the fingers intact.

The models in this section incorporate several features which are interchangeable. The vehicles themselves present no major problems and the methods should be largely apparent from the diagrams.

The **Wheelbarrow** is a simple box mounted between thick strips or wooden spills. If wooden beads are threaded on either side of the wheel, take note of the size of the beads when planning the box. They must not be so big as to force the struts away from the sides.

The **Perambulator** is a little more complicated. The wheel base is shown opposite, and the coach-work below. Construct the box a, and the side panels b and c. Assemble these first (i). The floor e, from thin card, is slightly wider than the chassis and is glued to the edges of the side panels completely enclosing one end of the pram (ii). The hood d, is made separately and glued to the side panels. The handle is mounted last. Note that small parts of the overhanging edge are folded up to permit the handle supports to lie flat on the side panels.

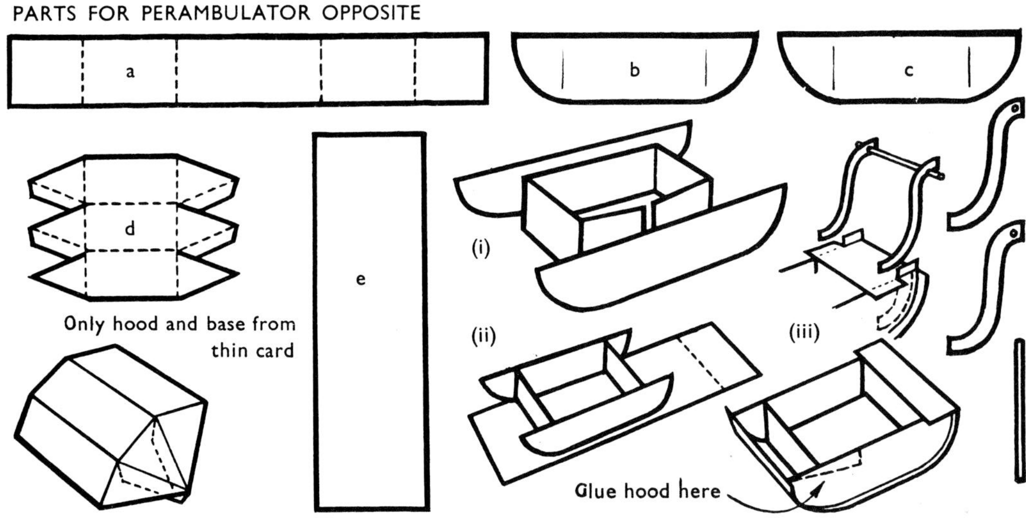

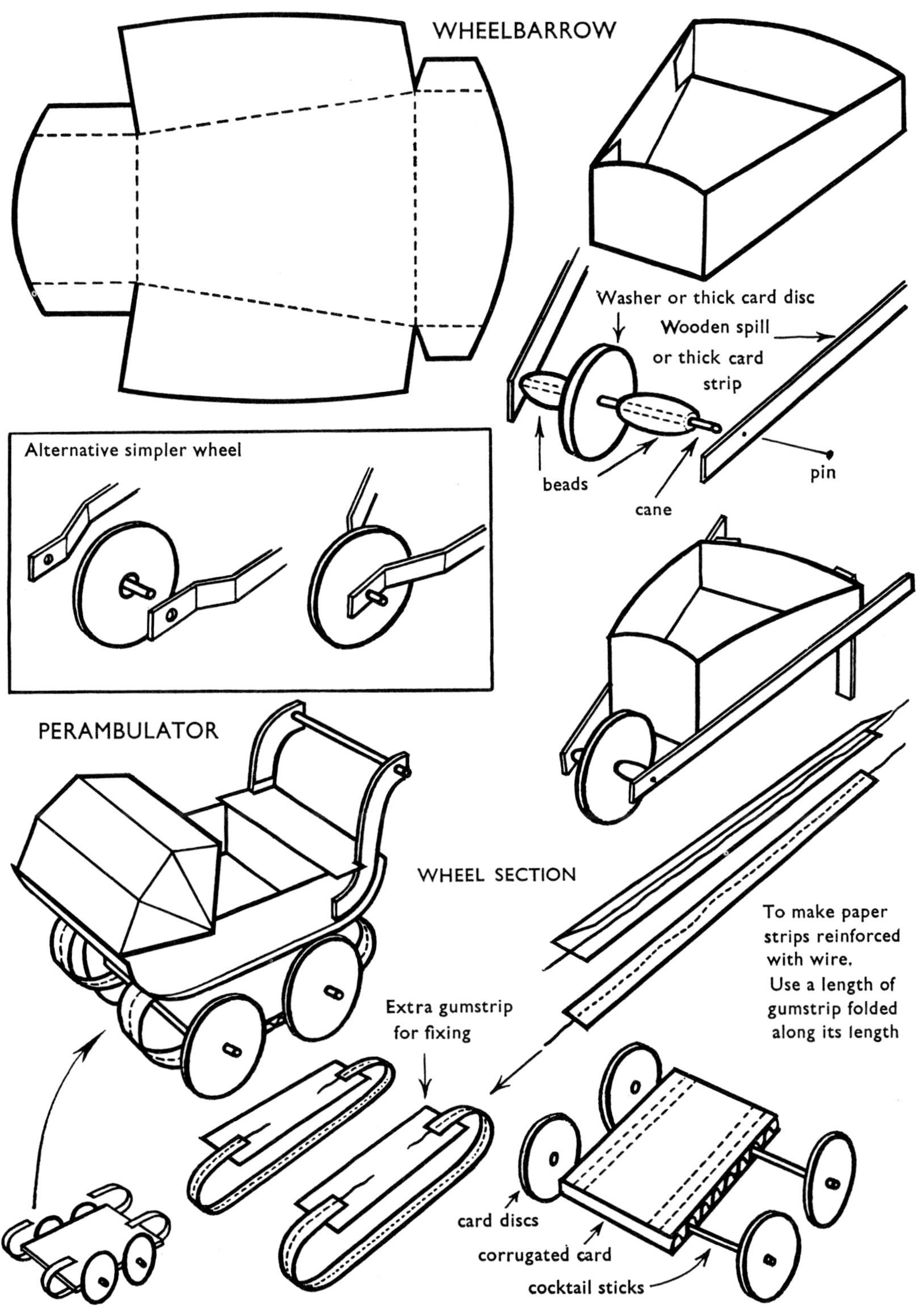
WHEELBARROW
Washer or thick card disc
Wooden spill
or thick card
strip
beads
cane
pin
Alternative simpler wheel
PERAMBULATOR
WHEEL SECTION
To make paper
strips reinforced
with wire.
Use a length of
gumstrip folded
along its length
Extra gumstrip
for fixing
card discs
corrugated card
cocktail sticks

The models below are built up on bases which must be cut from thick card. The wheels are fixed with pins, so there must therefore be sufficient thickness of card into which to push them. The front wheels should be smaller than the rear ones. This implies a difference in level between the wheel centres and this is not possible unless the base has been built up to a relatively good thickness. If there is difficulty in extending the thick card to form the shafts, then cut the shafts from a separate thinner piece and hinge them to the base. A piece of wire, bent to the shape of the shafts will steady them. Bind the wire and card together with gumstrip.

The models opposite have axles cut from basket-work cane. The wheels are attached with drawing pins driven through into the end of the cane. The cane must therefore be thick (at least grade 14). Moisten the ends to minimise the risk of splitting.

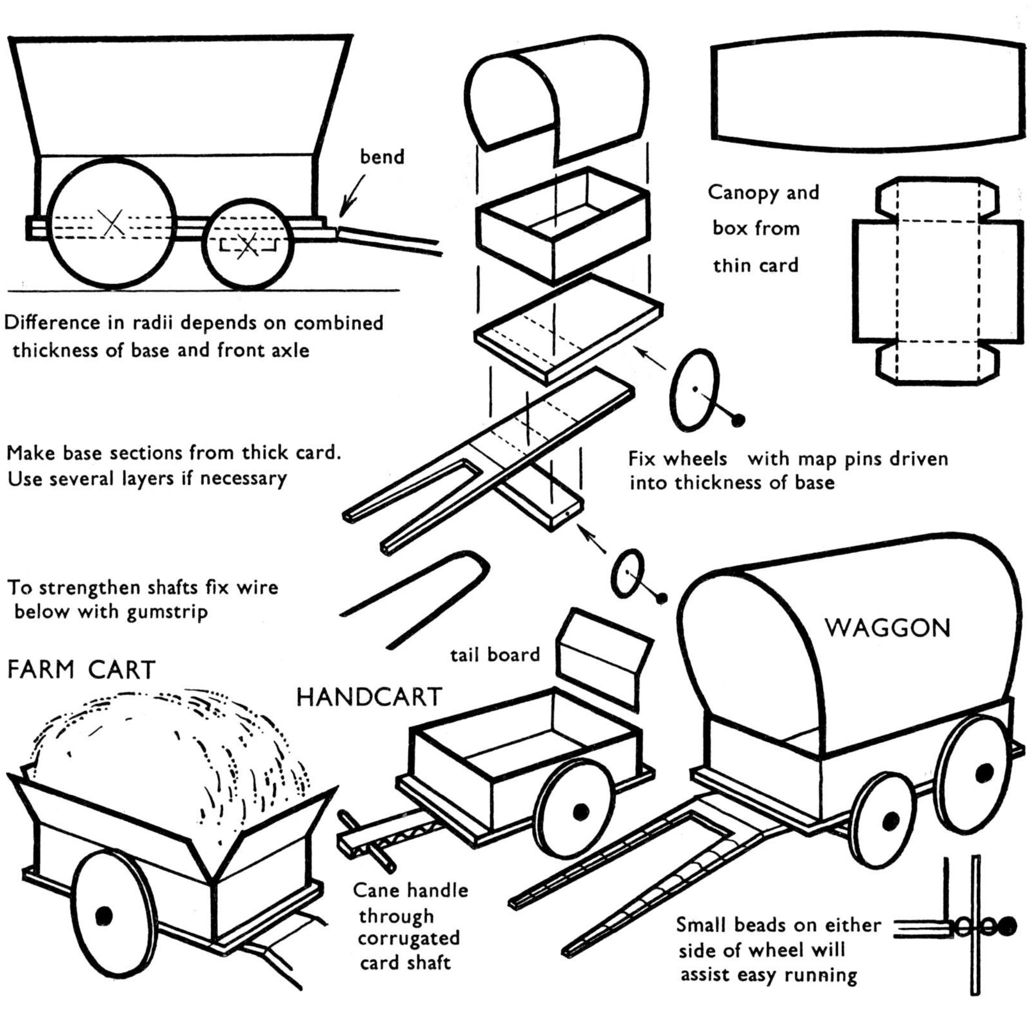

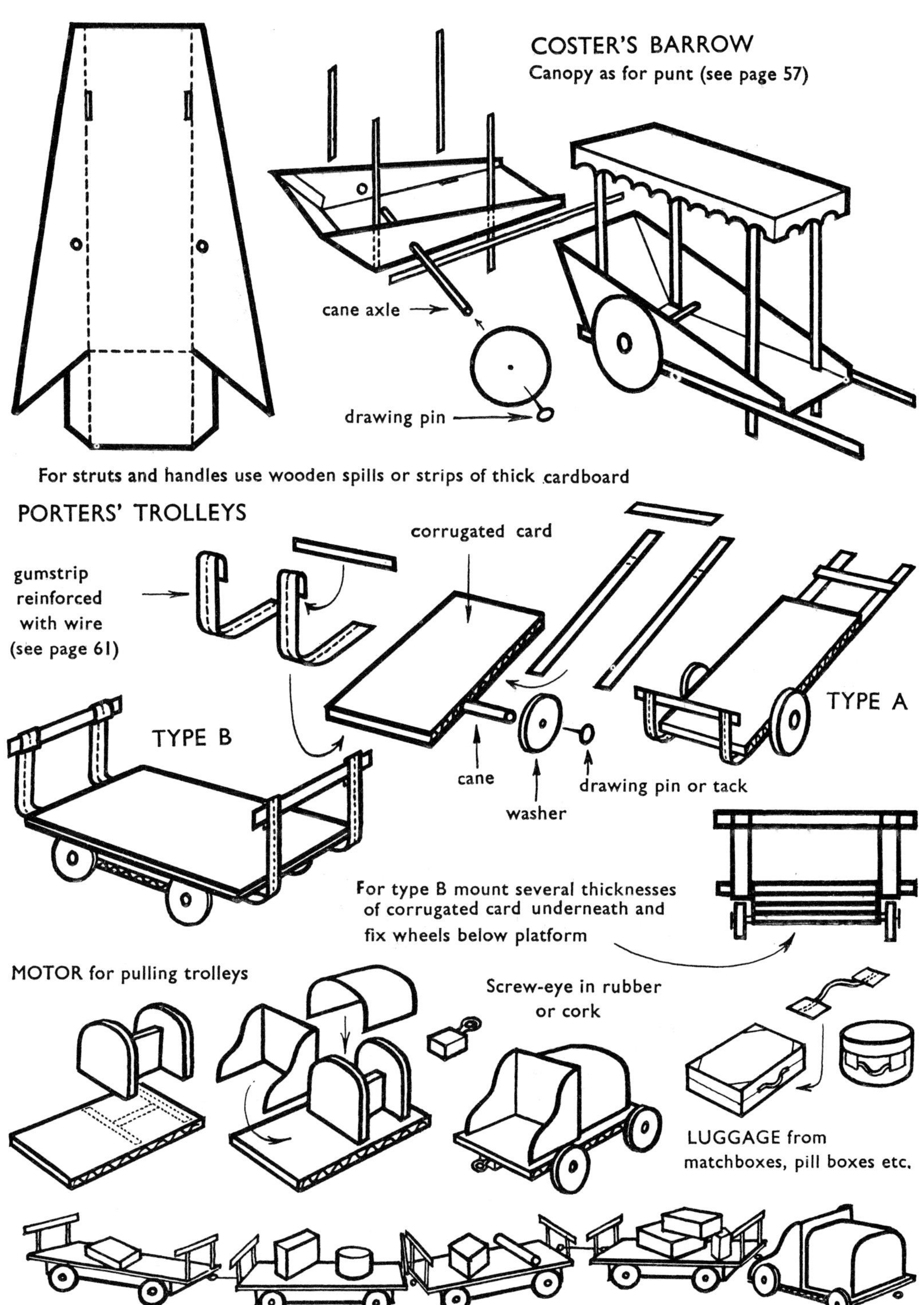
COSTER'S BARROW
Canopy as for punt (see page 57)
cane axle
drawing pin
For struts and handles use wooden spills or strips of thick cardboard
PORTERS' TROLLEYS
corrugated card
gumstrip
reinforced
with wire
(see page 61)
TYPE A
TYPE B
cane
washer
drawing pin or tack
For type B mount several thicknesses
of corrugated card underneath and
fix wheels below platform
MOTOR for pulling trolleys
Screw-eye in rubber
or cork
LUGGAGE from
matchboxes, pill boxes etc.

Saloon car. First draw the chassis on thin card. The layout must be perfectly symmetrical. The finger holes do not finally show. They are simply to provide a means of reaching into the model which, in its final stages, would otherwise be completely enclosed. The ends of the shape for the chassis should be made of ample length so that they may be trimmed later.

Next assemble the roof, see (i). This is formed from a square piece of thin card. For its actual dimensions refer again to the chassis. Bend up the sides of the chassis and glue them to the completed roof section, thus holding the roof section in a central position, see (ii). Note that the line A – B is exactly on a level with the top edge of each side. Then bend round the ends of the chassis, thus enclosing the ends of the vehicle at the front and back, see (iii). The free ends are tucked under and inside the roof section. The small V-shaped tabs are folded down over the sides and glued there. It may be necessary to cut off some of these tabs if there are too many. Try out the fixture before applying any glue.

Cut two identical wing sections from thick card (make one first and draw round it for the other). These should be slightly larger all round than the sides of the chassis. Ensure that the shapes for the mudguards are large enough to accommodate the wheels. Glue the wings flat on to the sides of the chassis. Cut strips of thin card for the mudguards. Bend these to fit, and glue them into the seating formed by the edge of the wings. Fit cane axles and pin on the wheels (see note on page 62).

The **Caravan** is considerably easier. Cut three identical shapes or 'walls' from thick card and draw a central line on each as a guide. The holes for the axle must be punched at the same point along this line in each piece. Make a box (or use a carton) which will not protrude beyond the edges of the three prepared shapes. Draw central guide lines inside the box. Place the side of the box against one of the walls making sure the centres are in alignment. Draw round it. Repeat on the other two walls. Cut slots as indicated in the middle wall. Cut corresponding slots in the ends of the box. To determine the base draw round the bottom of the box.

Stock car. Approx. 7in. long. Made in one piece from grey Sugar paper painted blue. Wheels of thick cardboard painted black and glued on.

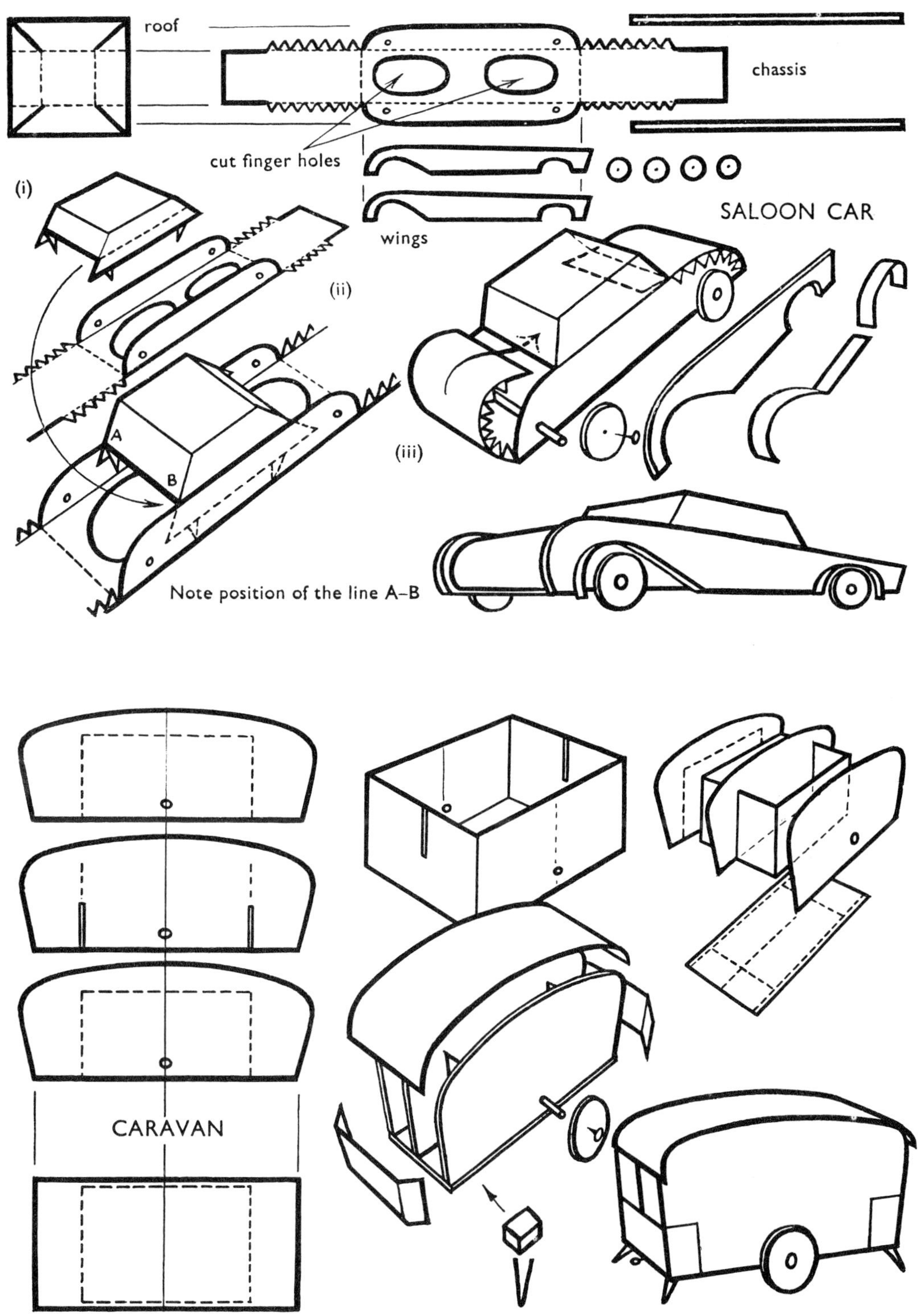
roof
chassis
cut finger holes
(i)
wings
SALOON CAR
(ii)
(iii)
A
B
Note position of the line A–B
CARAVAN

Punch axle holes in the sides of the box. Slot in the middle wall. Glue the other two on either side and the base underneath. Apply glue to the edges of the walls. Stick down the roof and end walls. Fix the wheels. A simpler version combines the roof and end walls in one continuous length folded under the base at each end, in which case the windows would be painted on the outside. The model may be further simplified by omitting the axle and fastening the wheels with pins into the edges of the base card, or by making the wheels fixtures. For corner supports glue pieces of cork underneath and push in pins or bent wire.

A miniature version may be easily built round a matchbox, in which case the middle wall may be ignored. Such a model, however, would probably be rather too obviously out of scale with the car above — page 65.

Another useful means of fixing wheels is introduced on this page. An axle cut from strong wire or cane passes through a tube. The tube is securely attached underneath the vehicle but the axle itself is left free. Thus the fixture between wheel and axle may be permanent. For the tube, use a length of drinking straw. The cane or wire must not fit too tightly. The wheels are best cut from cork because this provides a good thickness in which the axle may be embedded. First coat the end of the axle with glue.

For the **Racing car** below, wooden beads are also threaded on to the axle so that the wheels stand clear of the body. The body itself is quite straightforward provided that the base is made first and the other parts planned with reference to it. The supporting sections inside are all from thick card, and the covering sections from thin card.

The **Motor scooter** opposite is built on a base which must be firm, but also capable of being bent round to form the front. Thick Bristol board would be suitable. Form the bend round a pencil. Next mount the wheels. Then build the remaining sections from thin card, except for the steering column which is made from strong corrugated cardboard so that the handlebars may be pushed through. For handle grips bind the ends of the handlebars with coloured Sellotape.

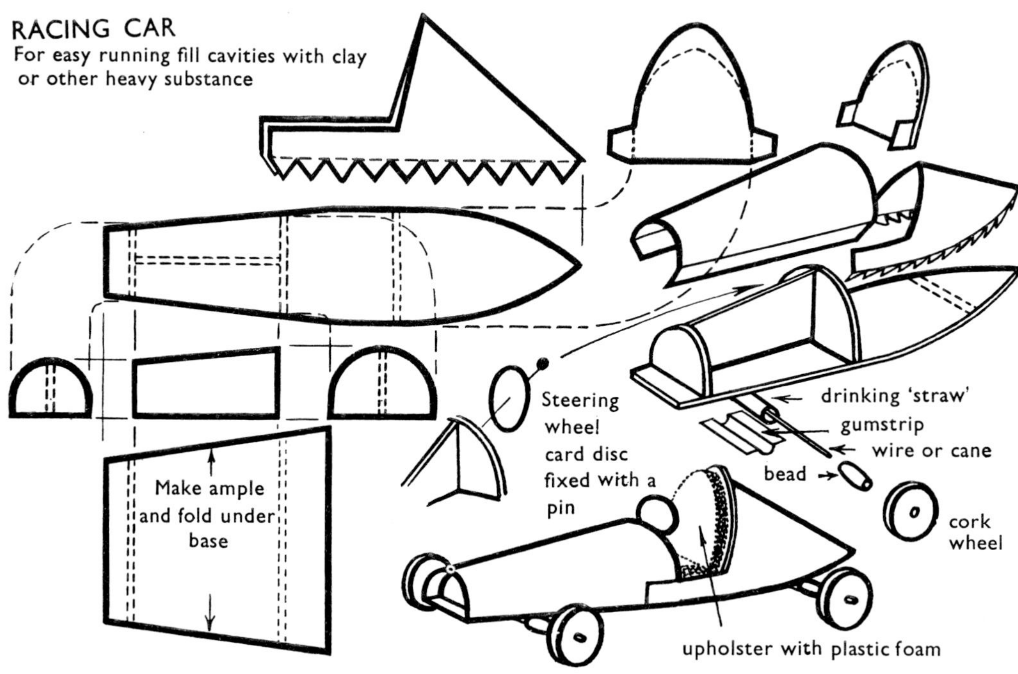

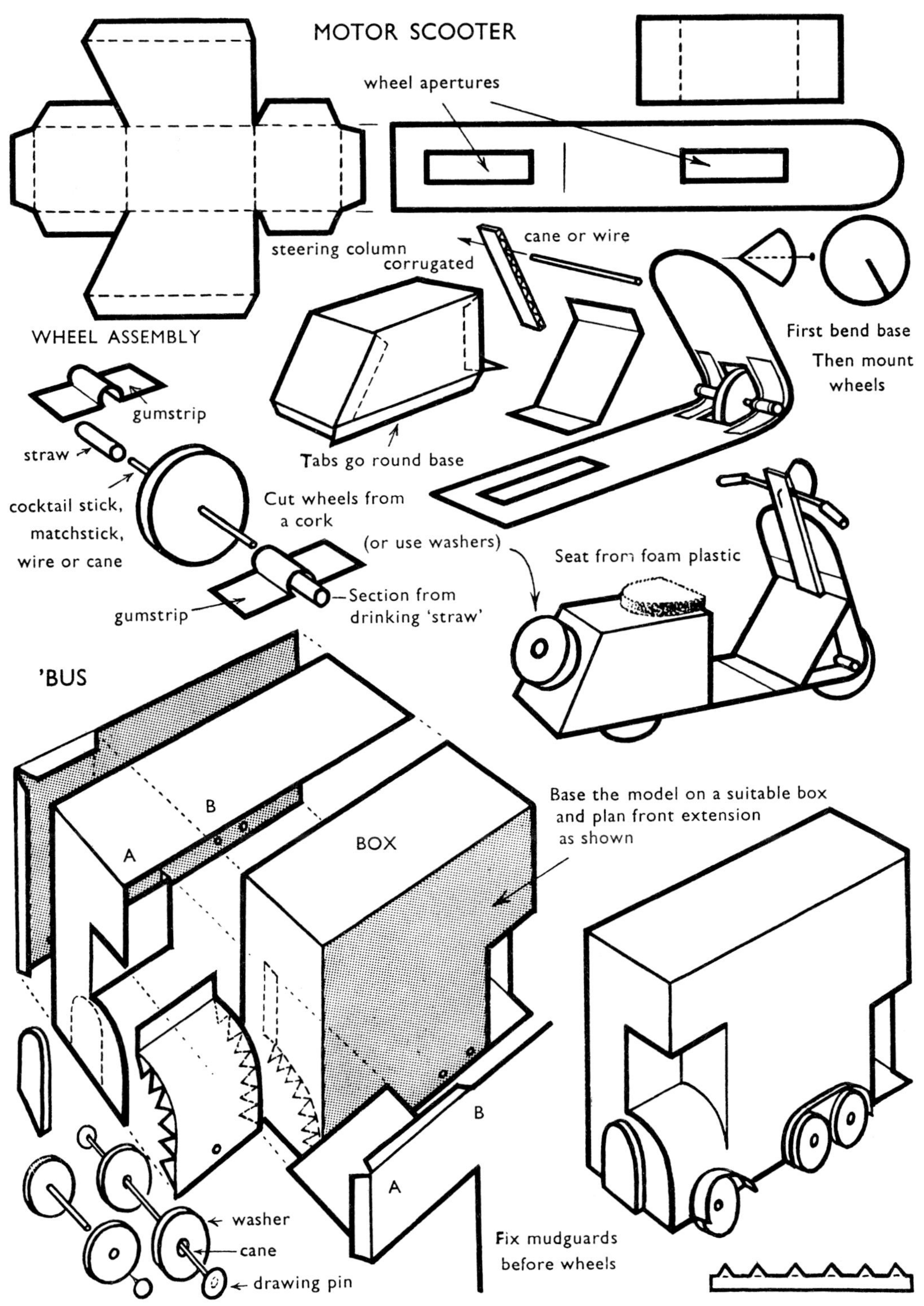
MOTOR SCOOTER
wheel apertures
steering column
corrugated
cane or wire
First bend base
Then mount
wheels
WHEEL ASSEMBLY
gumstrip
straw
Tabs go round base
cocktail stick,
matchstick,
wire or cane
Cut wheels from
a cork
(or use washers)
Seat from foam plastic
gumstrip
Section from
drinking 'straw'
'BUS
B
A
BOX
Base the model on a suitable box
and plan front extension
as shown
B
A
washer
cane
drawing pin
Fix mudguards
before wheels

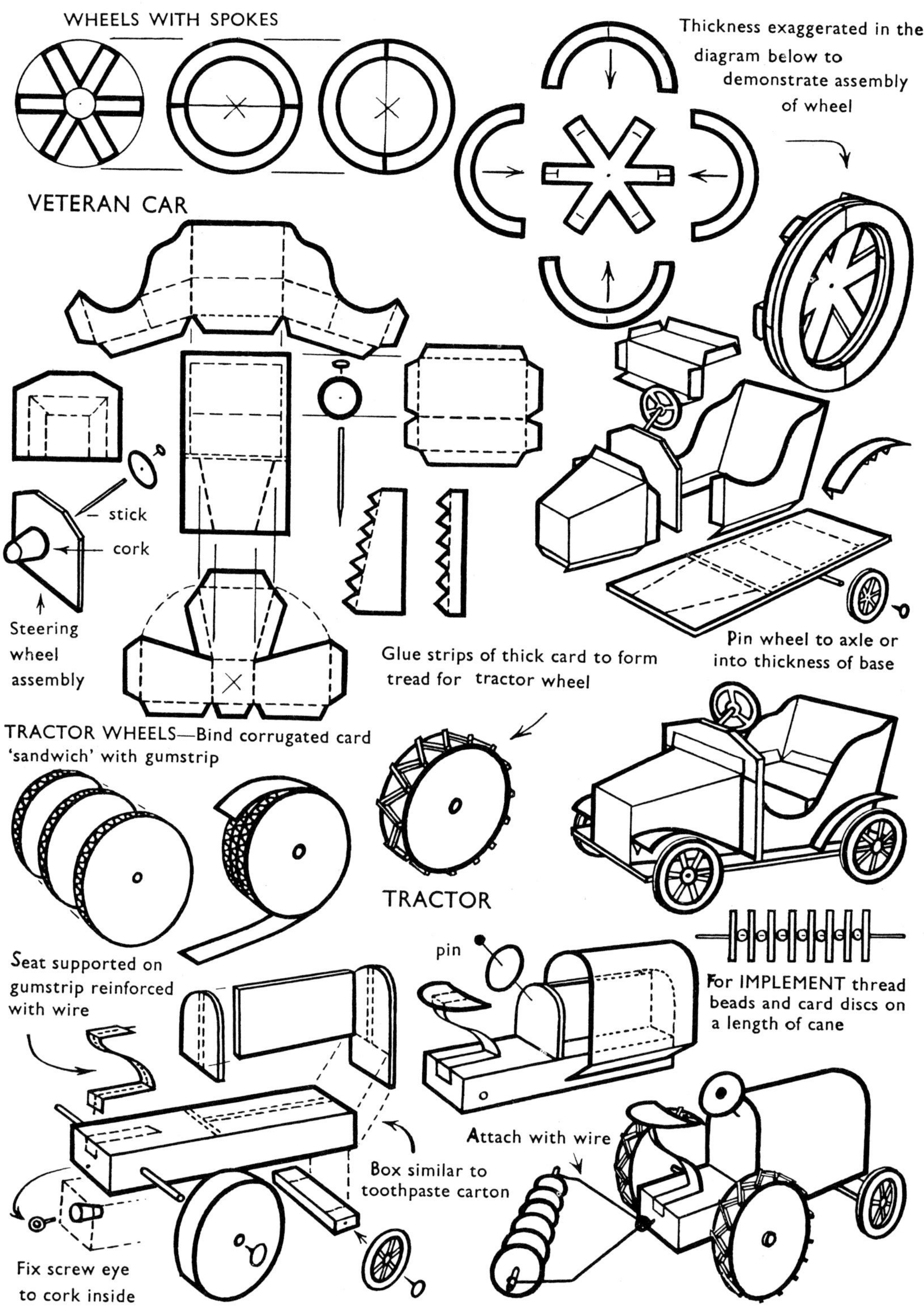
WHEELS WITH SPOKES
Thickness exaggerated in the diagram below to demonstrate assembly of wheel
VETERAN CAR
stick
cork
Steering wheel assembly
Glue strips of thick card to form tread for tractor wheel
Pin wheel to axle or into thickness of base
TRACTOR WHEELS—Bind corrugated card 'sandwich' with gumstrip
TRACTOR
pin
For IMPLEMENT thread beads and card discs on a length of cane
Seat supported on gumstrip reinforced with wire
Attach with wire
Box similar to toothpaste carton
Fix screw eye to cork inside

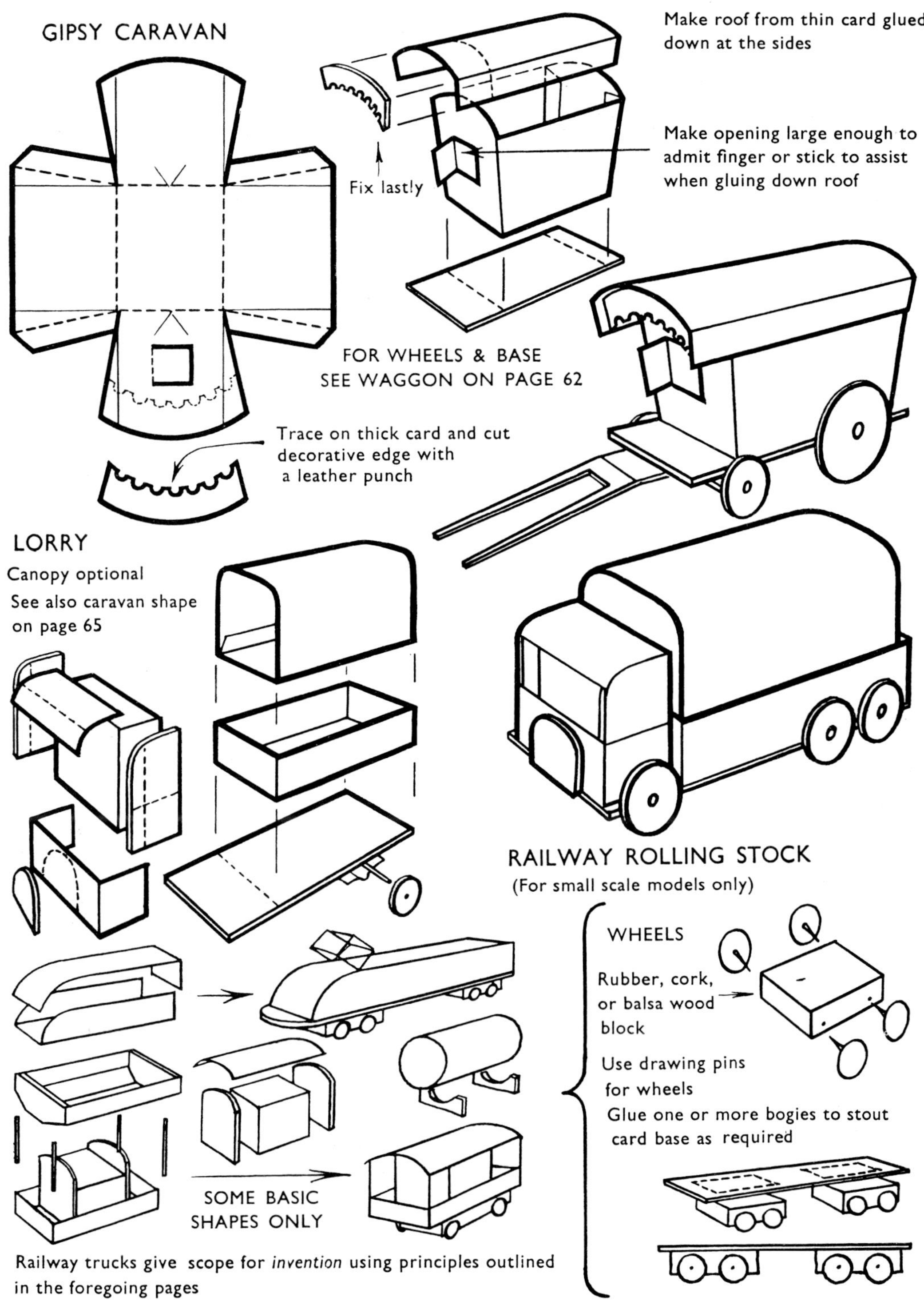
GIPSY CARAVAN
Make roof from thin card glued down at the sides
Make opening large enough to admit finger or stick to assist when gluing down roof
Fix lastly
FOR WHEELS & BASE SEE WAGGON ON PAGE 62
Trace on thick card and cut decorative edge with a leather punch
LORRY
Canopy optional
See also caravan shape on page 65
RAILWAY ROLLING STOCK
(For small scale models only)
WHEELS
Rubber, cork, or balsa wood block
Use drawing pins for wheels
Glue one or more bogies to stout card base as required
SOME BASIC SHAPES ONLY
Railway trucks give scope for *invention* using principles outlined in the foregoing pages

The **Bus** on page 67 is built round a box, preferably open at the base. The sides, top, and front of the box are all finally covered, and the covering pieces projected forward to form the driver's cabin. A careful scrutiny of the diagram should reveal the method of planning and assembling this front extension. Most children will enjoy cutting up magazines to glean advertisements with which to adorn the finished model.

Models on pages 68 and 69 should be clear from the diagrams alone.

Group models. In the miniature world of the model there need be no 'traffic problems'. Any congestion on the roads will only add to the general interest, and a busy model is usually more effective than one where all the components are static. Nevertheless, it is as well to plan the layout with plenty of 'parking space'.

The buildings in these three group models are explained in the next section except for the grandstand, which is only a simple box with the front cut away. The haystack is made from raffia (or hay!) glued on to a cone and cylinder base. The background effects are explained in chapter beginning on page 14.

The only difficulties which may arise in grouping models from different sections are minor problems of scale. Children, unless they are very fastidious, usually seem to attach little importance to such considerations. To make the combined models as authentic as possible, it would be advisable for the teacher to look ahead when planning the size of the individual pieces. Sandpaper and green felt are useful materials to bear in mind for road surfaces and grass verges.

Models of road junctions are sometimes useful aids when demonstrating to children the requirements of the Highway Code.

As a general rule, it is better not to plan the group in great detail beforehand so that everything has to conform to a rigid scheme. Rather accumulate a number of individual pieces and let them evolve naturally into a composite picture. Thus the children themselves will more easily play a part in the organisation of the design.

Cranes and construction. This short section is included as a logical introduction to the one that follows. Wherever buildings are going up there is usually plenty which will appeal to the imaginative model maker. Models of trim housing estates or town centres are very satisfying to make. They can be most impressive, but all the paraphernalia of the building site provides a no less fruitful source of ideas.

Wheelbarrows and lorries have already been described in the previous section. Likewise, it should not require much ingenuity to convert the tractor on page 68 into a bulldozer or an excavator. Caterpillar tracks can be made from strips of corrugated cardboard. The models shown opposite, in conjunction with the buildings on page 74, are intended to augment such a setting. The cranes will also be appropriate to docks or shipyards. In the latter case, see also pages 54-59.

Cranes. Type A is a working model which should be about 6 in. high and made from thick card. At the joints, instead of gumstrip, use bookbinder's cloth for strength. The upright column is a simple box with the back open. It should be wide enough to take a cotton reel. Note the slot in the front which permits the cotton reel to turn after projecting 'spokes' (map pins) have been fitted. The horizontal beam is made in one piece folded in two places. Note the paper fasteners to provide anchorage for the thread. Holes must be punched for the spindle which will connect both parts of the model. Ensure that the holes in the beam will correspond with the holes in the column. Holes must also be punched in the column for the spindle supporting the cotton reel. Attach one end of the thread to the cotton reel with a drawing pin. Mount the cotton reel inside the column. Spindles are cut from thick cane, and broad-topped drawing pins driven into the ends after assembly to keep them in position. Fit the beam to the column. Pass the other end of the thread through the top of the beam near to the paper fastener. Tie it on top to the paper fastener. Fix another thread to the end of the beam and add a cup hook. The complete model may be glued down on to its base, or better, if the base is wooden, fixed with a single nail through the floor of the column. A flat-headed nail, such as a roofing clout, is required. The crane will then turn on its base, and the beam may be raised or lowered by revolving the cotton reel with the aid of its projecting spokes.

Type B need not be quite so robust, and as it is a static model can be built to a greater height. The beam is the same as before but with box shapes mounted on top. The front of the operator's cabin should be closed in with clear acetate sheet or similar transparent material.

The **Scaffolding** method is very simple but very useful. It embodies a technique with all sorts of applications. (See diagram opposite.)

Ladders are made with matchstick rungs held between strips of thick card with holes punched along their length. Note that the holes must be punched (away from the edge) before cutting the strips.

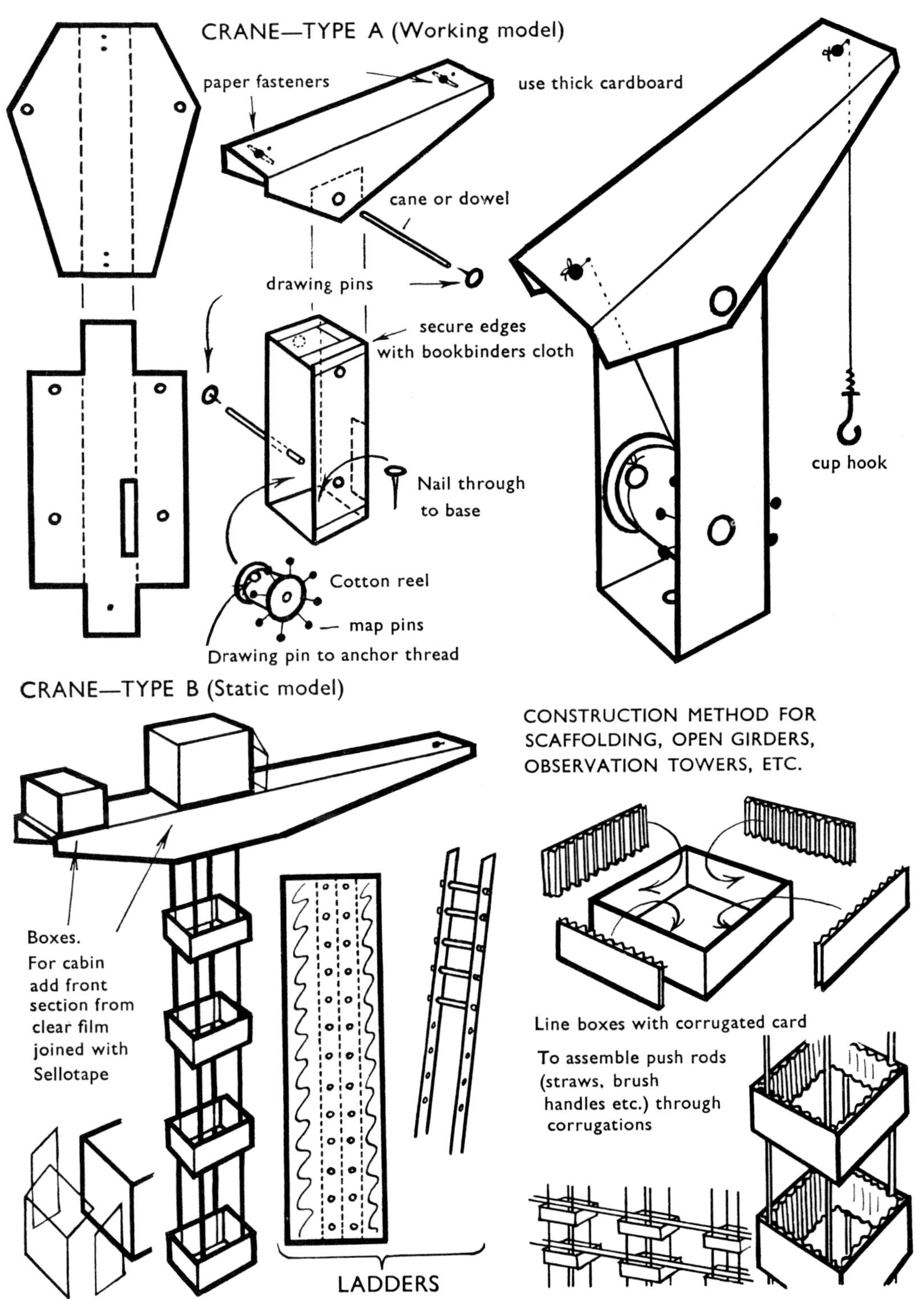
CRANE—TYPE A (Working model)
paper fasteners
use thick cardboard
cane or dowel
drawing pins
secure edges
with bookbinders cloth
Nail through
to base
cup hook
Cotton reel
map pins
Drawing pin to anchor thread
CRANE—TYPE B (Static model)
CONSTRUCTION METHOD FOR
SCAFFOLDING, OPEN GIRDERS,
OBSERVATION TOWERS, ETC.
Boxes.
For cabin
add front
section from
clear film
joined with
Sellotape
Line boxes with corrugated card
To assemble push rods
(straws, brush
handles etc.) through
corrugations
LADDERS

Buildings. Architectural models probably offer more scope than any other sort. There is scarcely another branch of model making more capable of individual treatment, yet originating from such simple foundations. All but a few buildings are box-like in construction. For this very reason, and because the basic fixing methods are covered elsewhere under 'Basic Shapes', many of the models in this section are presented in diagrammatic form only.

Pages 80 to 83 will be found to contain much of the information which is fundamental to the building of houses. Roofs are shown on squared paper so that the shapes most commonly required can be seen as flat sections and transferred more easily to cardboard. The supporting box structure is shown separately. Indeed, it is recommended that wherever practicable, roof and walls be regarded as separate shapes until the final assembly.

Except for the three gateways (pages 88, 89), the models make no serious pretensions to architectural style. Children are sometimes apt to do all sorts of outrageous things and television aerials crop up in the most unexpected places. Nevertheless, there has at least been some attempt to draw a clear distinction between the modern and the traditional. The teacher may find here some useful material for the History lesson, but the models make no great contribution to architectural appreciation.

The simplest of buildings, however, provided there are enough of them, will give the class an opportunity to express their ideas, however naïve, on town and country planning.

The models opposite are quite elementary.

The **Sentry Box** uses thin card for the front, and for the side walls. The diagram shows how these two sections may be planned together with the aid of compasses. For the back, draw round the front section on thick card. These three pieces are then assembled and two pieces of overhanging thick card added for the roof.

The **A.A. Box** is the same as the above except that no opening is cut in the front. Small dormer roofs are made from squares (provided the main roof slopes at 45°), and sign boards mounted on top with a berry pin.

The **Police Box** has upright sides, but a rather distinctive roof. Plan the shape like a Maltese cross as in the diagram. Make a narrow strip marked off in four sections (each section equivalent to the straight tab on each arm of the cross). Set up this strip as a shallow four-walled enclosure and mount the cross on this framework (each tab covering one wall of the enclosure). The completed roof is fixed with gumstrip to a thick cardboard square which is glued to the main box. The plinth is formed from strips of thick card.

The **Chicken coop, Garage, or Kennel** are all made from separate sections of thick card joined with gumstrip. The garage has a cardboard finial attached with a pin. For the boarded effect on the kennel roof overlap strips of thick card. The slope to the door of the coop has matchsticks glued at intervals.

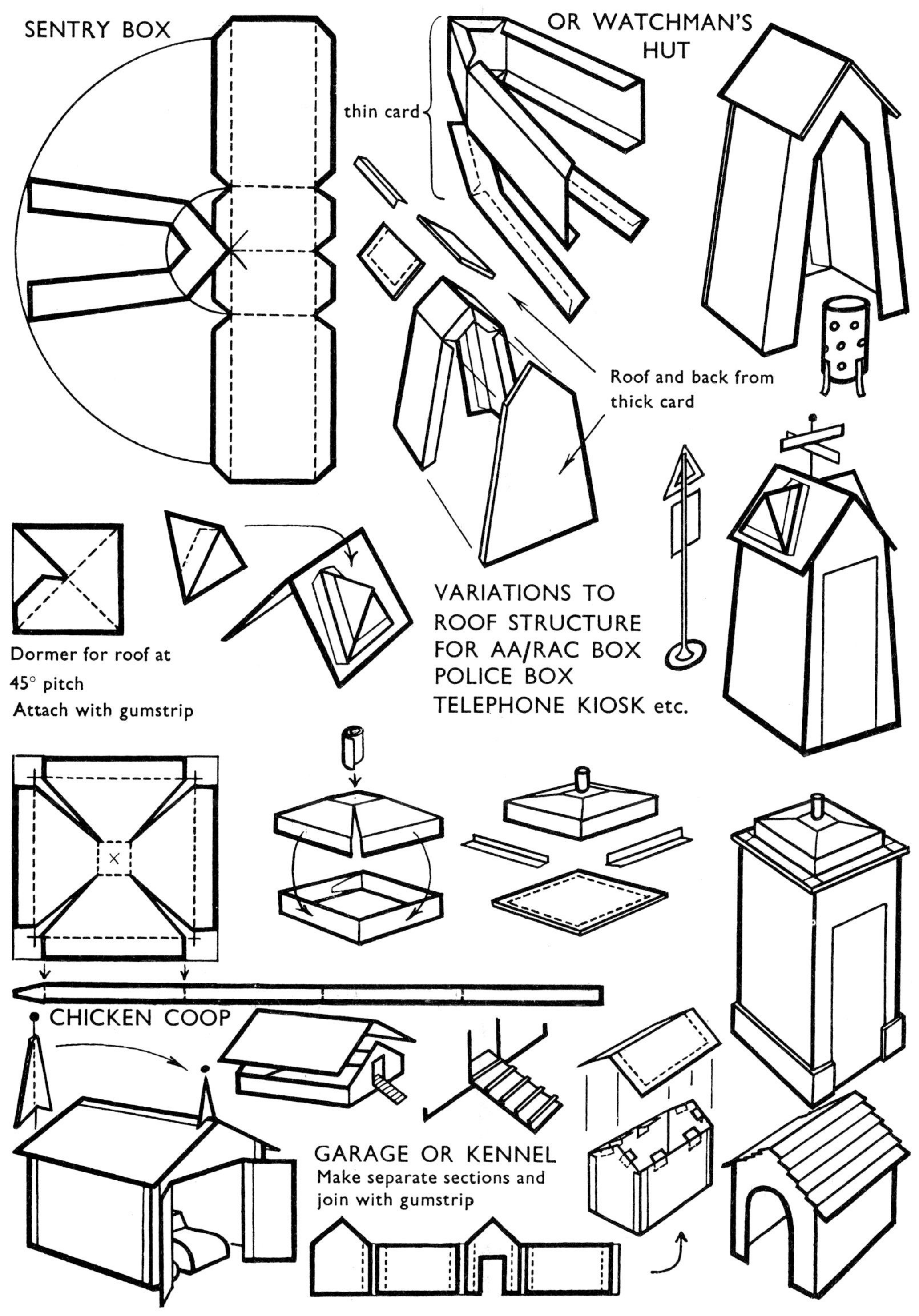
SENTRY BOX
OR WATCHMAN'S HUT
thin card
Roof and back from thick card
Dormer for roof at 45° pitch
Attach with gumstrip
VARIATIONS TO ROOF STRUCTURE FOR AA/RAC BOX POLICE BOX TELEPHONE KIOSK etc.
CHICKEN COOP
GARAGE OR KENNEL
Make separate sections and join with gumstrip

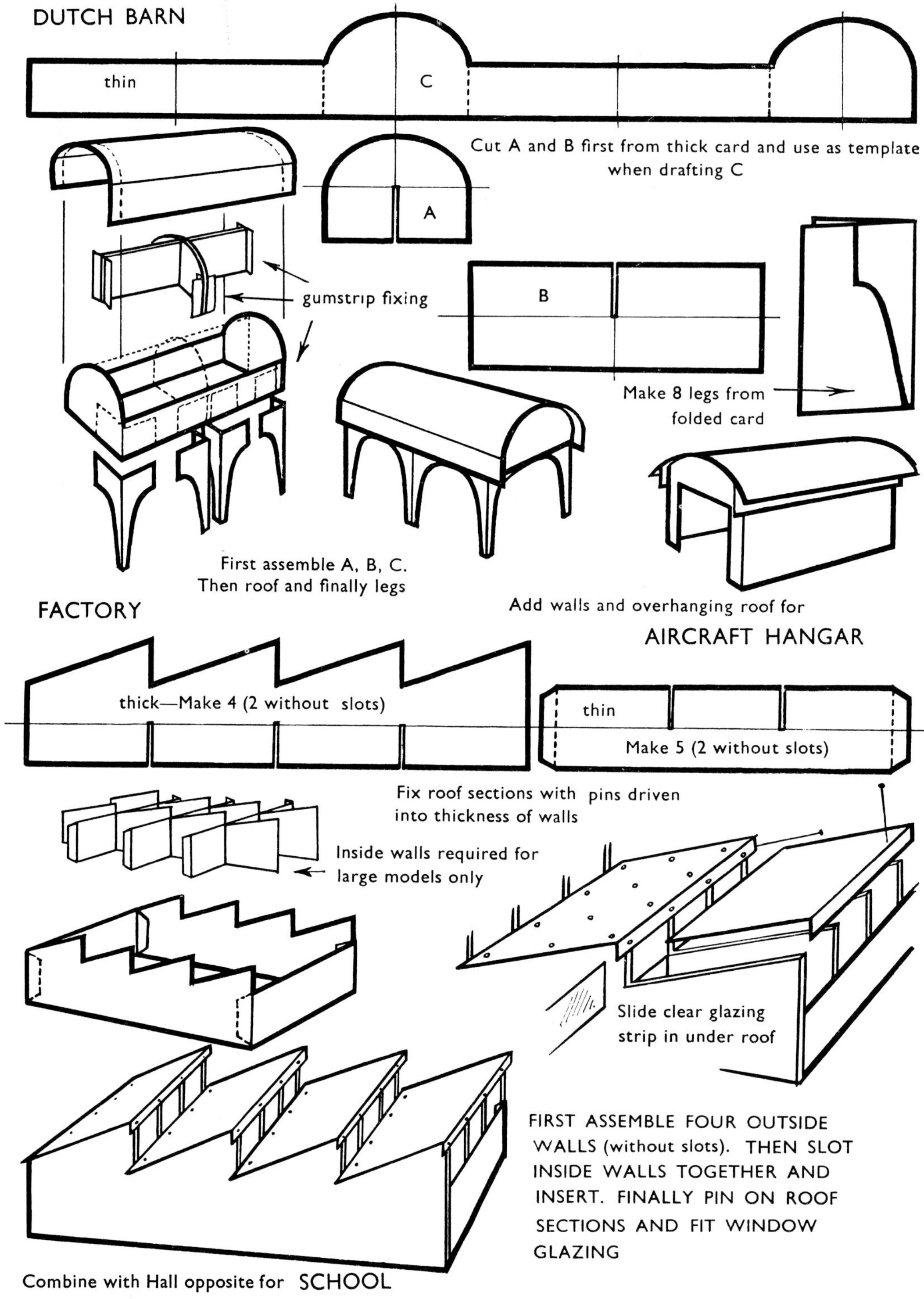
DUTCH BARN
thin
C
Cut A and B first from thick card and use as template when drafting C
A
gumstrip fixing
B
Make 8 legs from folded card
First assemble A, B, C. Then roof and finally legs
FACTORY
Add walls and overhanging roof for
AIRCRAFT HANGAR
thick—Make 4 (2 without slots)
thin
Make 5 (2 without slots)
Fix roof sections with pins driven into thickness of walls
Inside walls required for large models only
Slide clear glazing strip in under roof
FIRST ASSEMBLE FOUR OUTSIDE WALLS (without slots). THEN SLOT INSIDE WALLS TOGETHER AND INSERT. FINALLY PIN ON ROOF SECTIONS AND FIT WINDOW GLAZING
Combine with Hall opposite for SCHOOL

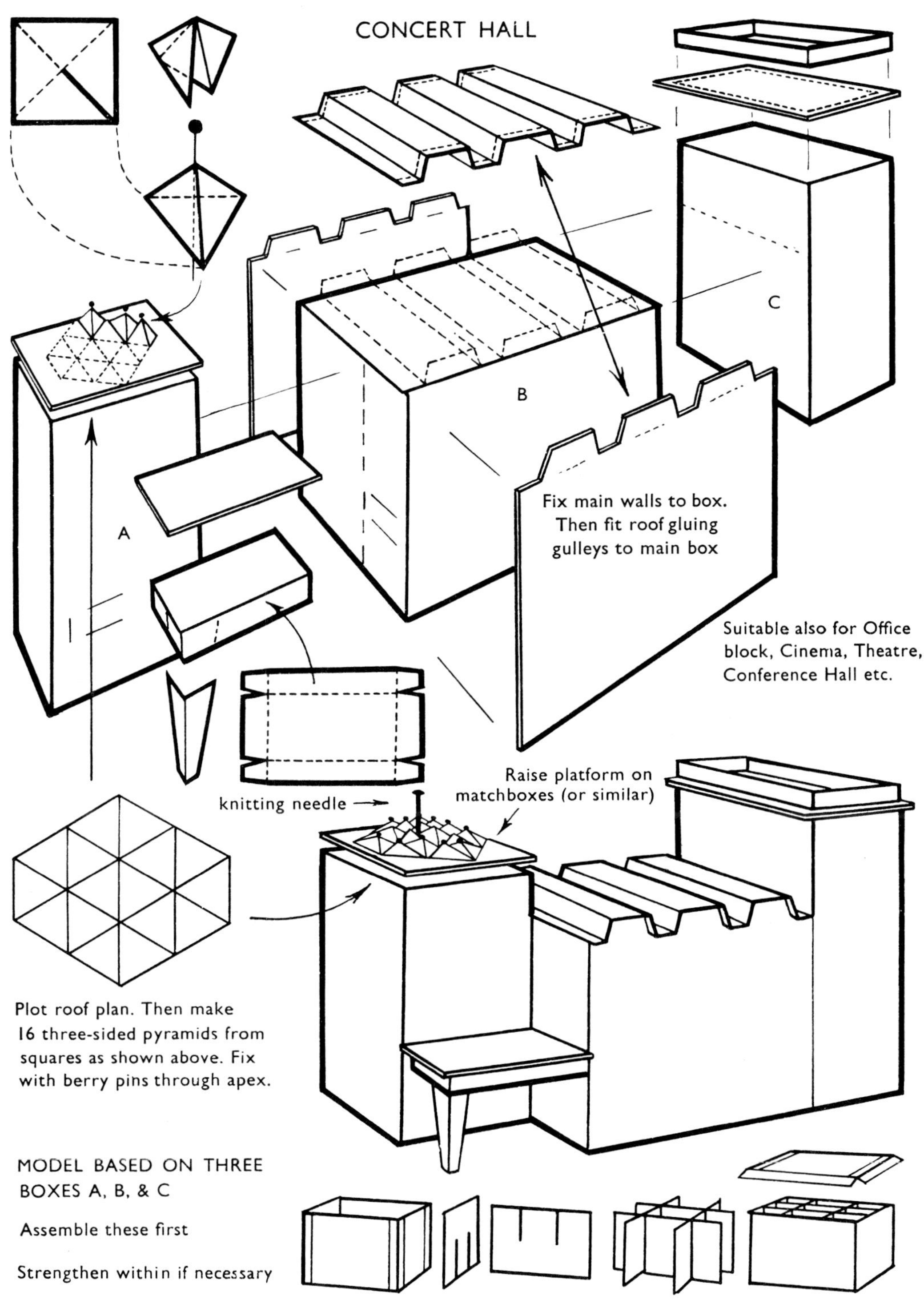
CONCERT HALL
C
B
A
Fix main walls to box. Then fit roof gluing gulleys to main box
Suitable also for Office block, Cinema, Theatre, Conference Hall etc.
Raise platform on matchboxes (or similar)
knitting needle
Plot roof plan. Then make 16 three-sided pyramids from squares as shown above. Fix with berry pins through apex.
MODEL BASED ON THREE BOXES A, B, & C
Assemble these first
Strengthen within if necessary

The order of assembly for these models is summarised below.

Bandstand. Construct the roof from a disc of thin card. (See also page 34). Note that there are six divisions. Cut six double supporting sections from thick card (each of these may be cut from a folded piece or formed from two pieces hinged together). Open each of these to an angle of 60° and assemble as shown. Assemble roof and supports with a hat pin (see diagram). If the pin will not grip, try a knitting needle coated with glue, or if it protrudes beneath, drive the point into a cork. Cut the platform from thick card (Radius = length of one side). Cut radiating slots and insert the roof supports. Add a loose collar below the platform. Enclose the platform with a wall and add steps.

Pavilion. Take a suitable box. Mount it on a stout platform with a front extension. Punch holes for flag poles. Mount the platform on cotton reels directly beneath the holes. Glue back and end walls to the box. Form the roof and punch holes for flag poles. Attach roof to walls. Insert flag poles. Erect a fence round the front of the platform. Assemble and mount the clock. Add steps.

Engine shed. Prepare a suitable box. Noting its width, draw out (a). In relation to (a) draw out (b), noting distance between slots on the side of the box. In relation to (a) and (b), draw out (c). Cut shapes (a) and (b) from thick card. Cut shape (c) from thin card. Form (a) and (b) into a rectangular enclosure and slot on to the box. Mount (c) allowing shapes (a) to extend through slots. Fix narrow roofing section to these extensions.

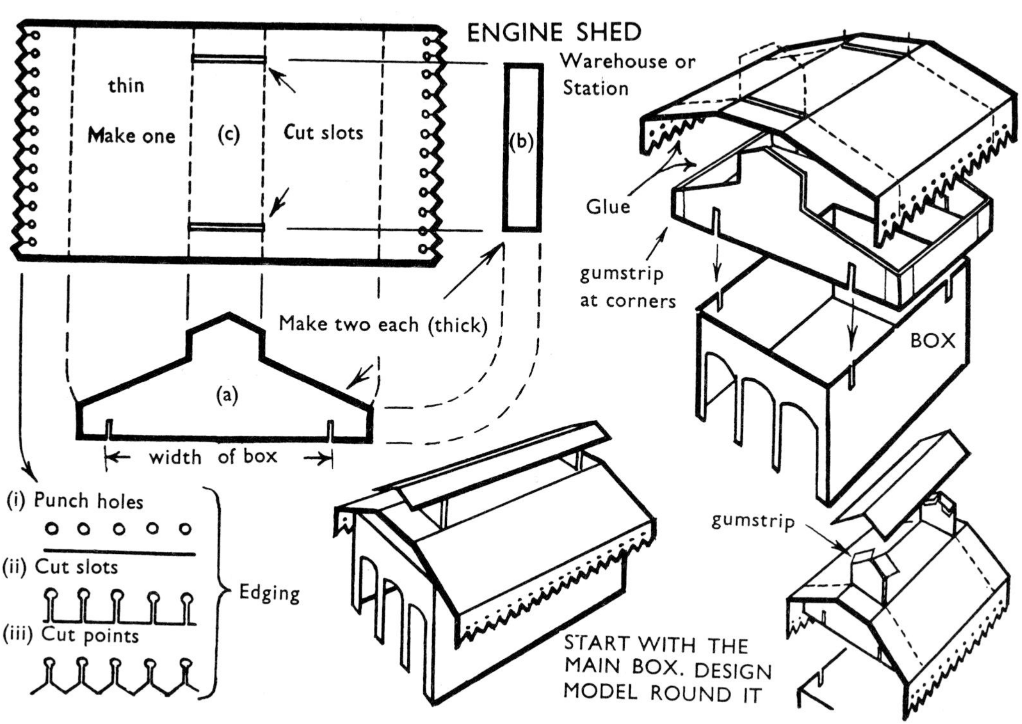

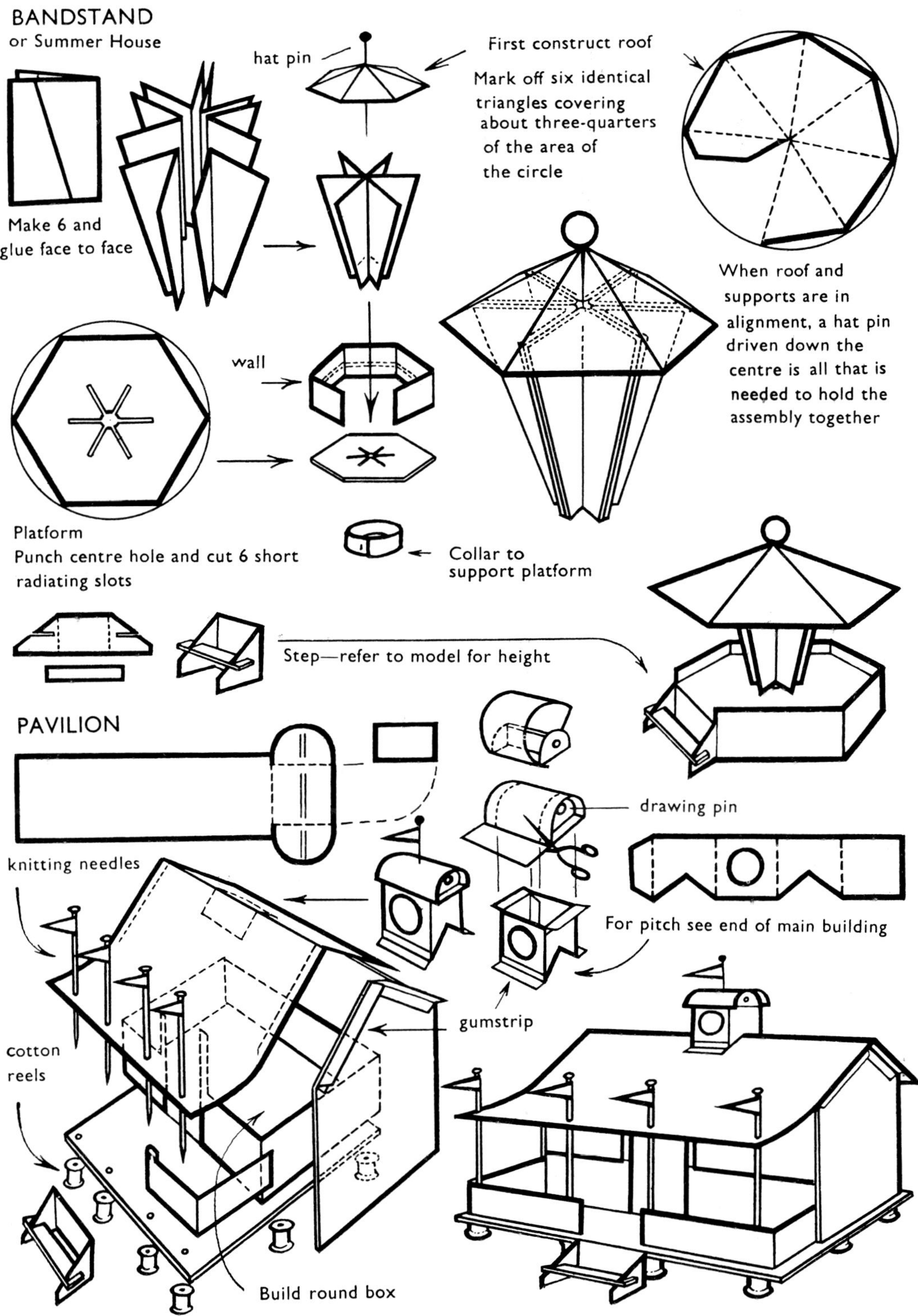
BANDSTAND
or Summer House
hat pin
First construct roof
Mark off six identical triangles covering about three-quarters of the area of the circle
Make 6 and glue face to face
When roof and supports are in alignment, a hat pin driven down the centre is all that is needed to hold the assembly together
wall
Platform
Punch centre hole and cut 6 short radiating slots
Collar to support platform
Step—refer to model for height
PAVILION
drawing pin
knitting needles
For pitch see end of main building
gumstrip
cotton reels
Build round box

SOME USEFUL BASIC CONSTRUCTIONS ROOFS ETC.

Using squared paper or thin card

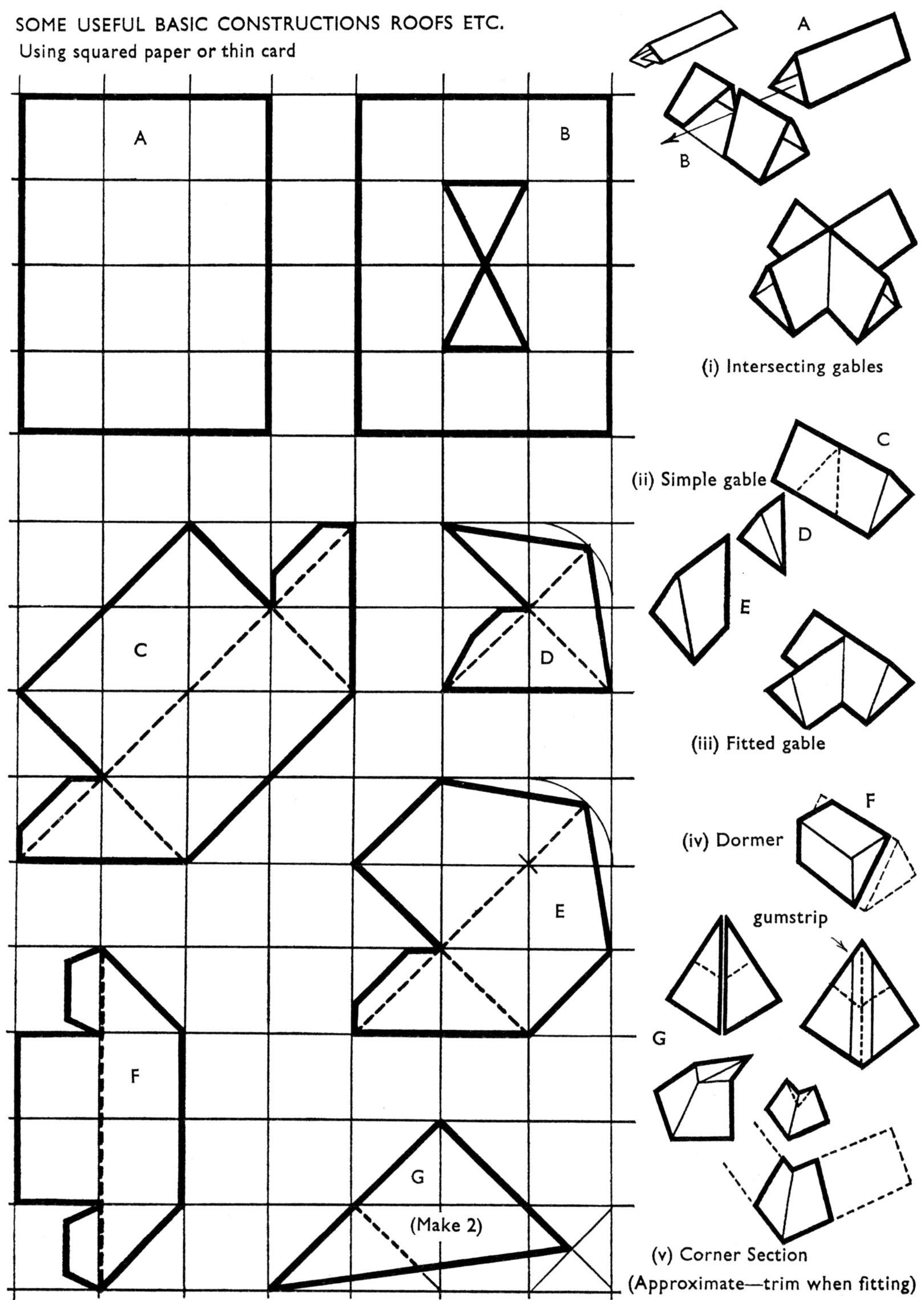

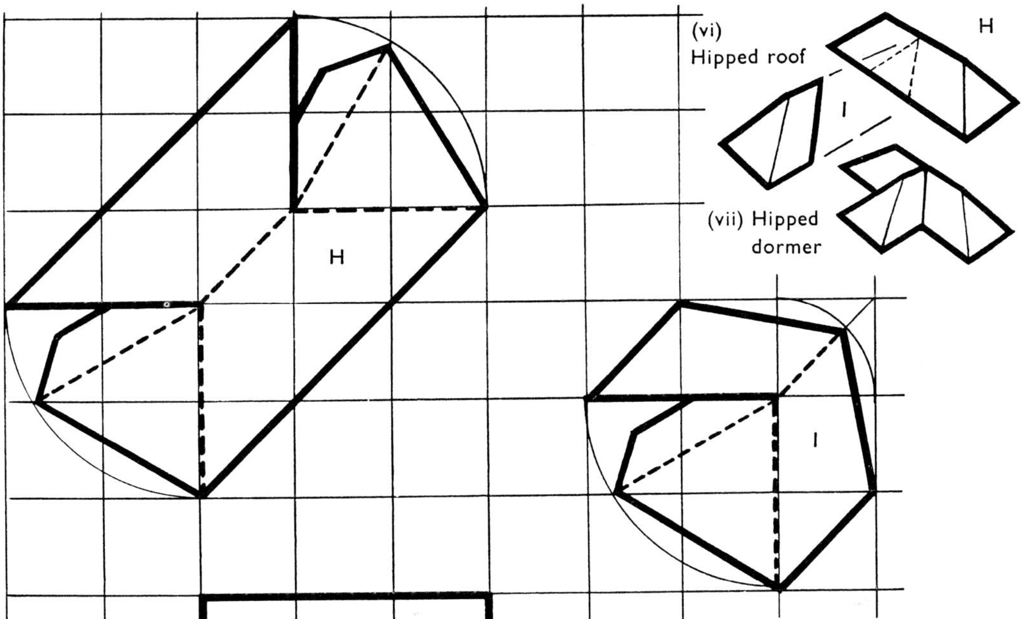

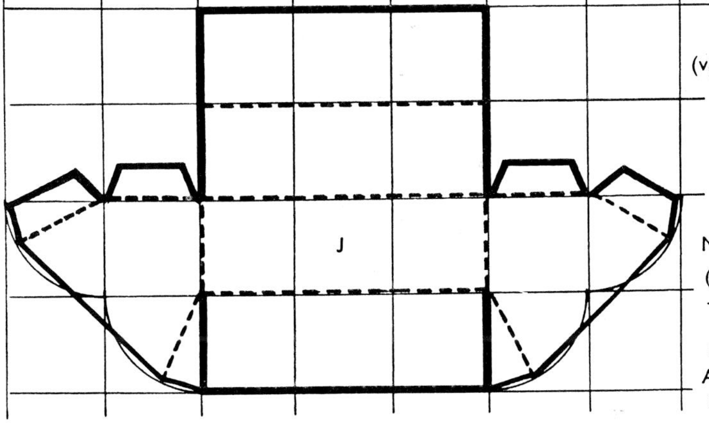

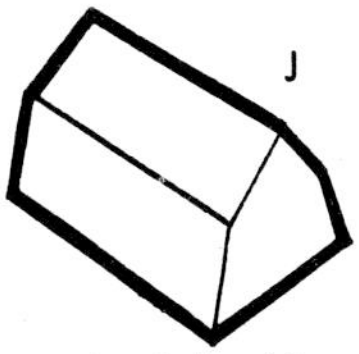

(vi) Hipped roof

H

I

H

(vii) Hipped dormer

I

(viii) Mansard roof

J

J

METHODS (ii) (iii) (iv) (v) (vi) (vii) ONLY APPLY TO ROOFS OF 45° PITCH

METHOD (i) Opposite ONLY APPLIES TO ROOFS OF 60° PITCH

IT IS OFTEN SIMPLER WHEN USING THESE METHODS TO *START* WITH THE ROOF, DRAW ROUND THE COMPLETED SECTION, AND DESIGN THE REST OF THE BUILDING TO FIT

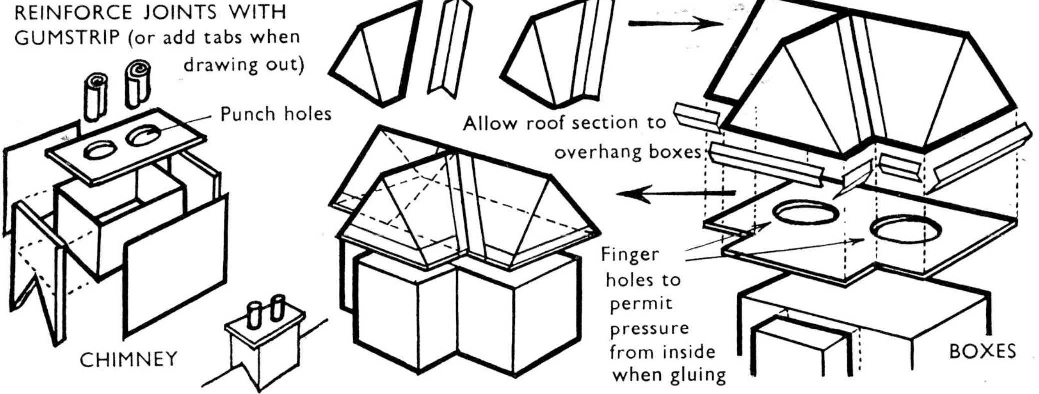

HOUSES—MORE BASIC CONSTRUCTIONS

Alternative Roofing—A longer method for large models, or where a different pitch is required—May also be used in conjunction with the shapes on the previous two pages. Use thick card

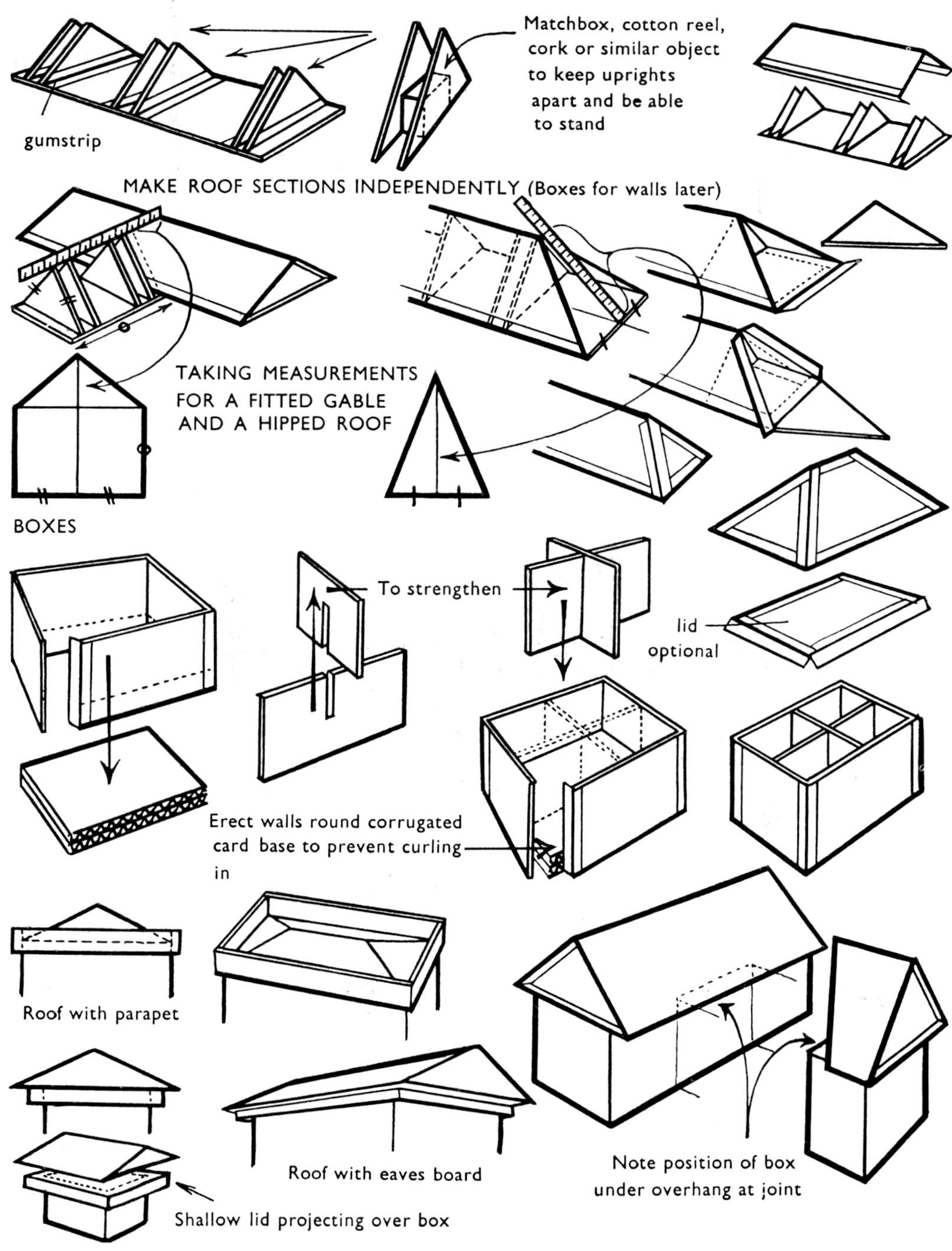

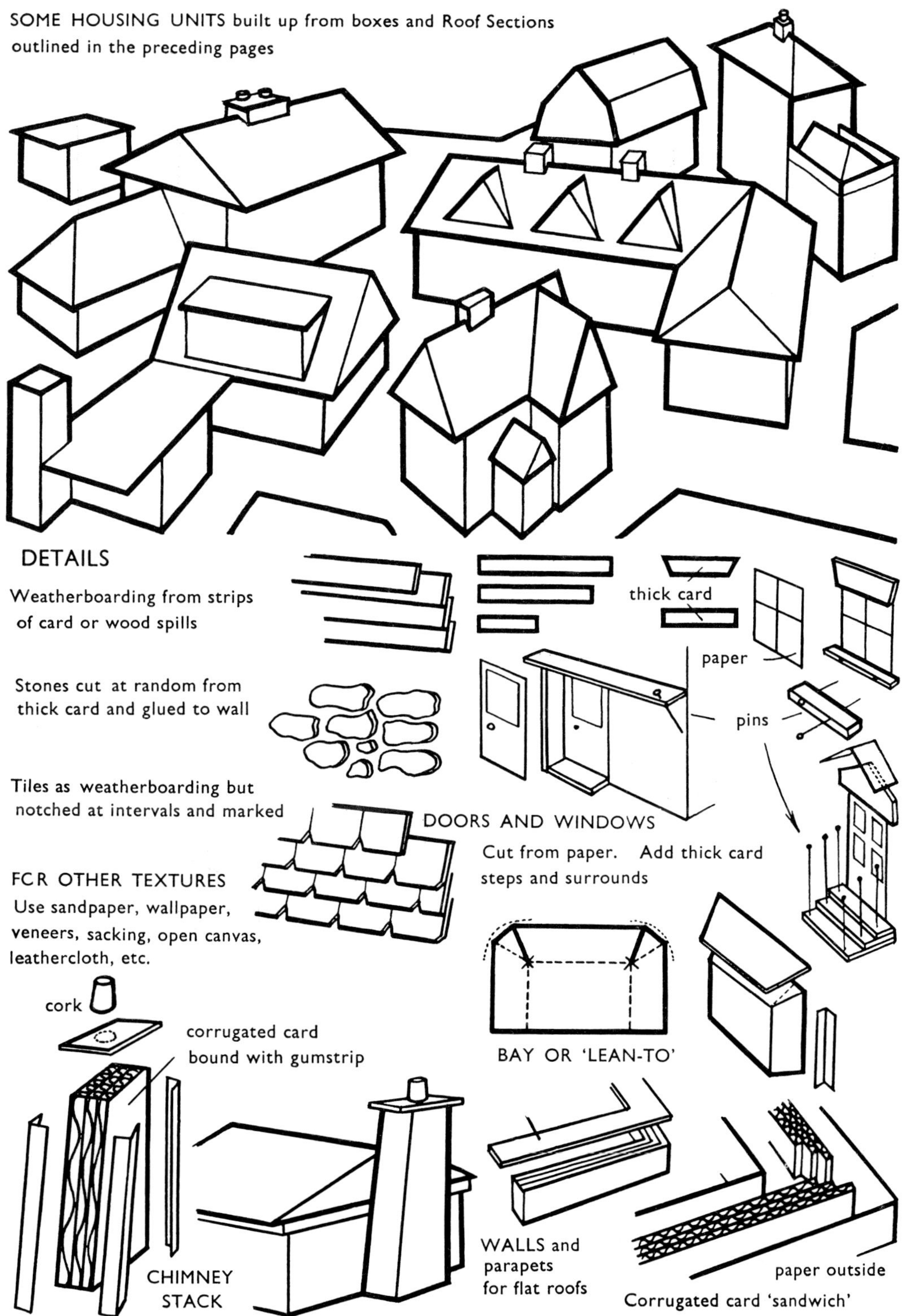
SOME HOUSING UNITS built up from boxes and Roof Sections
outlined in the preceding pages
DETAILS
Weatherboarding from strips
of card or wood spills
thick card
paper
pins
Stones cut at random from
thick card and glued to wall
Tiles as weatherboarding but
notched at intervals and marked
DOORS AND WINDOWS
Cut from paper. Add thick card
steps and surrounds
FCR OTHER TEXTURES
Use sandpaper, wallpaper,
veneers, sacking, open canvas,
leathercloth, etc.
cork
corrugated card
bound with gumstrip
BAY OR 'LEAN-TO'
CHIMNEY
STACK
WALLS and
parapets
for flat roofs
paper outside
Corrugated card 'sandwich'

For other styles of church architecture see also the temple on page 33, and the church on page 37.

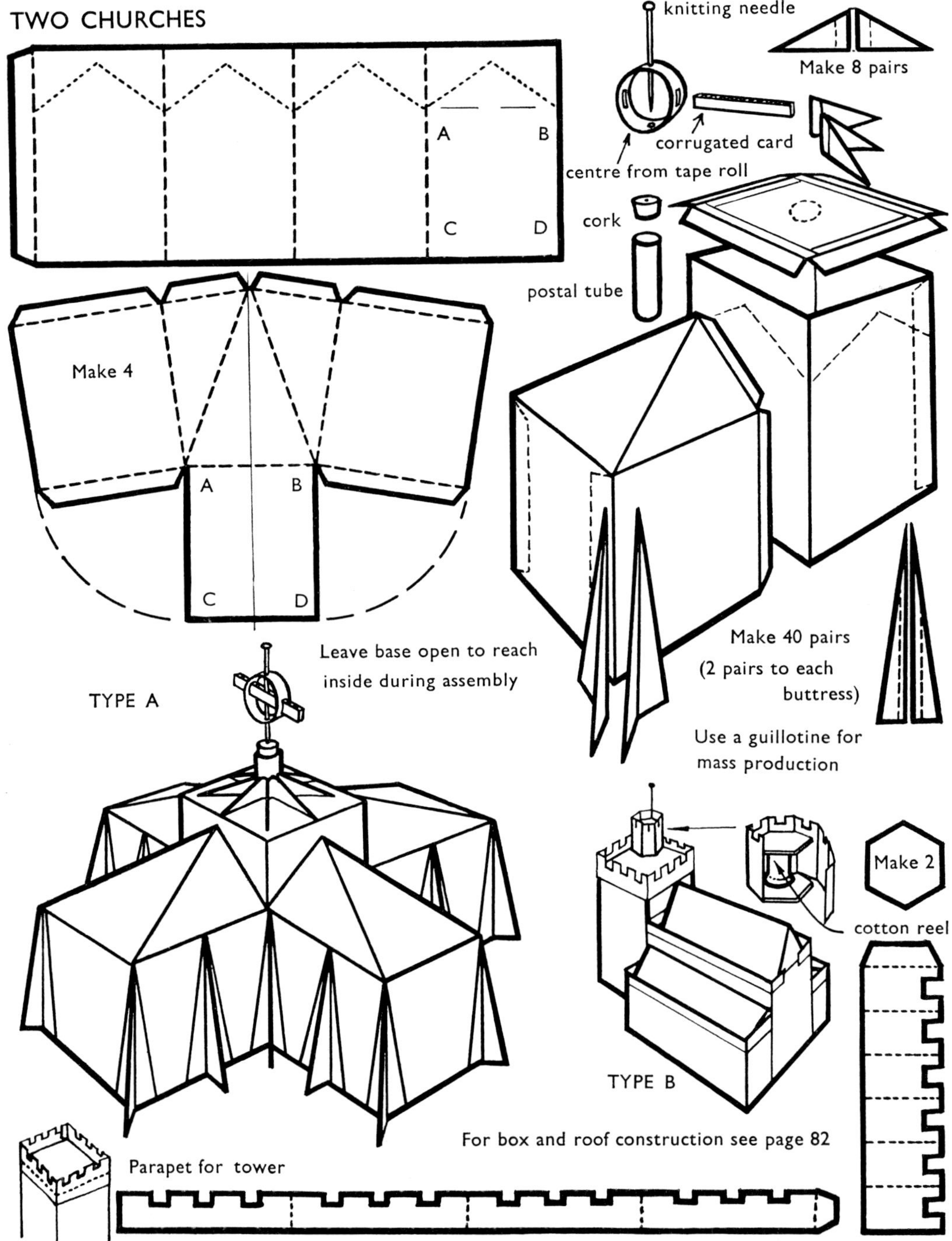

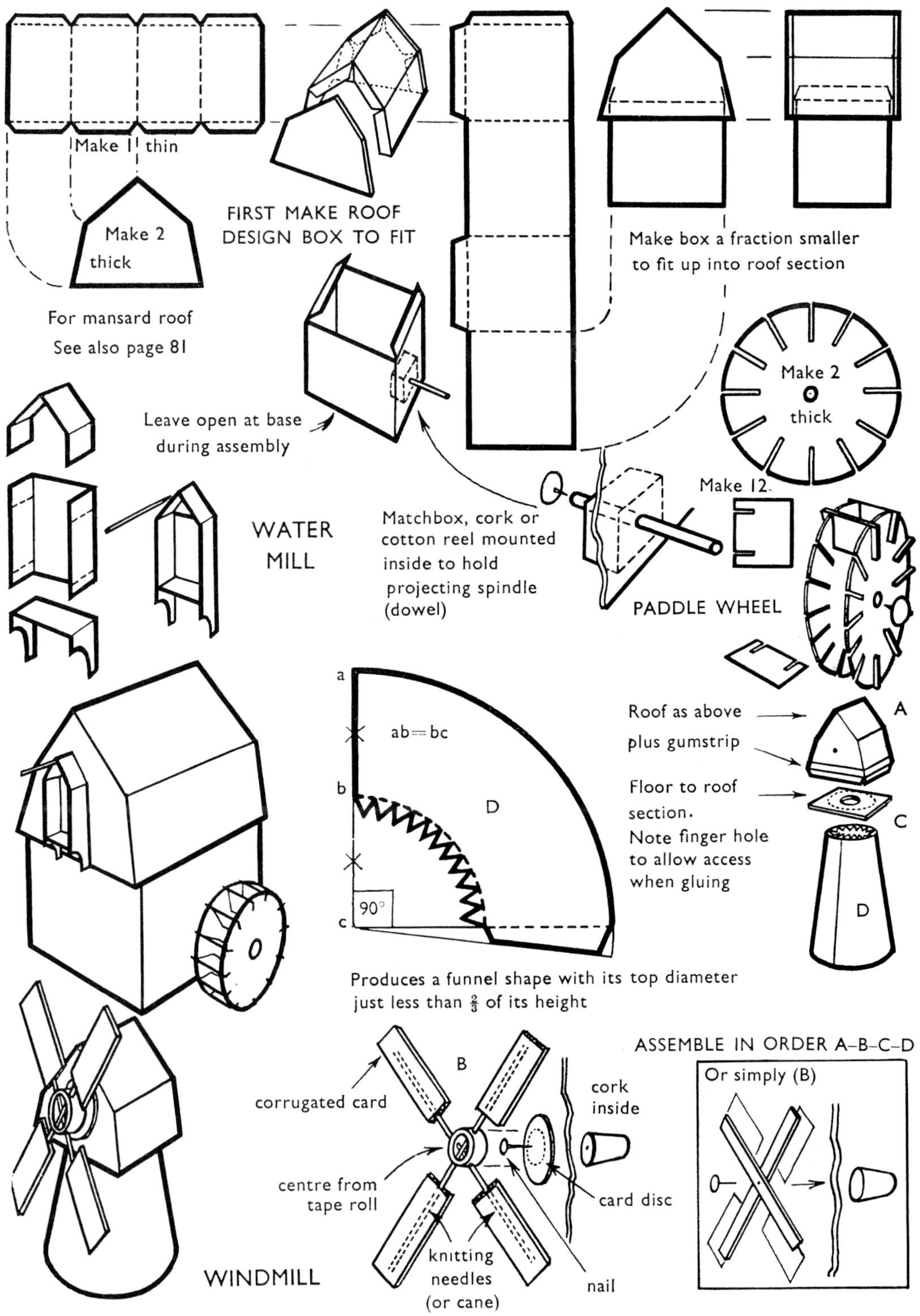
Make 1 thin
Make 2 thick
For mansard roof
See also page 81
FIRST MAKE ROOF
DESIGN BOX TO FIT
Make box a fraction smaller
to fit up into roof section
Make 2
thick
Leave open at base
during assembly
WATER
MILL
Matchbox, cork or
cotton reel mounted
inside to hold
projecting spindle
(dowel)
Make 12
PADDLE WHEEL
a
ab = bc
b
D
c
90°
Roof as above
plus gumstrip
A
Floor to roof
section.
Note finger hole
to allow access
when gluing
C
D
Produces a funnel shape with its top diameter
just less than ⅔ of its height
ASSEMBLE IN ORDER A–B–C–D
B
corrugated card
cork
inside
centre from
tape roll
card disc
knitting
needles
(or cane)
nail
Or simply (B)
WINDMILL

It will have been noticed that many model buildings originate at the top and grow downwards. In the case of the **Timber-frame house** it is probably more convenient to be a little more orthodox and start on ground level.

Boxes again form the main fabric of the building. They should be made from thick cardboard, not only for strength, but in order to provide a good bearing surface at the edges for gluing. The boxes need not have lids (the base of the box above serves to cover in the one beneath). Each box must have a floor. The boxes are all of the same width but the distance from front to back increases slightly with each successive floor. The building begins to look ridiculous after about the fourth floor. The children may need to be instructed that in medieval times the building of skyscrapers was the exception rather than the rule. A reasonable approach is to construct in advance a number of boxes of the same width but in three or four stock sizes. Then experiment freely with these building units before deciding upon the final arrangement. By this means some rambling mansions may be constructed which would be impressive if not stately.

Each box requires an inside supporting division running from side to side. It must fit exactly. Two small slots are cut into the top of this division. Two corresponding slots are also cut in the front and back walls of the box. Two supporting beams are sunk into these slots. Note the half slot intersection, see (i). The beams project at front and back. Their tops should lie flush with the top of the box. The three triangular roof supports fit over the beams and are positioned alongside the back wall, the centre division, and the front wall respectively. They may be glued to these sections where they overlap. The roof is made to overhang at the eaves. The chimney is cut from card marked out in squares (6 squares by 7 squares). It will adapt itself to the pitch of the roof. With this style of building the chimneys usually look better in groups.

When representing old buildings, an impeccable finish is hardly required but if the model really looks as though it is falling apart at the seams it is advisable to cover the sides with new walls cut from one continuous sheet. This model, in fact, requires some careful measurement, and is best regarded as a precision job like any other. The effects of age may be imparted by strips of cardboard glued to the outside to indicate more beams. Some of these could be quite irregular.

A model village. The arrangement, on a clay base, has been allowed to evolve freely from the personal wishes of the builders.
A picturesque, though somewhat uneconomical, use of land space; the model retains the individual character of the buildings.

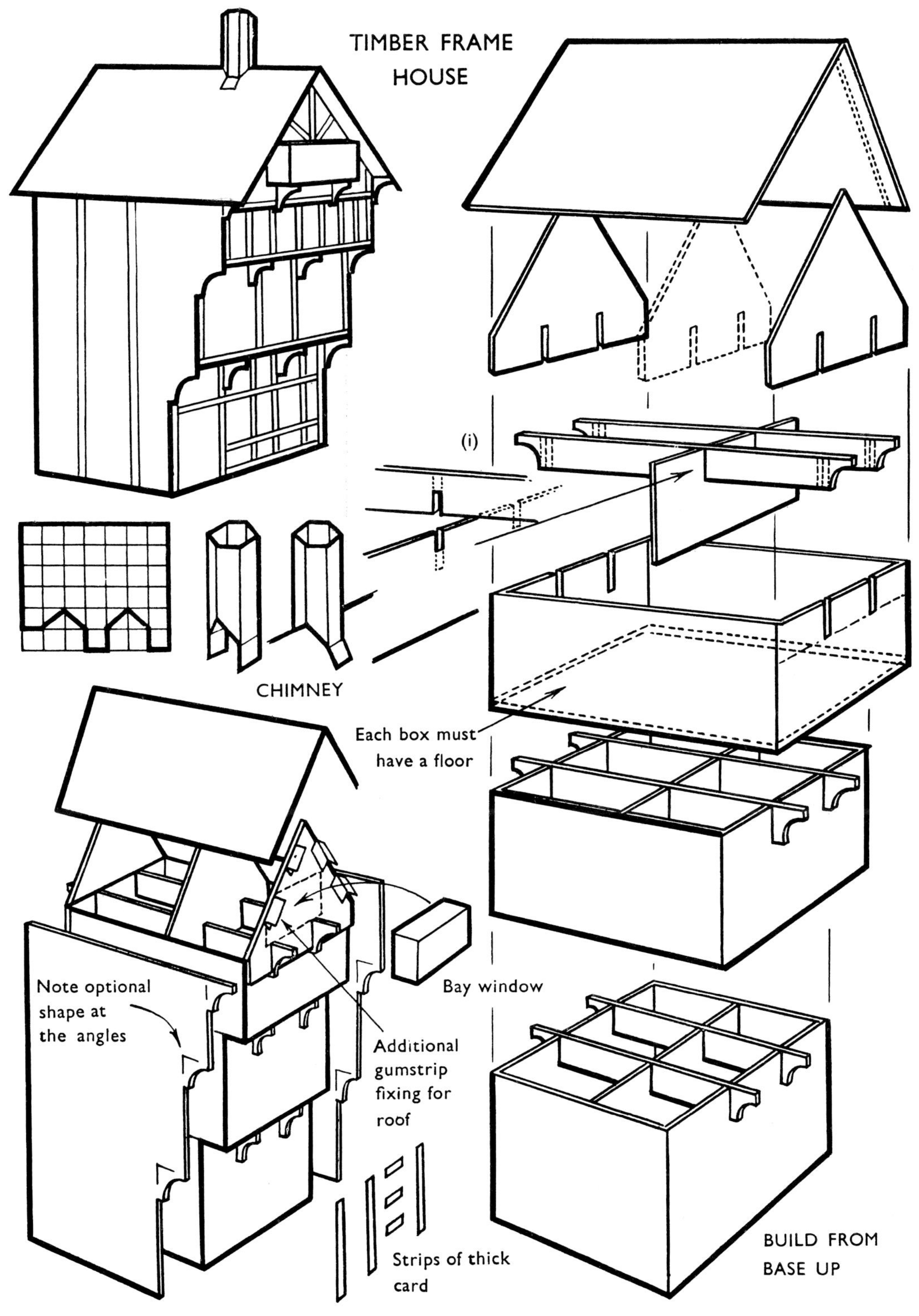
TIMBER FRAME
HOUSE
(i)
CHIMNEY
Each box must
have a floor
Note optional
shape at
the angles
Bay window
Additional
gumstrip
fixing for
roof
Strips of thick
card
BUILD FROM
BASE UP

The diagrams opposite give all the necessary information for the assembly of these three gateways.

They may be effectively combined to form continuous arcades, or to enhance the facade of a building. The architectural styles have been interpreted quite freely and other modifications may suggest themselves. For example, the top of the Norman gateway could be mounted on square columns. The top of the Classic gateway could then be mounted on top of this and the result would be a triumphal arch of quite a different order. The Tudor gateway is perhaps the most adaptable. Six-sided turrets, used as independent building units, will be found to produce a variety of composite structures. Quite a presentable castle may be formed by using simple wall sections instead of the open gateway. These may be repeated round an enclosed space with turrets at intervals. The addition of a drawbridge and a painted moat should not present any great difficulty. (See pages 105 and 115).

The Tudor style is best painted to represent red bricks. The other styles should be painted white.

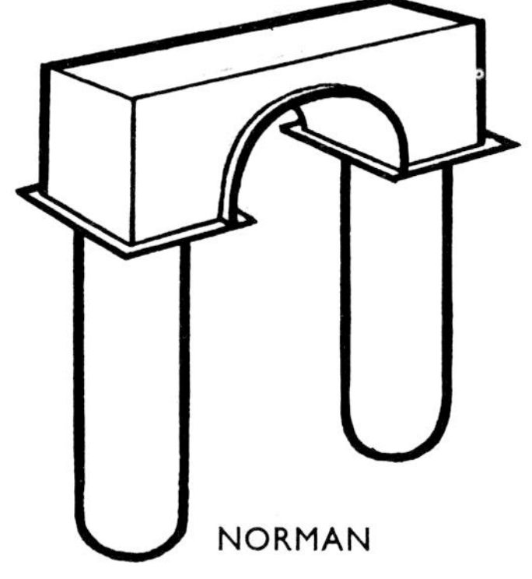

THREE GATEWAYS

See also the arch on page 21

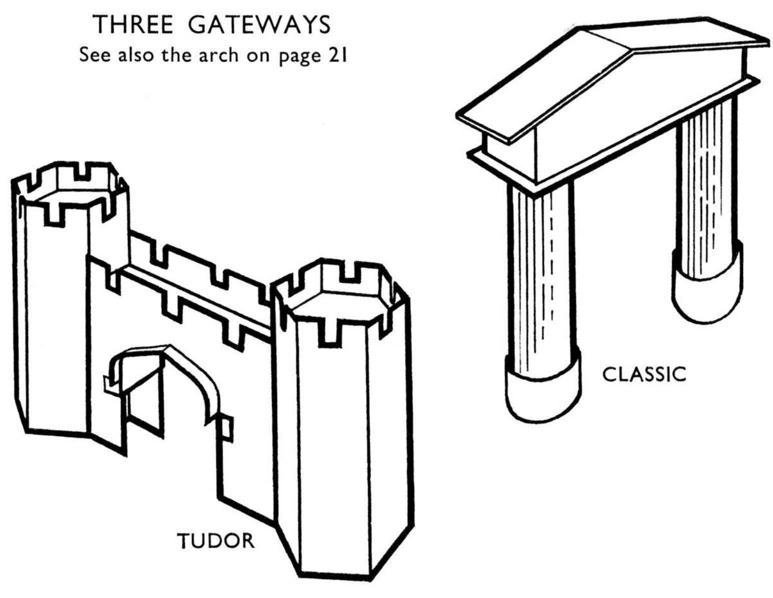

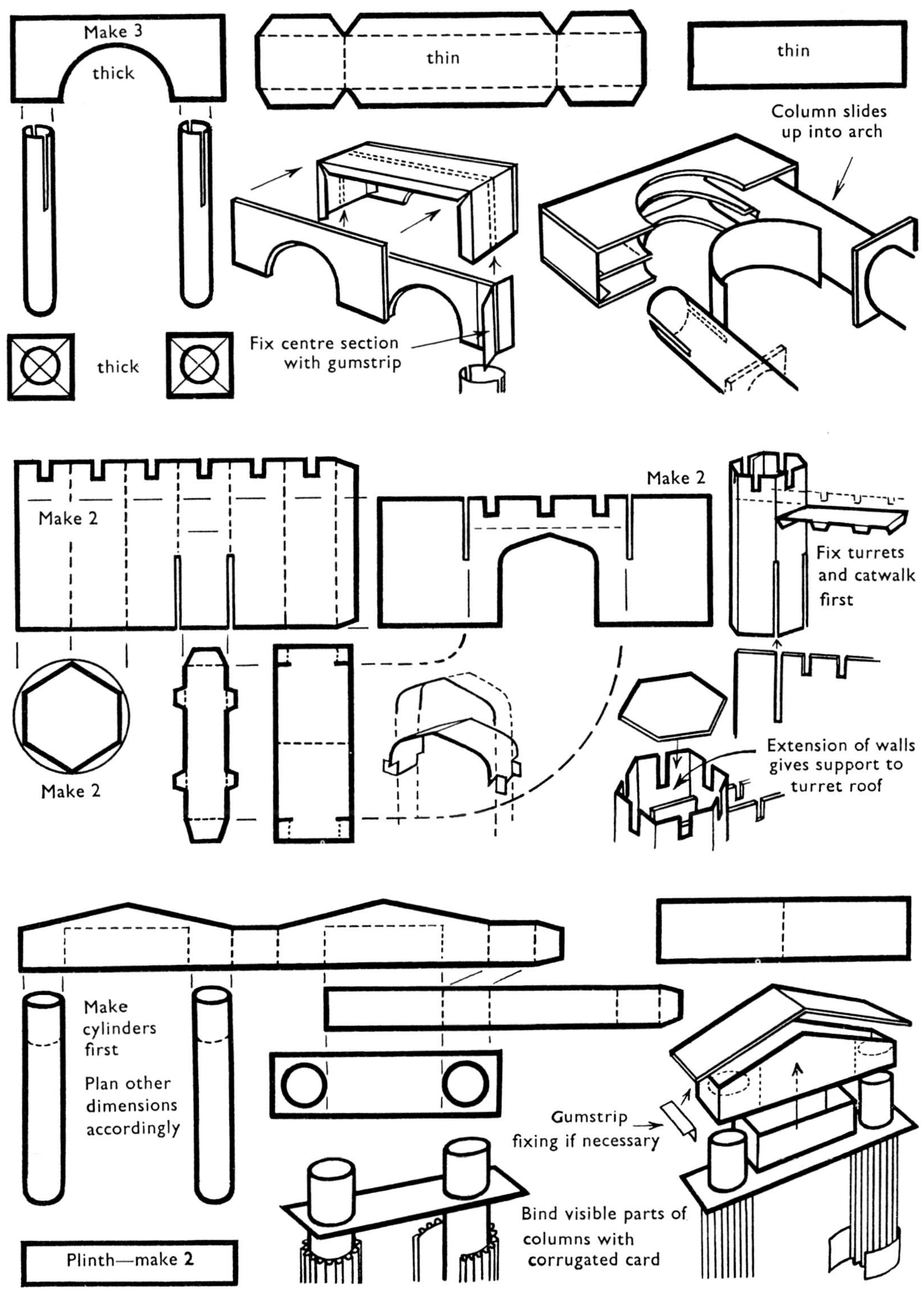
Make 3
thick
thin
thin
Column slides up into arch
thick
Fix centre section with gumstrip
Make 2
Make 2
Fix turrets and catwalk first
Make 2
Extension of walls gives support to turret roof
Make cylinders first
Plan other dimensions accordingly
Gumstrip fixing if necessary
Bind visible parts of columns with corrugated card
Plinth—make 2

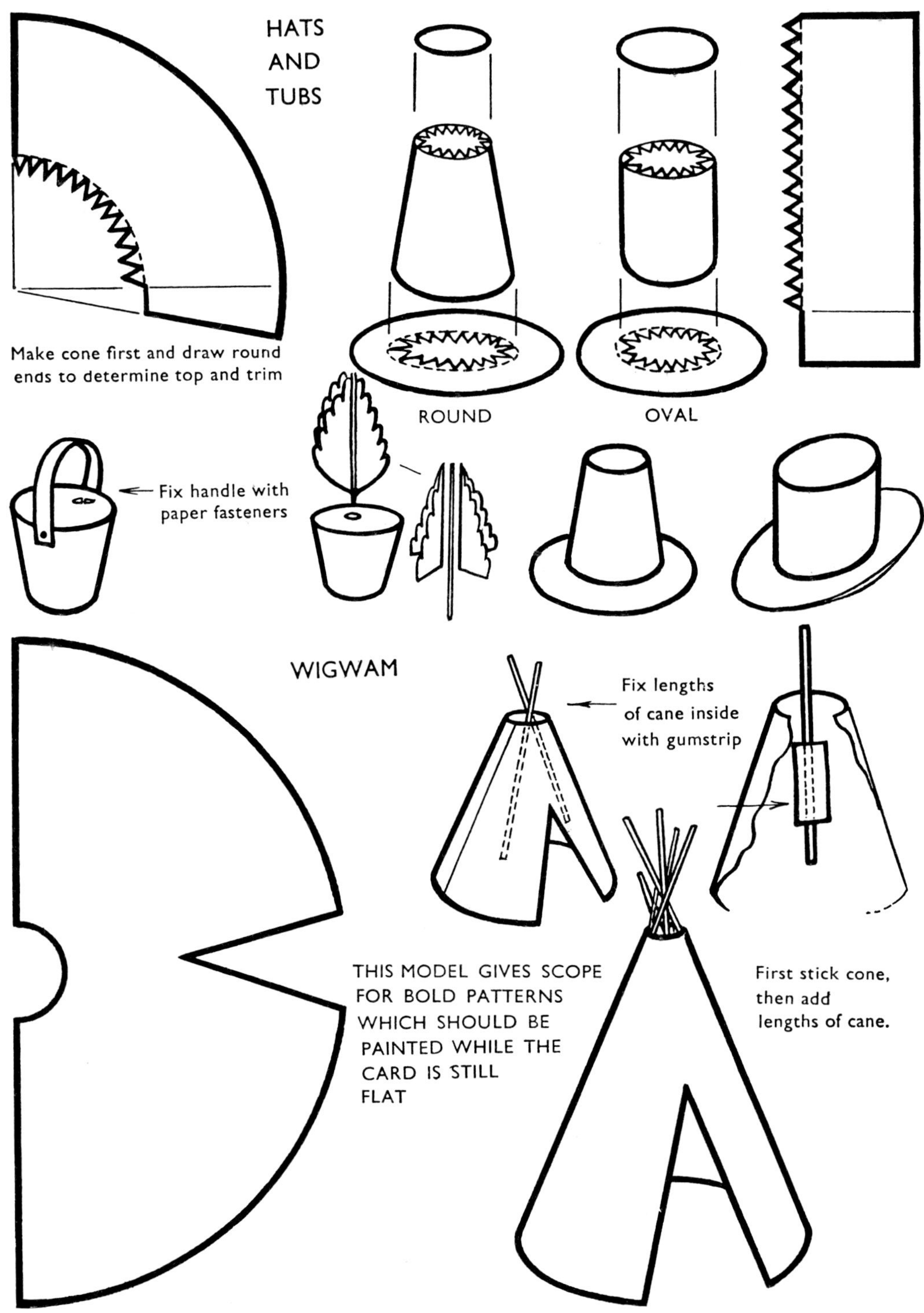
HATS
AND
TUBS
Make cone first and draw round ends to determine top and trim
ROUND
OVAL
Fix handle with paper fasteners
WIGWAM
Fix lengths of cane inside with gumstrip
THIS MODEL GIVES SCOPE FOR BOLD PATTERNS WHICH SHOULD BE PAINTED WHILE THE CARD IS STILL FLAT
First stick cone, then add lengths of cane.

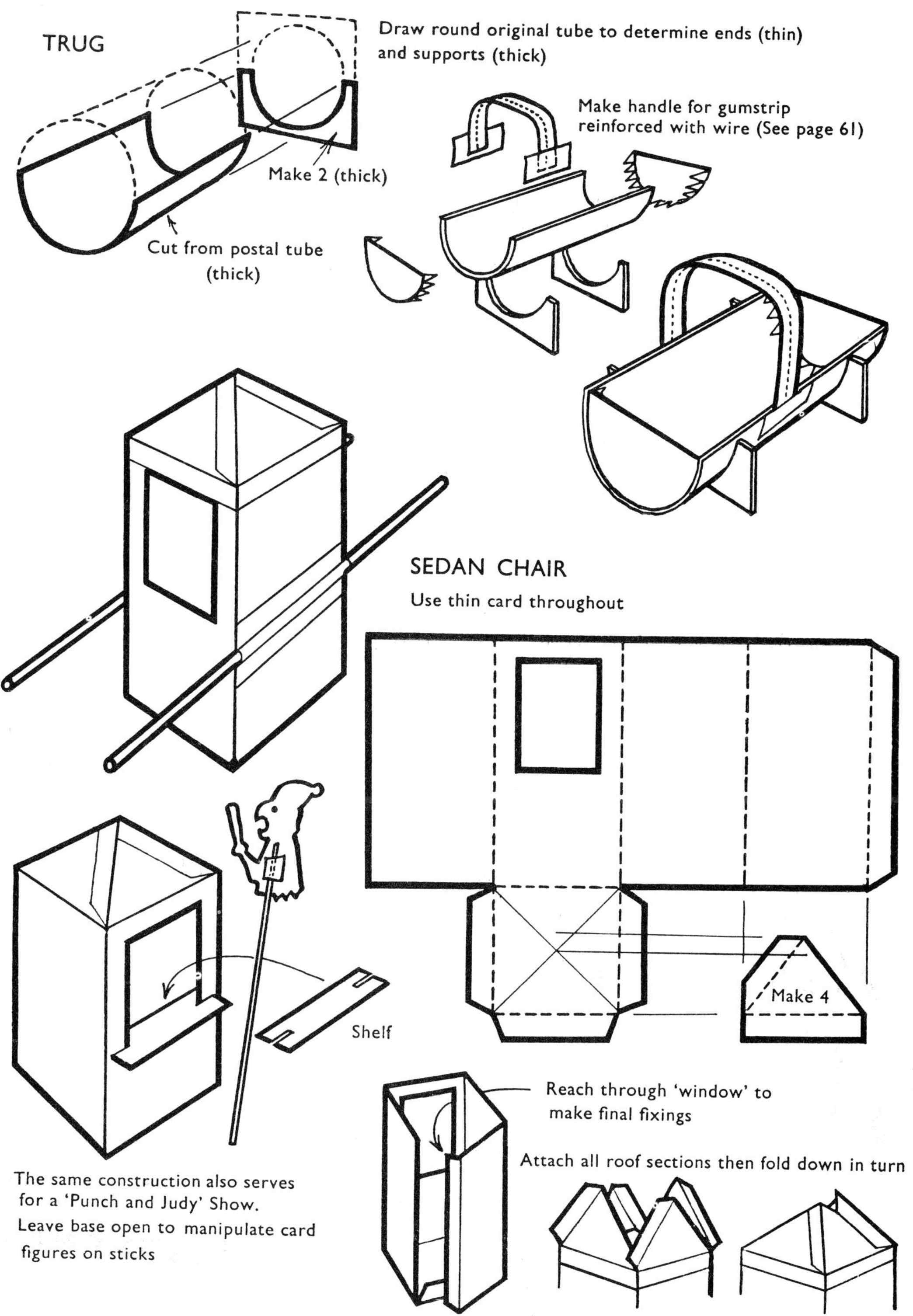

The same construction also serves for a 'Punch and Judy' Show. Leave base open to manipulate card figures on sticks

Right: Lighthouse. 5in. high. Made from cotton reels. Top section from celluloid fastened with Sellotape round a tap washer glued to reel. Conical roof from red paper. Crane cut from parts of a match box.
Cargo vessels. Both 7in. long. Formed round match boxes on a thick cardboard base. Quayside platform raised on match boxes covered with white cartridge paper.

Below: Dinghy. Height about 7in. Hull from corrugated cardboard painted with white poster colour; trimmed at bows and stern with pieces from red wooden spills. Mast from two plain wooden spills glued together.

Below right: Yacht. Height about 6in. Hull from thin blue tinted card. Deck thick grey cardboard. Flag white. Mast of cane sandwiched between two sail thicknesses of white cartridge paper.

Right: Refectory table and bench. 8in. long. Unpainted strawboard. Sections slotted and pegged either side of uprights with matchsticks. Uprights secured below top with gumstrip.

Below: School desk $4\frac{1}{2}$in. from front to back. Frame from two lengths of galvanised wire. Seat, back-rest, foot-rest, and box from unpainted strawboard. Box hinged and bound with brown gumstrip. Wires attached with gumstrip beneath seat and box.

Light training 'plane. 7in. wingspan. Fuselage of thin blue tinted card. Wings, cockpit, and tail-plane of thick grey cardboard. Propeller from thin white card pierced with a pin driven into cork inside nose.

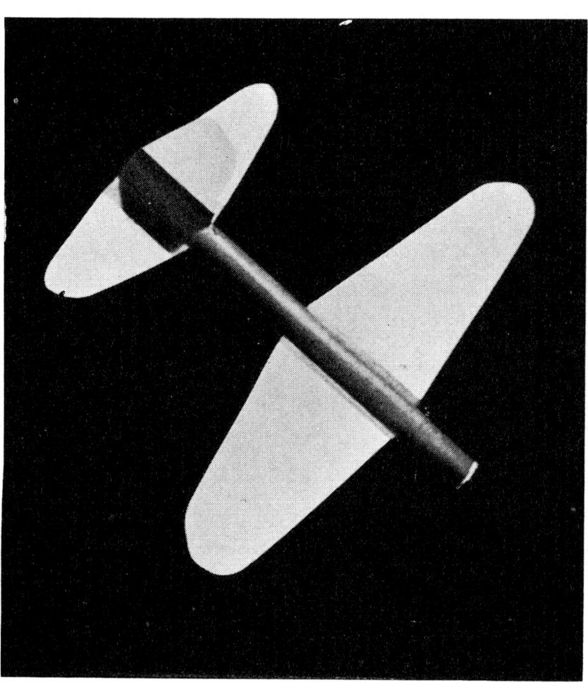

Small glider. 6in. wingspan. Fuselage of rolled-up Sugar paper bound with red gumstrip. Wings and tail section of thin white card passing through fuselage and secured with gumstrip.

Above: Suburban house and bus. House $3\frac{1}{2}$in. long from strawboard faced with various materials. Roofs open canvas; walls wood veneer, corrugated cardboard, and wall-paper in neutral shades; chimney of balsa wood; doors and windows ink on white paper glued on.
Bus 3in. long from thin card painted red and varnished.

Right: Housing units. Independent roof sections are made from thin card marked out in squares, attached with gumstrip to a thick cardboard base. Walls are box-like, made slightly smaller to allow overhanging eaves. Walls and roof are painted separately with opaque colours, details added, and the two parts glued together.

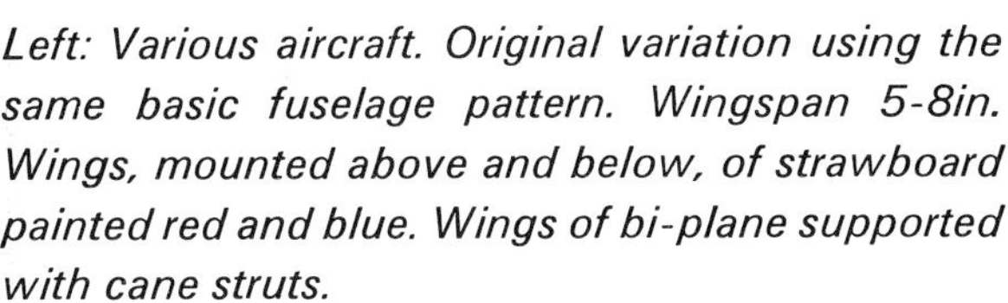

Left: Various aircraft. Original variation using the same basic fuselage pattern. Wingspan 5-8in. Wings, mounted above and below, of strawboard painted red and blue. Wings of bi-plane supported with cane struts.

Composite models

It has been said that 'it is better to make a simple thing well than to make a complex thing badly'.* Obvious though this may be to the craftsman, it could easily be misinterpreted by the teacher. It does not mean, for example, that a child should only be allowed to make pictures of inanimate objects because they are easier to draw than his own friends and relations. Similarly with a model – an interesting subject is worth any number of precision-made exercises. There will be a more active response from the children if the model is important enough to arouse their imagination as well as the skill required to build it. The result may be ramshackle in places, but the real value of the enterprise lies not in the excellence of the product so much as in the interest inspired by the making of it. Like many educational processes, it is all a plot to encourage some original thinking on the part of the pupil. A few technical blunders will not seriously upset the stratagem unless the children are made to feel self-conscious about their efforts by an over critical teacher.

Cardboard model making by young children is not one of the 'utilitarian' crafts. In a creative sense it might be compared with picture making. Some of the results are just as impermanent. Therefore it would be inappropriate to impose the same standards as apply to the traditional crafts like weaving or pottery where the purpose is expressed in the finished article.

At the same time, however, even the simplest cardboard model requires that sort of care which is the basis of all craft work. Some degree of draughtsmanship is inherent in every example. An over insistence on precision would tend to defeat the purpose of these early models, but the children should be given every facility to exercise to the utmost the skill they have. The models in the preceding chapters and the variations which follow are all built on sound principles. The careful pupil will find in them ample foundation for real craftsmanship.

For the professional approach to model making every serious student should study *Model Making in Cardboard* by Thomas Bayley, published by Dryad Press.

This final chapter brings together many of the individual models explained earlier and indicates broadly how they may be incorporated in larger settings. In most cases it will be necessary to form a general picture, and then turn up the appropriate sections for detailed instruction. Sometimes, however, if individual models have been allowed to accumulate, they will themselves suggest suitable group arrangements.

The planning and organisation of such models provides an excellent opportunity for some valuable discussion. Likewise the division of the class into groups and the allocation of the work among them is itself an experiment in 'industrial relations'. Comparatively few crafts afford this sort of combined approach. As a rule the composite idea seems to hold the child's attention for only so long as he can recognise his own special part in it. At first he tends to be rather undemocratic about it. The problem is, therefore, to apportion the work so that individual talents are neither wasted nor allowed to dominate others.

* *Handbook of Suggestions for Teachers*—H.M. Stationery Office.

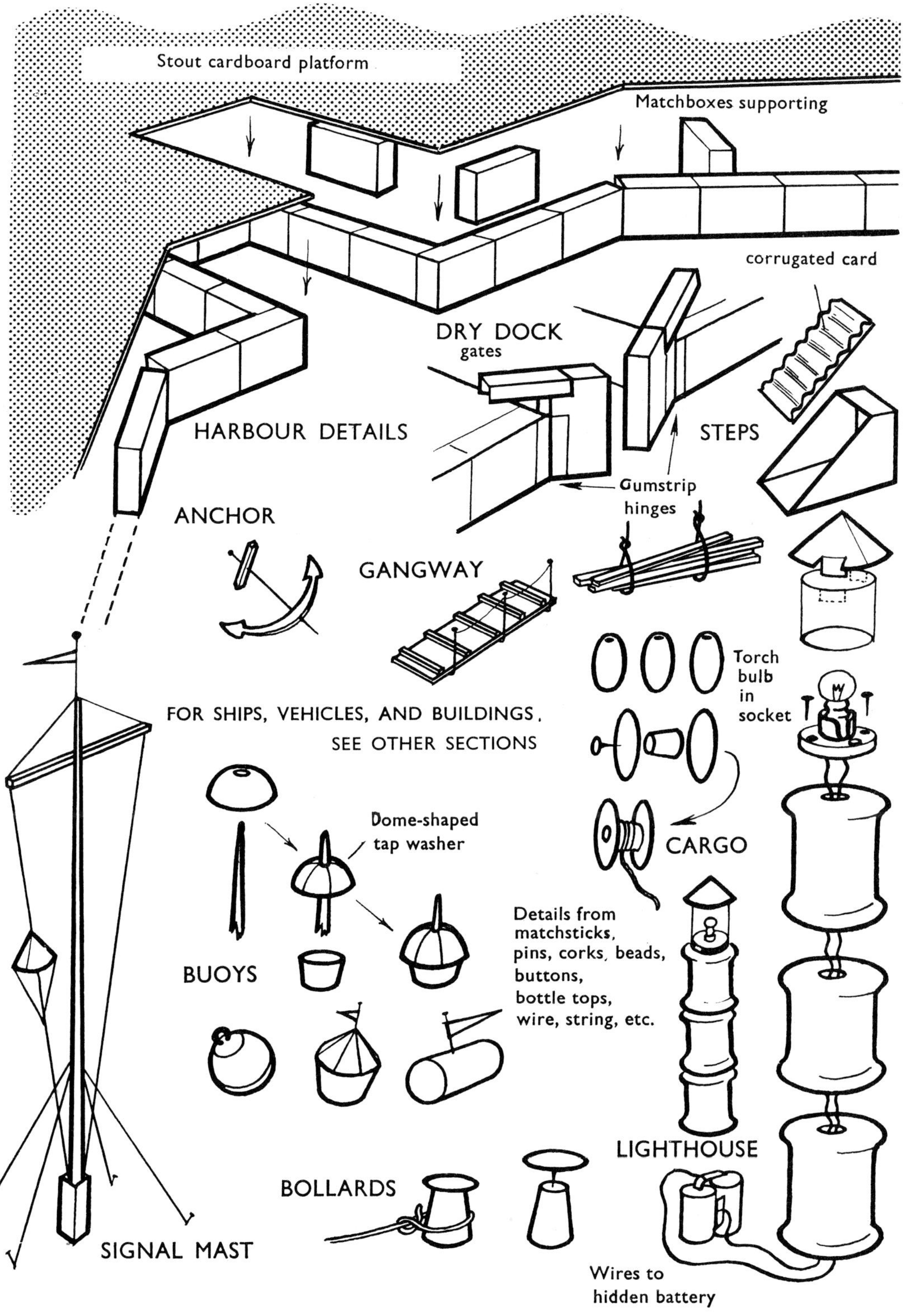
Stout cardboard platform
Matchboxes supporting
corrugated card
DRY DOCK
gates
HARBOUR DETAILS
STEPS
Gumstrip
hinges
ANCHOR
GANGWAY
Torch
bulb
in
socket
FOR SHIPS, VEHICLES, AND BUILDINGS,
SEE OTHER SECTIONS
Dome-shaped
tap washer
CARGO
Details from
matchsticks,
pins, corks, beads,
buttons,
bottle tops,
wire, string, etc.
BUOYS
LIGHTHOUSE
BOLLARDS
SIGNAL MAST
Wires to
hidden battery

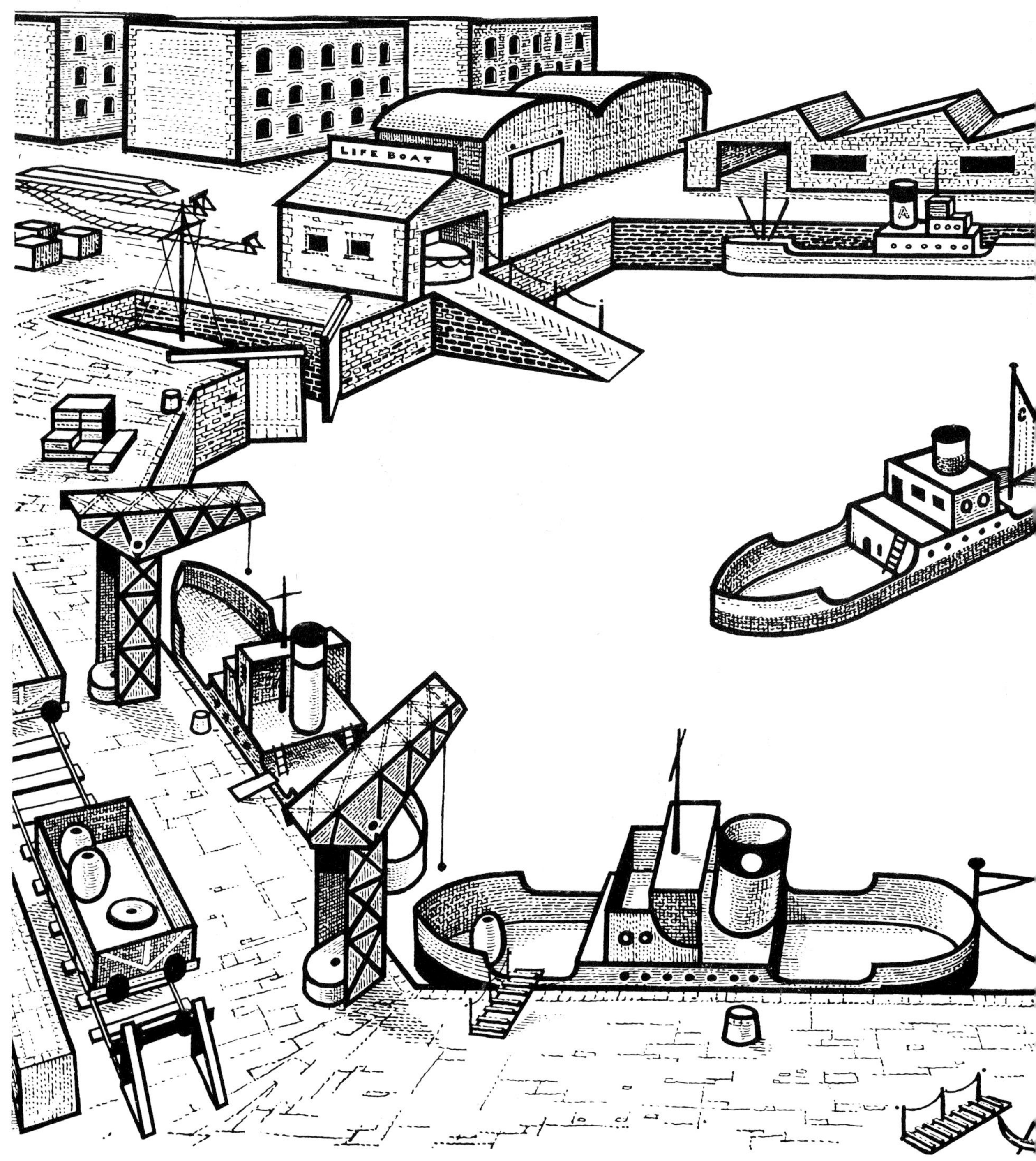
LIFE BOAT

A part of the docks. Approx. 3ft. 6in. long. A composite model arranged within a picture frame. Harbour platform of strawboard raised on match boxes covered with grey paper. Sea painted blue on hardboard base. Factory walls of thick cardboard; roofs of thin card in various colours. Buoys from wooden beads. Trucks mounted on rubbers with drawing-pin wheels. Shipping brightly coloured from thin tinted card with cane masts and bookbinding thread.

Right: Complete harbour. On hardboard base 6ft. long against a painted background on frieze paper. Made by a group of 28 children. Factories assembled from identical cardboard units. Painted with poster and powder colours. Dark colours for buildings, trucks, and background. Bright colours for shipping. Lighthouse and cranes black and white.

Ship in dock 5in. long. Painted with opaque water-colours bright yellow with black markings and blue band round funnel. Built round thick cardboard base. Harbour wall grey Sugar paper over match boxes. Trucks painted dark green, brown and black.

To prepare the harbour a portion must be raised for the land. Cut this floor from thick card. Lay it down on the base board and draw round it. Remove the floor and erect a wall of matchboxes (or similar supports of uniform height) along this line. Replace the floor on these supports. Extra matchboxes will be required at random to support the main expanse. (See page 97).

The lighthouse (also page 97) is similar to the tower on page 31 but with an actual torch bulb for illumination. The socket for this costs only a few pence from an electrical supplier. The lamp assembly is housed in a cylinder of clear acetate sheet to which the conical roof is also attached. The signal mast (also page 97) is made from an old brush handle driven into the harbour floor and lashed with thread or fuse wire. Cut notches to prevent the thread from slipping.

The diagrams on this and the opposite page are self-explanatory.

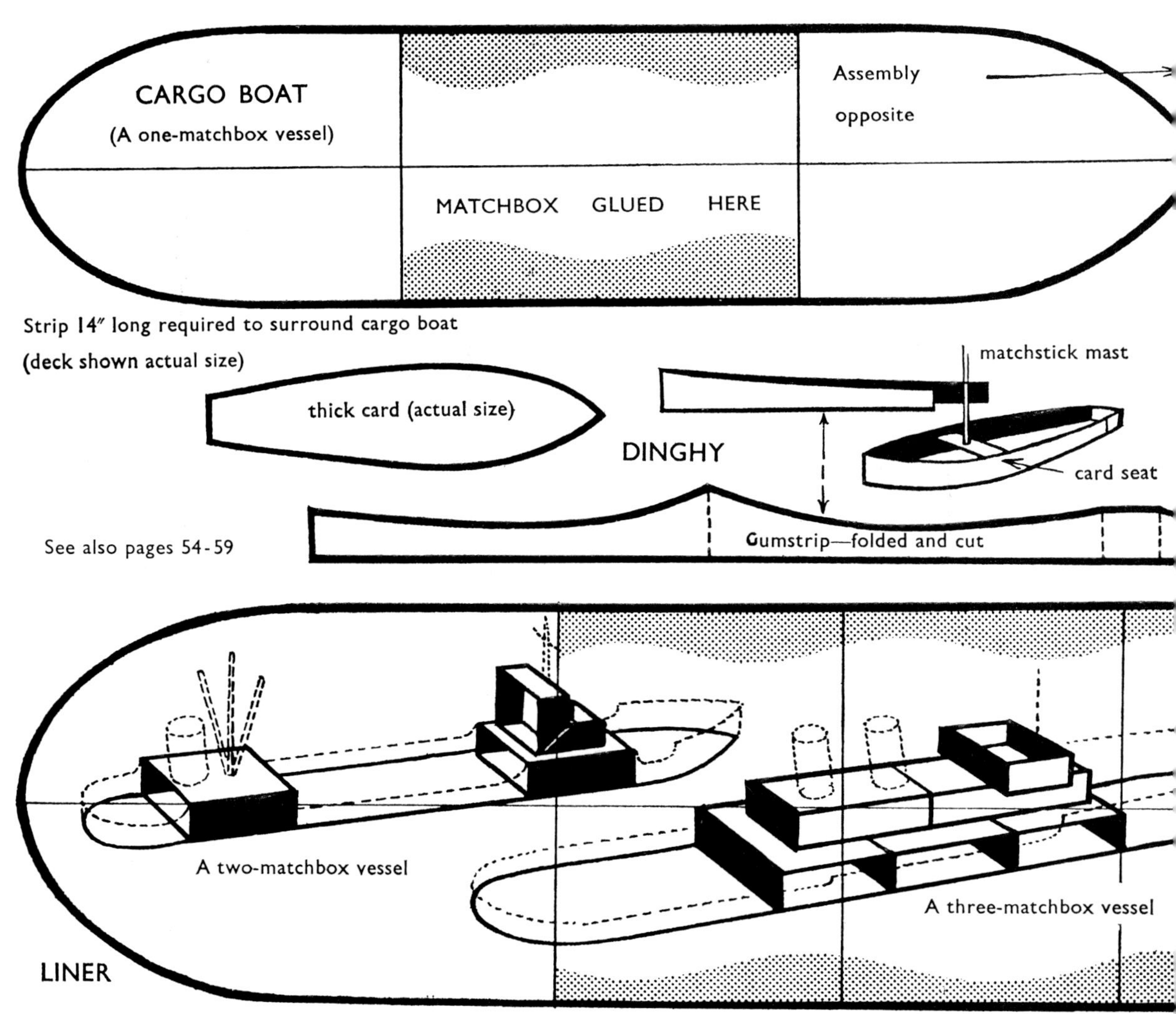

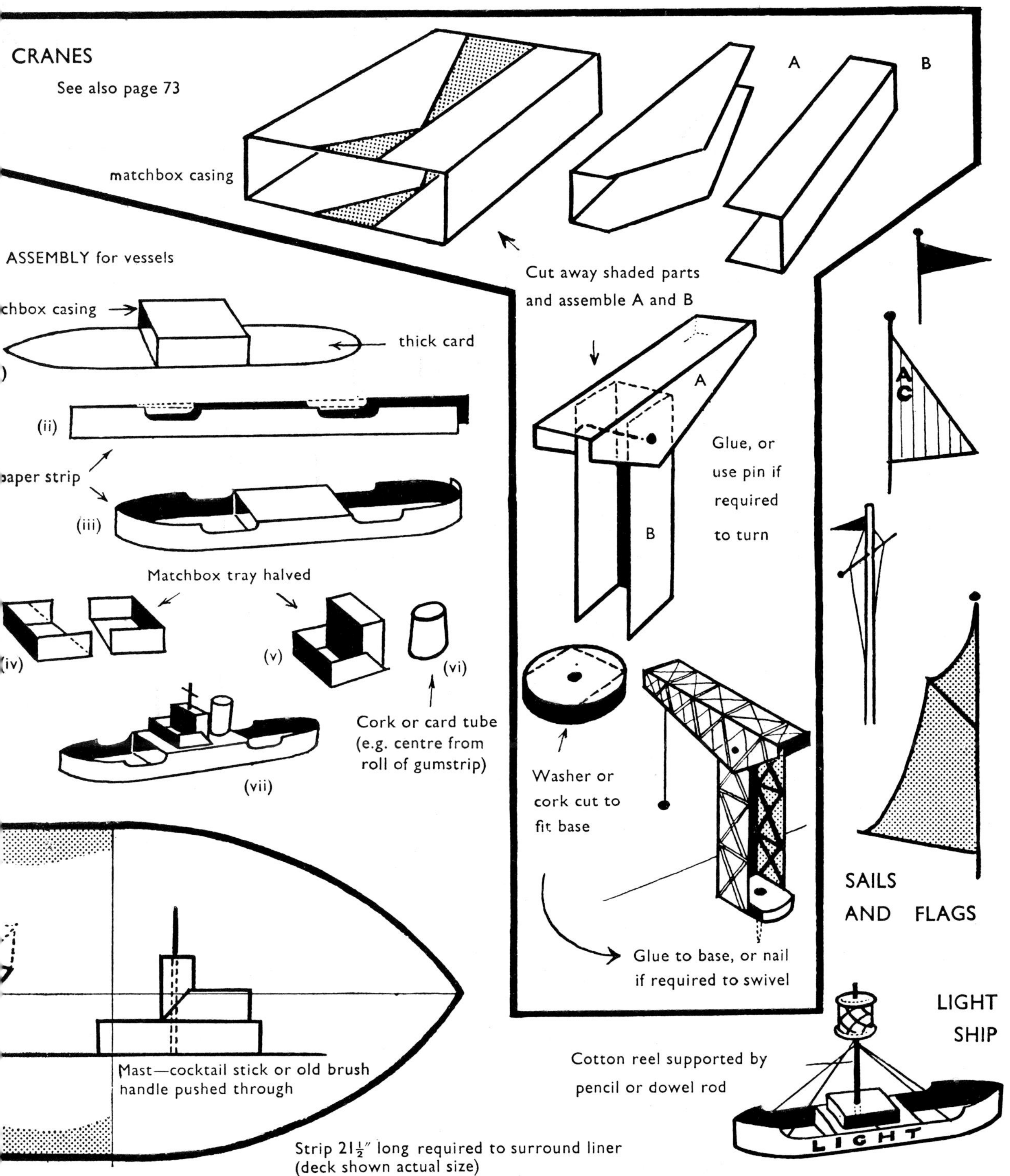
CRANES
See also page 73
A
B
matchbox casing
ASSEMBLY for vessels
chbox casing
thick card
Cut away shaded parts
and assemble A and B
A
(ii)
Glue, or
use pin if
required
to turn
B
paper strip
(iii)
Matchbox tray halved
(iv)
(v)
(vi)
Cork or card tube
(e.g. centre from
roll of gumstrip)
(vii)
Washer or
cork cut to
fit base
SAILS
AND FLAGS
Glue to base, or nail
if required to swivel
LIGHT
SHIP
Mast—cocktail stick or old brush
handle pushed through
Cotton reel supported by
pencil or dowel rod
LIGHT
Strip 21½″ long required to surround liner
(deck shown actual size)

Bridges. The models shown opposite and on the following two pages are particularly suitable for group construction because they employ repetitive features (i.e., the towers). One set of instructions is thus sufficient to start off a whole group making a number of these and assembling them in pairs. Sectional models like these are adaptable for groups of different sizes. If any children are without a job, the bridge simply grows another span. The bigger the class, the longer the bridge.

The two models opposite are both *working* models. In the case of the lifting bridge the centre span can be made to open, and in the case of the swing bridge the whole span can be made to turn on its support.

For towers of a different pattern see pages 31, 73 and 89.

Lifting bridge may be easily adapted as a castle drawbridge. Notice that for this model the moving span is counterbalanced by means of a cotton reel (or similar weight) concealed within the tower. This and the string attaching to it should be threaded in place before the tower becomes inaccessible from beneath. Otherwise the diagram should be clear enough.

Swing bridge is very straightforward, but its support may need a word of explanation. A cotton reel is glued securely underneath (use a strong 'impact' adhesive). The support itself is simply a box, but within this box, and protruding slightly from the lid, is a postal tube or toilet roll cylinder. This must be held steady by means of a shelf within the box. Make sure that the cotton reel will drop down into the top of the tube, thus enabling the bridge to turn.

Suspension bridge requires no further explanation, except perhaps with regard to the suspension itself. This is the last part to be erected after the towers and roadway have been fixed in position. (The roadway having already been punched with holes for the vertical wiring). Unlike the real thing the model bridge would stay put without any suspension. The main cables are lengths of basketwork cane fixed at three points with paper fasteners. First bend the two prongs of the paper fastener round the cane, making sure that the cane fits as snugly as possible up against the head of the fastener. Then open the prongs so that they always tend to splay out. Bring them together and push both prongs into the tower so that they will open out again inside. This will hold the cable while the vertical wires are being attached.

For each pair of wires cut an ample length and bend into shape with pliers. Push the ends through the holes in the road from beneath. Twist the free ends once round the cane and snip off any surplus, but leave sufficient wire on which to thread a wooden bead. Fill the bore of the bead with glue.

Another simple bridge may be found on page 16. Pages 21 and 88 may also be consulted.

Models of bridges have more interest if there is a river (if only a painted one) which needs to be spanned.

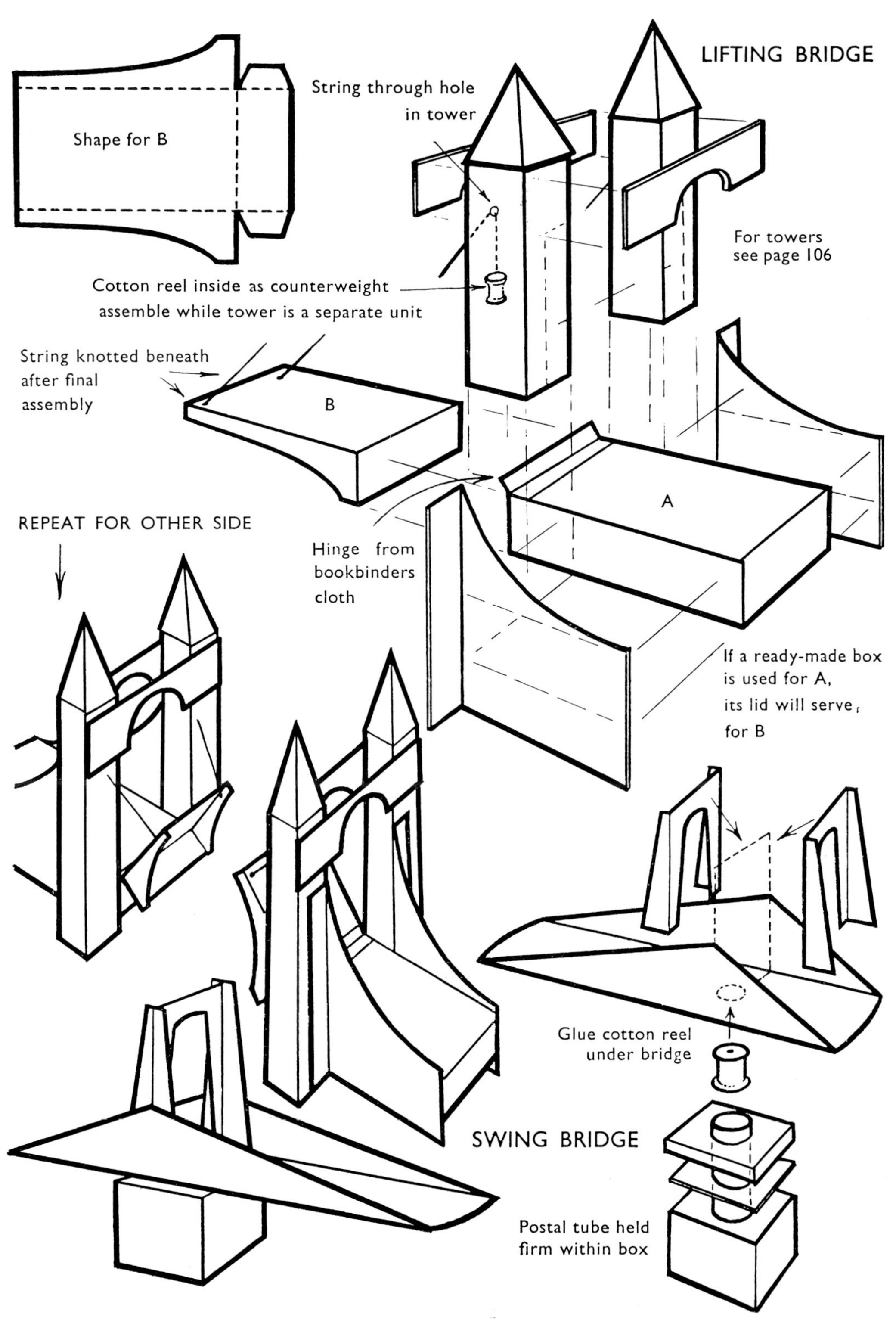
LIFTING BRIDGE
Shape for B
String through hole
in tower
For towers
see page 106
Cotton reel inside as counterweight
assemble while tower is a separate unit
String knotted beneath
after final
assembly
B
A
REPEAT FOR OTHER SIDE
Hinge from
bookbinders
cloth
If a ready-made box
is used for A,
its lid will serve,
for B
Glue cotton reel
under bridge
SWING BRIDGE
Postal tube held
firm within box

SUSPENSION BRIDGE

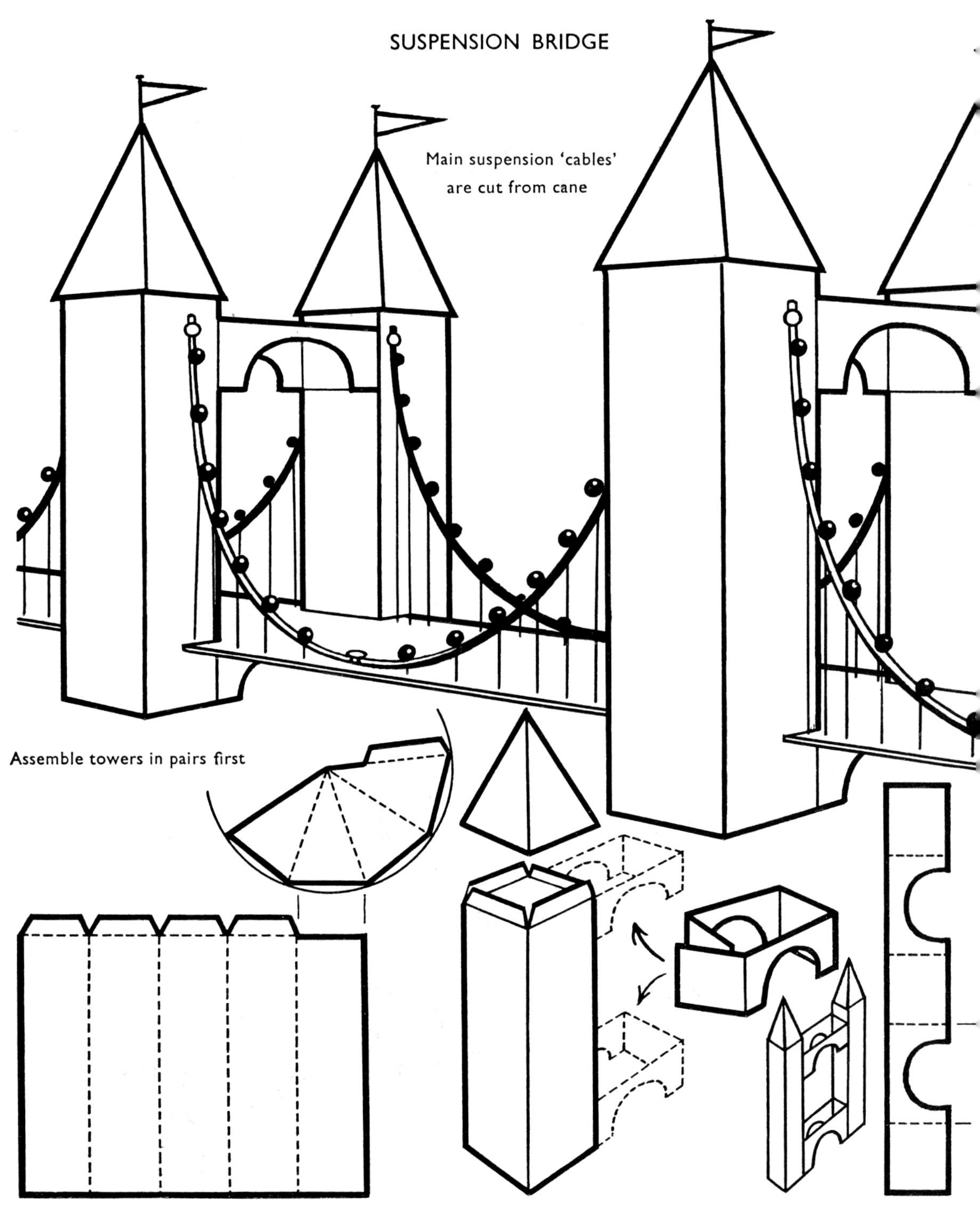

Attach cane to tower and road with paper fasteners
Vertical wires inserted from below
Twist round cane
bead
Insert on edge and lower into position
Make roadway from thickest card
Punch holes before assembly

In contrast with the functional examples on the previous two pages, this bridge is included for its decorative qualities. The basic construction is simple but the model would be greatly enhanced with painted details. Ornate balustrades can be applied with a brush to the flat sections before they are assembled. There are usually some children who are happier with a brush than with a pair of scissors and this is just the sort of opportunity for them to show what they can do. Although it does not properly fall within the scope of this book, painting is nevertheless an important aspect of composite model making which it would be a pity to overlook.

Other models with which the ornamental bridge might be effectively combined are the classic temple on page 33, or the arcades suggested on pages 88 and 89. Even when there is no water, the bridge sometimes makes an interesting feature when applied to the facade of a building. As an architectural extravagance it might not be out of place in a formal garden. A Venetian setting is also indicated. The gondola may be found on page 55, and the punt on page 57 might also be appropriate.

A large mirror, lying flat on the table, makes an extremely effective base for models of lakes or canals. Be sure the underneath of the model is painted black so that the reflection does not reveal any parts which are perhaps supposed to be hidden.

A rectangular box, A, forms the foundation of the model. A shoe box would do. The main arch is cut from opposite sides of this box. The opening should not extend too close to the edges or there will not be room to mount the sloping sections, B, on either side. Parts A and B must first be drawn out and the overlap noted before the length of part C can be accurately determined, or the small side arches safely cut out. The method of assembly can then be seen from the diagram. The surmounting structure in the middle can be designed quite freely provided that it conforms to the width of the main box.

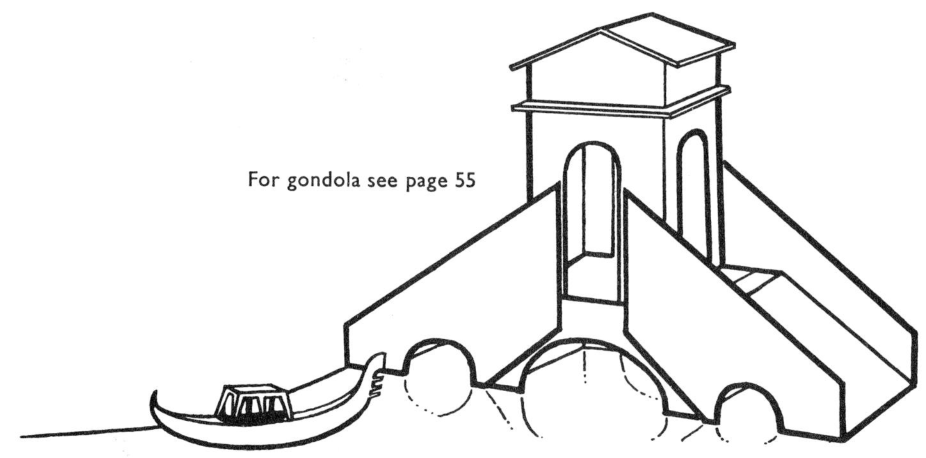

ORNAMENTAL BRIDGE

For various arches see also pages 21 and 88

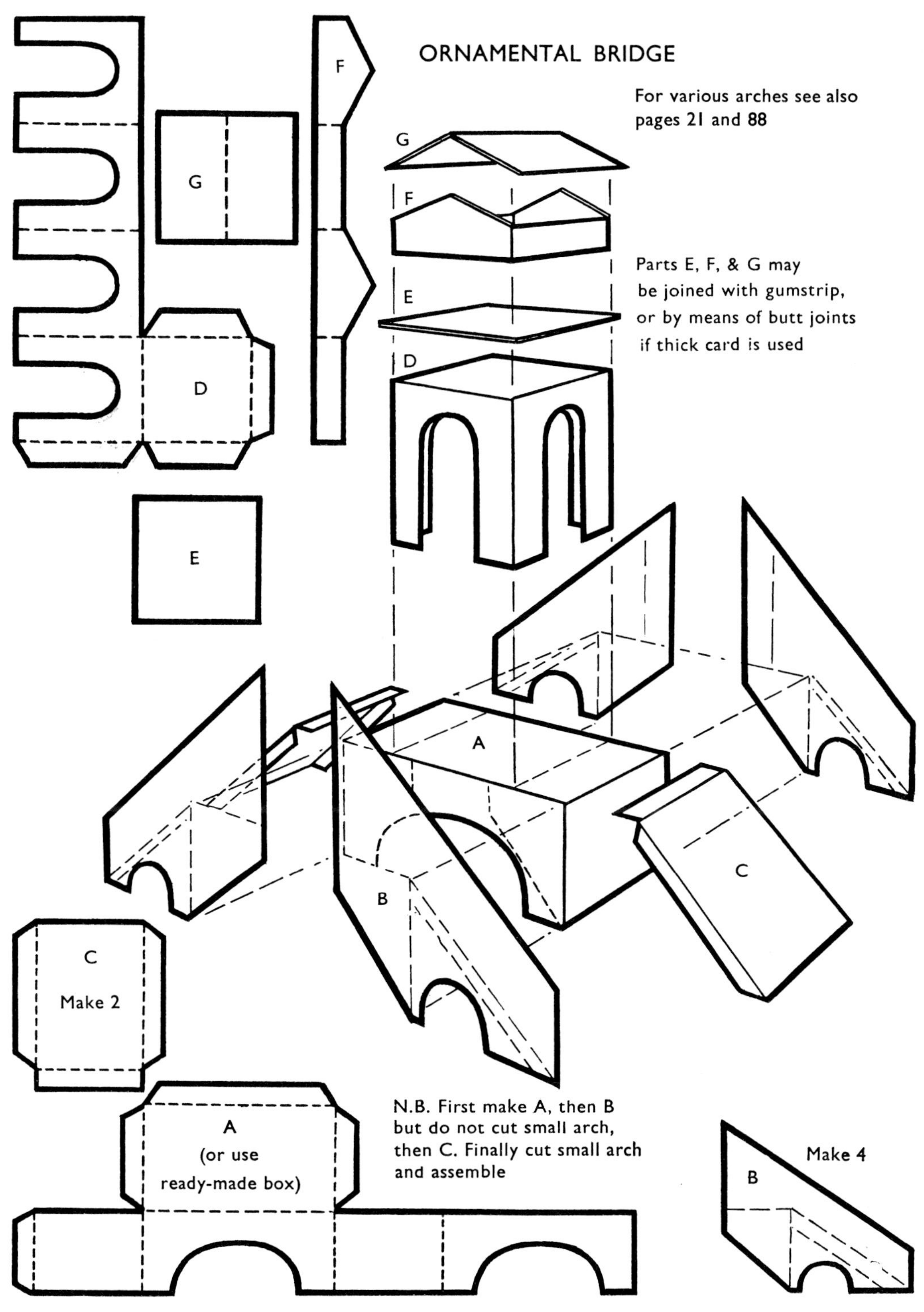

Parts E, F, & G may be joined with gumstrip, or by means of butt joints if thick card is used

N.B. First make A, then B but do not cut small arch, then C. Finally cut small arch and assemble

Marshalling yard. It would be a mistake to adhere too slavishly to the layout on pages 112 and 113 when the available materials and the children's own ideas may suggest otherwise. There is sure to be some expert in the class who will be quick to point out that signal arms and water towers belong only to the bygone age of steam locomotion. A 'modernisation programme' might, therefore, be indicated. Coloured lights may supersede the signals, and the gantries used to support overhead electric cables. Signal boxes may have flat roofs instead of sloping ones. Unfortunately diesel electric railway systems do not provide nearly the same structural variety as the traditional types. There is no reason why features from both eras might not be combined in the same model.

The details opposite merely augment existing material. The gantry is a shallow box formed round matchboxes (or similar strengthening sections) within. The signals are rectangular columns identical to the gantry supports. Shape the cardboard round a wooden former (about $\frac{1}{2}$ in. x $\frac{1}{2}$ in.). This former is also used to rule out the flat card, (i) (ii) (iii). At the corners the columns penetrate the floor of the box and are glued to the inside of its walls. The matchboxes provide convenient angles in which to mount the signals. Signal *lamps* may be represented by coloured-topped drawing pins. The ladders have sides of thick card punched at intervals, their rungs are wire, cane, or matchsticks. It is important that the side struts should be marked out and the holes punched before being cut from the sheet, otherwise the punching of the holes may ruin the strip. See also page 73.

The signal box, as might be expected, is in fact a box. Part of the front is cut away and replaced with perspex or clear acetate sheet. For the roof either use a flat box lid or refer to the varieties on pages 80-82. The steps are pieces cut from wooden spills supported by slots in the end wall, and by an additional cardboard section similarly slotted. For other useful buildings see particularly pages 75 and 76; also the engine shed on page 78. For the water tower refer to the appropriate sections dealing with cones and cylinders. A cheese box would be useful when forming the larger cylinder, and a postal tube would serve for the supporting column. Ladder as above.

The turntable is of simple construction. Fix through the centre with a paper fastener to a thick cardboard disc, which may then be glued flat on to the base of the model.

The loading platform and buffers need no further explanation except that drawing pins form the buffers themselves. This applies also to the trucks. Ideas for trucks are given on page 69 but a variation is shown opposite. A matchbox tray would provide the truck itself, while the undercarriage is formed from a single piece of card, folded round to accept axles of thick cane, into the ends of which drawing pins are fixed for wheels.

For the crane see page 73 or 103, for the fence page 19, for the lorry page 69, and for the observation or lighting tower page 73. Ideas for freight are shown on page 97. There is, of course, no end to the stuff which might be carried by rail!

As for the permanent way, 'permanent' is probably too optimistic a word. The track is best just painted on the base, unless anyone is sufficiently painstaking to cut individual sleepers from card in which case the rails could be represented by means of string glued on top.

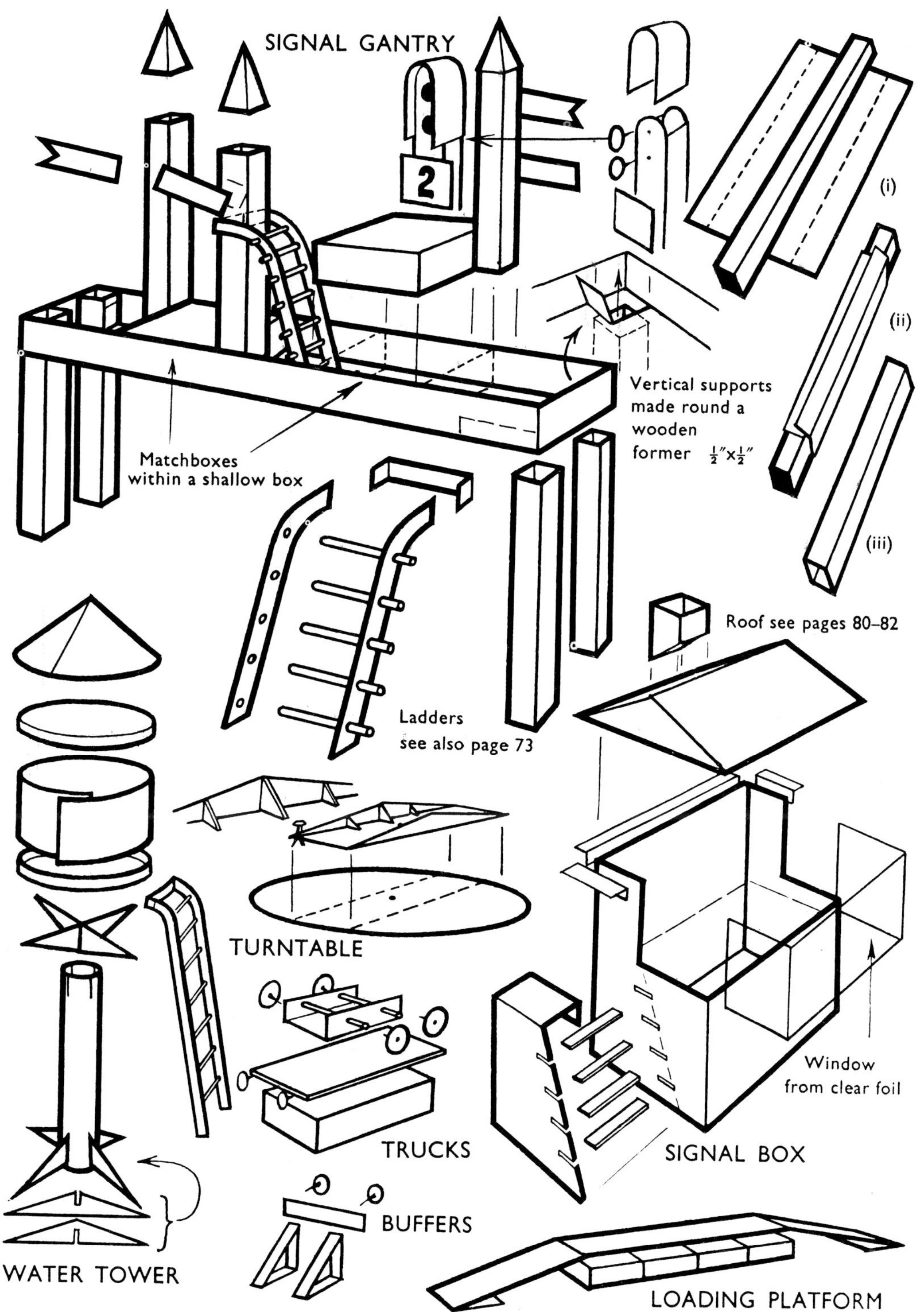
SIGNAL GANTRY
2
(i)
(ii)
(iii)
Vertical supports
made round a
wooden
former $\frac{1}{2}''\times\frac{1}{2}''$
Matchboxes
within a shallow box
Roof see pages 80–82
Ladders
see also page 73
TURNTABLE
TRUCKS
Window
from clear foil
SIGNAL BOX
BUFFERS
WATER TOWER
LOADING PLATFORM

2
1

Castles. Young children frequently demand quick results. The castle affords an opportunity to make an impressive model in a short time. It is adaptable with regard to scale. The towers, for example, may be anything from a few inches to a foot in height provided that the thickness of the card is chosen accordingly. For small scale sectional models, postcards are often useful as their uniform dimensions provide a convenient basis for repetitive building units.

One set of instructions is again sufficient for a whole group of children, all making identical towers to be assembled later.

The completed units need not be glued together. They simply slot into one another with the advantage that the final assembly of the model may safely be left until the end of the lesson. This also permits the arrangement to be modified as it grows. Individual children can paint and finish their own section before it is incorporated with the others.

The model lends itself to drawing out on card which has been marked in squares. Let one crenel of the battlement conform to one square. If a ground plan is to be painted, do this after the model has been assembled so that it can be allowed to take up its own position. For storage purposes a collapsible model has advantages.

Various outbuildings and surrounding fortifications may be devised. See the timber frame house on page 87 , and the drawbridge on page 105.

Of the variations opposite, type A has been selected for detailed treatment on the following two pages. All the towers conform to the same square base pattern, but are of three different heights according to their place in the model. The vertical slots are in adjacent faces of the corner towers for the keep, but in opposite faces of the towers which occur at intervals along the perimeter wall, and on either side of the gateway. The size and shape of the wall sections is shown in relation to the towers which they are designed to fit. All wall sections are made in pairs, thus producing a cavity wall. If only one thickness of wall is used the model will still stand but will lack stability.

Note that for the perimeter wall the two sections of each pair are exactly the same shape, but the slots in the outer section are slightly further apart than those in the inner section. This causes the towers to be mounted at an angle to the wall. When about eight towers and the gateway have been slotted together the wall should have come round to the first tower again to form a continuous rampart. The exact degree of turn depends upon the position of the slots and some special adjustment may be needed on the last section, or another section may need to be added.

Type B is easier to assemble, but the hexagonal towers may take longer than square ones. The keep requires no wall sections. The perimeter wall is made from identical connecting sections. No adjustment need be made to the slots as the hexagonal shape of the towers itself effects a change of direction in the wall. When painting the sections for the keep, remember that only three faces of each hexagonal unit will finally show. This method of construction is limited to multiple groupings of six.

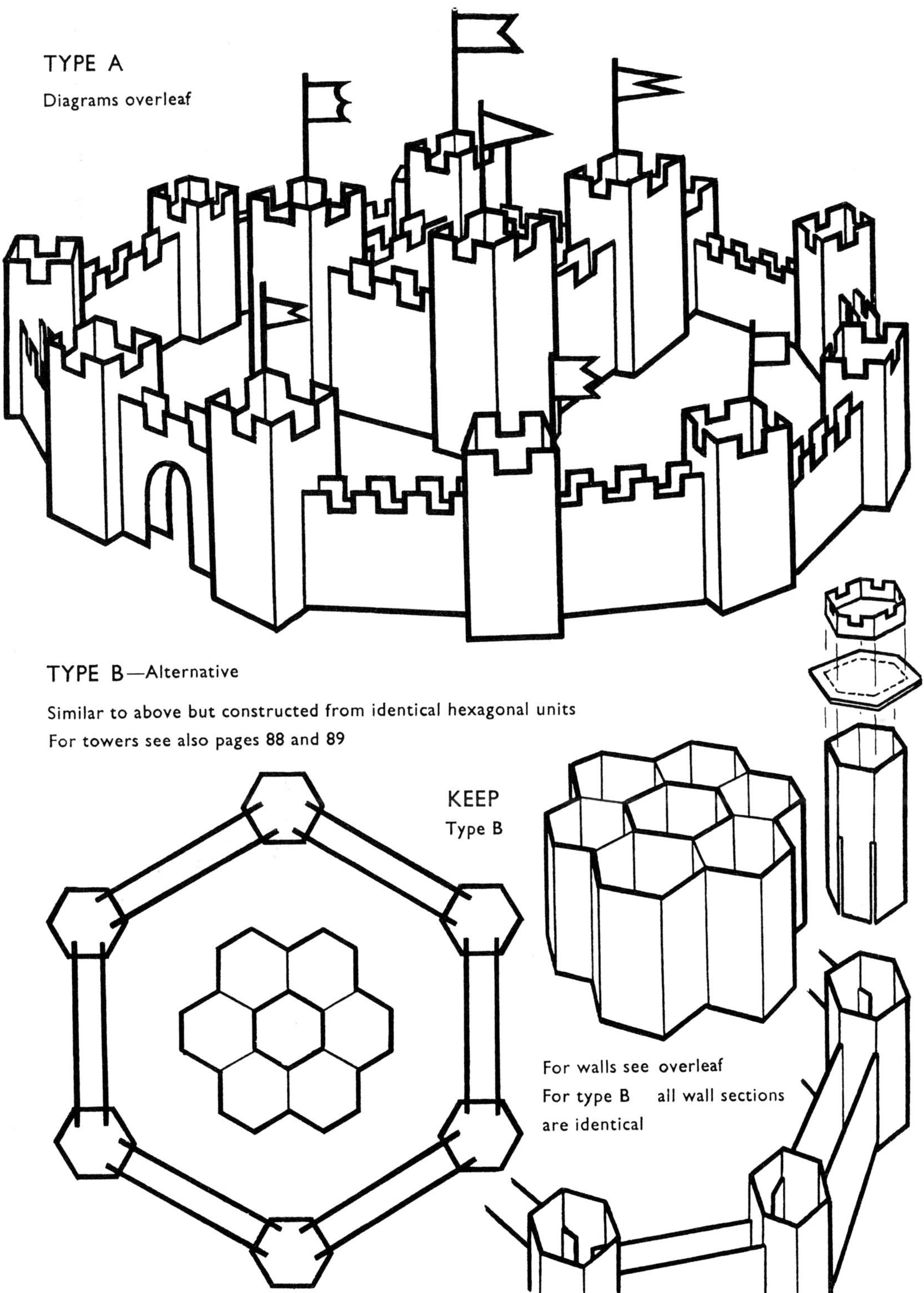
TYPE A
Diagrams overleaf
TYPE B—Alternative
Similar to above but constructed from identical hexagonal units
For towers see also pages 88 and 89
KEEP
Type B
For walls see overleaf
For type B all wall sections
are identical

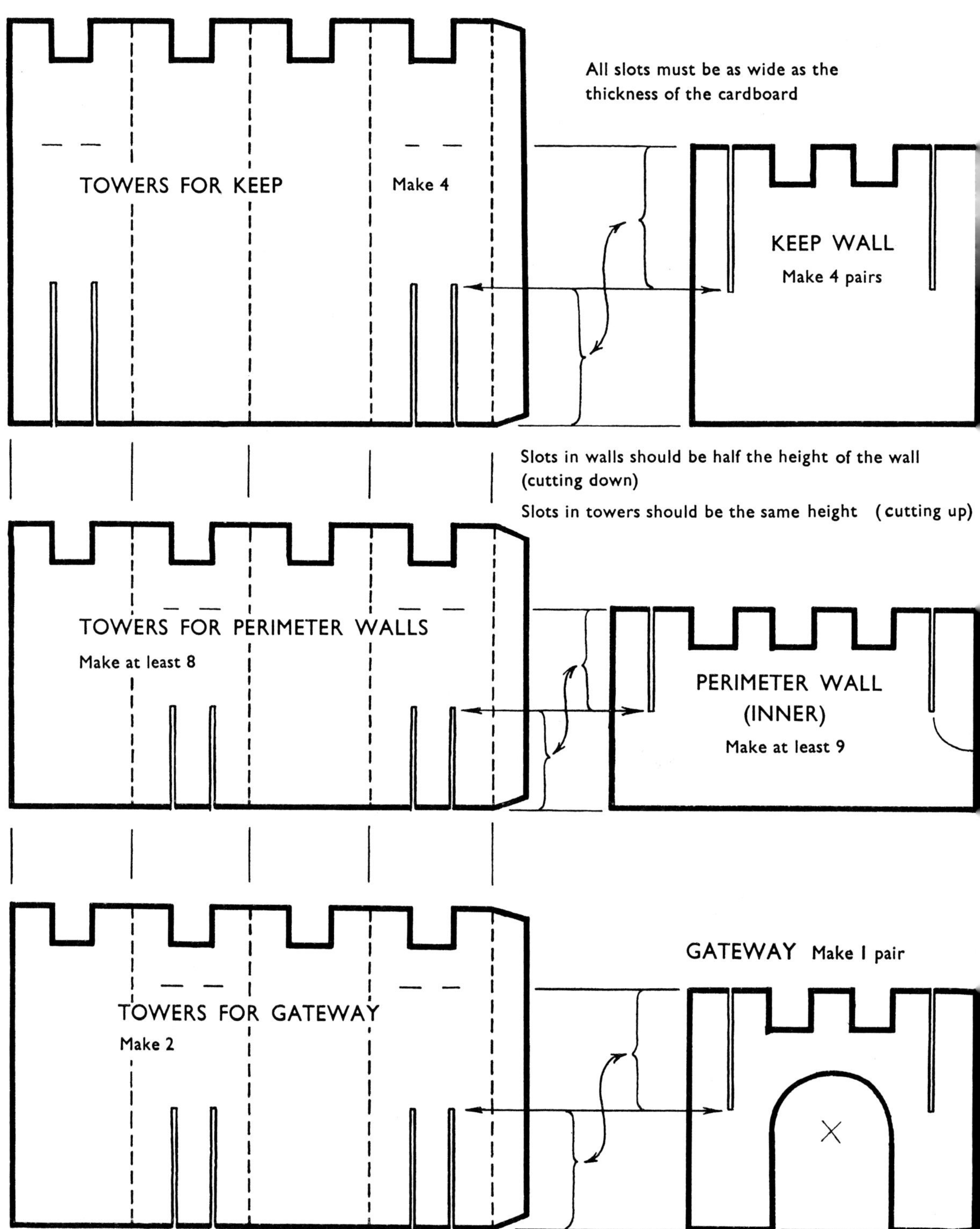

All slots must be as wide as the thickness of the cardboard
TOWERS FOR KEEP
Make 4
KEEP WALL
Make 4 pairs
Slots in walls should be half the height of the wall (cutting down)
Slots in towers should be the same height (cutting up)
TOWERS FOR PERIMETER WALLS
Make at least 8
PERIMETER WALL
(INNER)
Make at least 9
GATEWAY Make I pair
TOWERS FOR GATEWAY
Make 2

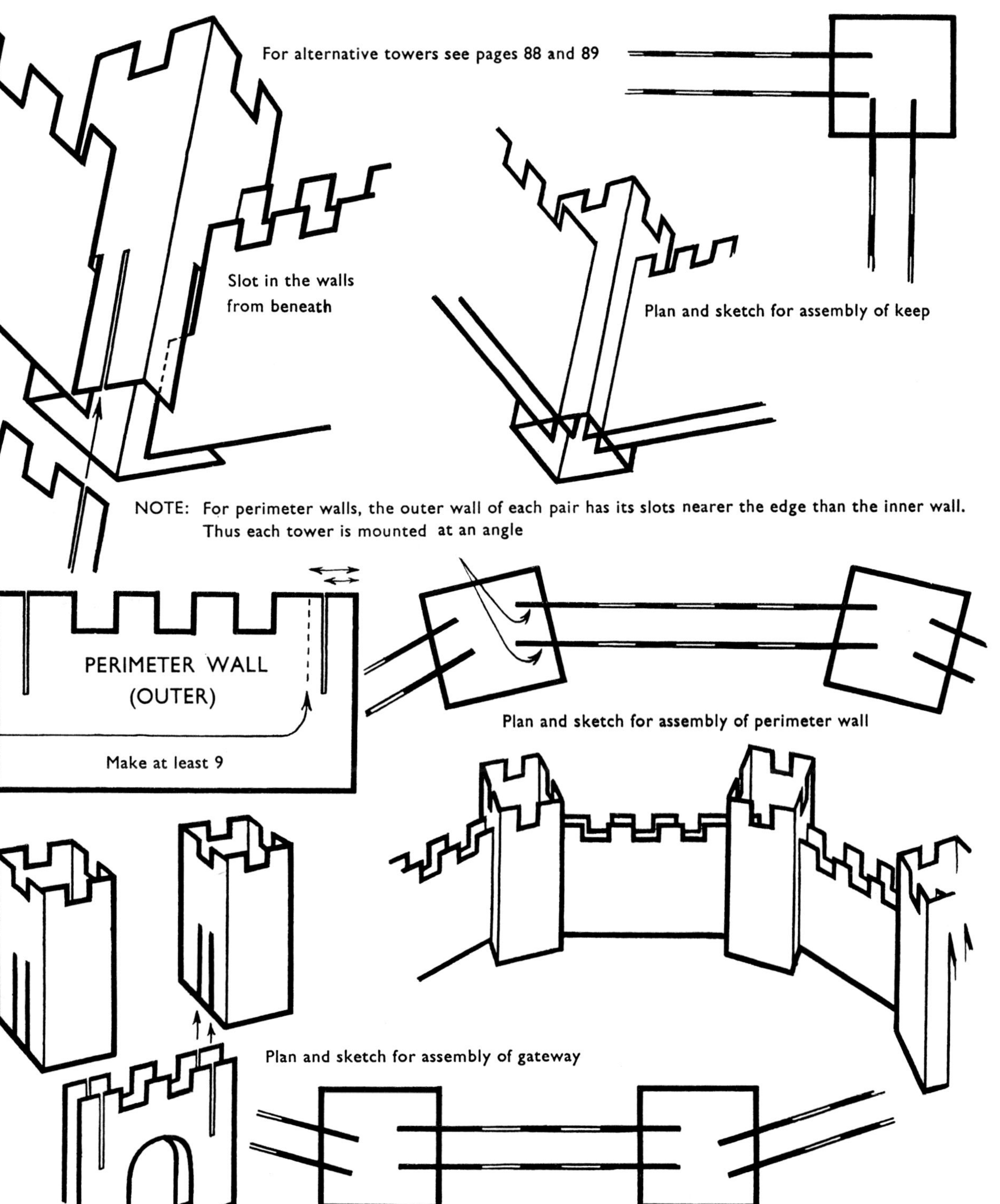

For alternative towers see pages 88 and 89
Slot in the walls
from beneath
Plan and sketch for assembly of keep
NOTE: For perimeter walls, the outer wall of each pair has its slots nearer the edge than the inner wall.
Thus each tower is mounted at an angle
PERIMETER WALL
(OUTER)
Make at least 9
Plan and sketch for assembly of perimeter wall
Plan and sketch for assembly of gateway

Right: Castle. Constructed throughout from post-cards. Height to top of flags $3\frac{1}{2}$in. Flag poles from match sticks. Towers of three standard sizes. Wall sections of two standard sizes and gateway. Unpainted.

Bottom right: Suspension bridge. Length about 3ft. Made by a group of eight children. Towers from medium thick card painted grey with black markings. Roofs from thin card painted red. Arches thin card painted grey. Roadway from thick straw-board punched along edges. Main suspension cables of cane. Vertical cables of wire topped with red wooden beads.

Below: Castle seen from above. Showing arrangement of keep and perimeter walls. Standard units slotted together without gluing. Distance across courtyard 8 in.

Pier and Funfair. This double model comprises two associated features. Either the Pier or the Funfair could be taken as complete in itself, but children usually welcome the chance to display a little initiative in these matters, and the combined model will offer them more scope.

The illustration on pages 122 and 123 is not intended as some sort of cryptic blueprint, but simply to suggest in a general way the character of the model. The more freely the basic shapes are interpreted the more varied will be the final arrangement. Some of the more hazardous pieces of modern fairground machinery would demand a certain daring on the part of the model maker, but the traditional shapes of roundabouts and side-shows are not complicated. Reference to the appropriate sections on cones and cylinders, and to some of the simple buildings, will supply all the necessary information. Then it remains only to apply individual details and plenty of that garish brand of decoration apparently peculiar to children and travelling showmen. Strings of beads would not look out of place, or screwed up tinsel toffee papers threaded on thin wire. Berry pins and hat pins may adorn the roof tops, and lots of flags are required. These may be fixed to coloured sticks or knitting needles bound round with coloured tape like barbers' poles. The pier pavilion is really the dutch barn on page 76 in disguise, and the mat slide is adapted from the windmill on page 85. Other shapes will be found to originate in similar easy beginnings.

In all original model making small constructional problems are bound to arise. They constitute a challenge to the inventive faculties of the children and enable them to apply the principles learned from earlier examples.

The platform for the pier must be made from very thick cardboard, or several layers glued together. It is supported on cylindrical piles cut from a postal tube, or from those tubes which are often found inside rolls of cloth. These supports should not be too far apart.

The big wheel is made from six equilateral sections. The outside of each section is formed with two strips of corrugated card so that a spindle may be pushed through on which to hang a matchbox. The matchbox must first be fitted with wire loops. Ensure that there is room between the corrugated strips for the box to swing freely. The main spindle at the centre of the wheel is a skewer or length of stout wire with corks pushed on each end. The cheesebox discs are not absolutely essential but afford extra support for large models. The wheel should be free to revolve.

For the base of the roundabout it would be wise first to draw a plan in order to determine the exact dimensions of the wedge-shaped components. The cardboard animals could be fitted with seats of plastic foam. They stand on a separate disc of card mounted within the roundabout.

The spiral for the slide is not an easy shape to draw and should be prepared by the teacher. The dotted lines are concentric circles included as a guide.

The walls of the scenic railway are of corrugated card with the corrugations running vertically so that sticks may later be pushed down into them to form the railing on top. The cars are matchboxes, suitably decorated, with drawing pins or washers for wheels (see 'Things on Wheels' page 60).

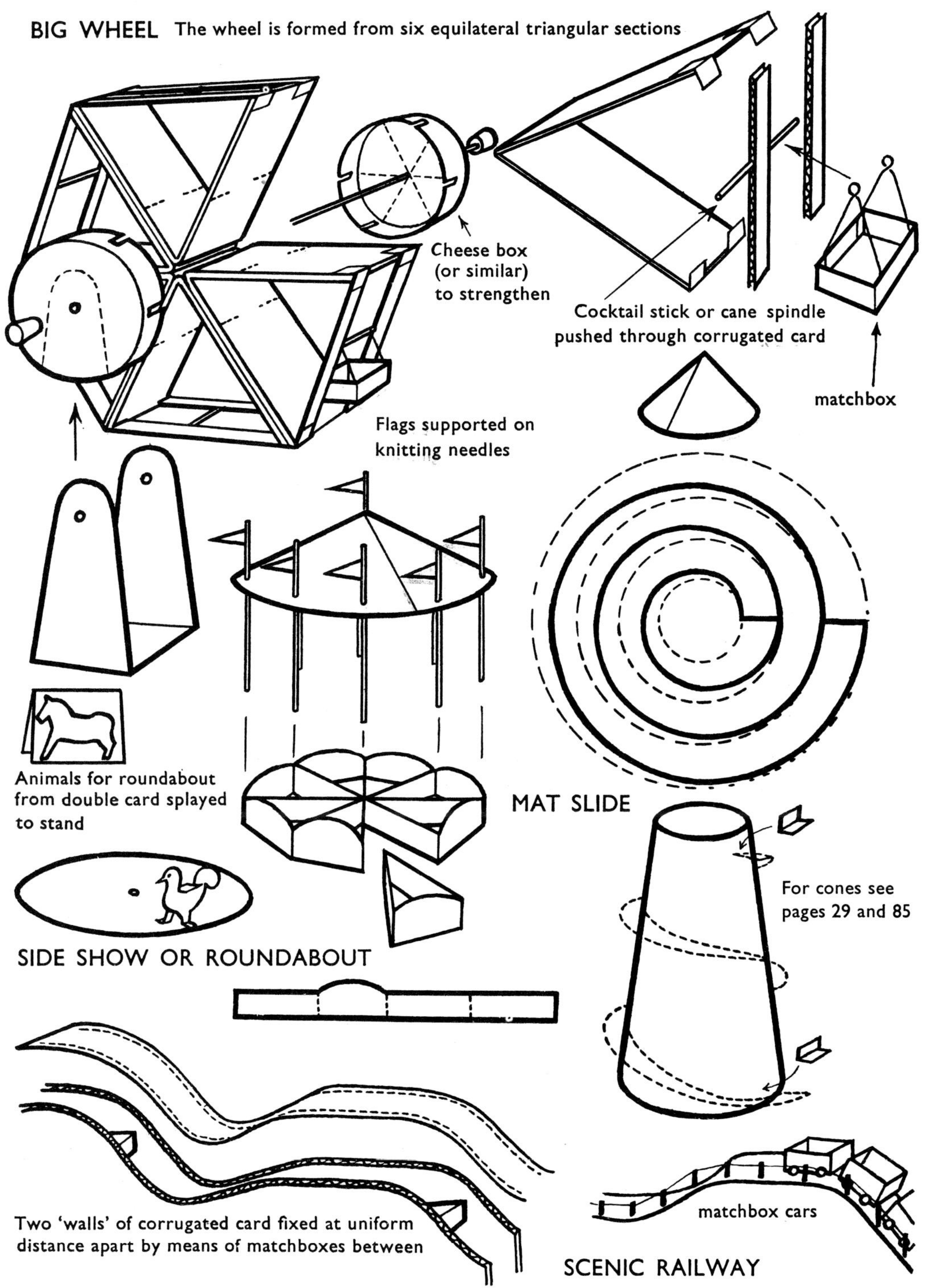
BIG WHEEL The wheel is formed from six equilateral triangular sections
Cheese box
(or similar)
to strengthen
Cocktail stick or cane spindle
pushed through corrugated card
matchbox
Flags supported on
knitting needles
Animals for roundabout
from double card splayed
to stand
MAT SLIDE
For cones see
pages 29 and 85
SIDE SHOW OR ROUNDABOUT
matchbox cars
Two 'walls' of corrugated card fixed at uniform
distance apart by means of matchboxes between
SCENIC RAILWAY

Circus. The central feature of the travelling circus is, of course, the big-top itself, and the diagrams in this section are devoted to it almost entirely. A solitary tent, however, would hardly convey the atmosphere of the circus field with all its attendant vehicles and side-shows. The reader is therefore invited to consult the appropriate earlier sections of the book where individual models will be found which could easily be adapted to the present composite idea.

It is a wise precaution, when organising large groups, to have available some very easy repetitive jobs for those who find themselves out of work. In this case the 'labour exchange' party could manufacture lengths of bunting, flags on poles, cages for the animals, and even a few clay animals to go inside.

The diagrams opposite show the construction of the circus ring and the seating arrangements. Obviously, it will only be possible to put all this inside if the tent is fairly large. Even so, much of it may be hidden. Nevertheless children are often intrigued to incorporate 'secrets' into their models, and if one or two electric torch bulbs are dangled inside, then the big-top immediately takes on some of the excitement of a peep-show. Each seating terrace and the segments bordering the ring may be set up without gluing. There will then be more chance of getting them out through the tent opening if necessary. The initial arrangement should be set up before the tent is lowered into position. Storage is simplified if the model can be easily dismantled.

Alternatively, the circus interior may be taken as a distinctly separate model in which case the scale of the tent may be disregarded. The seating arrangement has other applications e.g. open air theatres, grandstands, arenas, etc. The exact shape for the big top is given on page 126. It is not vitally important to use card marked out in squares, although it is helpful when enlarging from a small diagram. If the model is to be really large, i.e. more than 18 in. across, then a fairly stout material such as a light strawboard should be used. When drawing out, plot the centre points first. All the folds must be scored and bent sharply before the final shape is glued. It should be sufficiently rigid to stand alone without poles or guy ropes, which are added later. Coloured beads may be used on top of the poles.

A miniature version, only a few inches across, may be easily made from strong paper. Although this would be too small to contain any inside construction, it is an effective little exercise and quite an easy one because the folds need no scoring and hat pins, etc. could be used as tent poles.

The shape can be modified by altering the number of panels, or by bringing the two centres together so that only one main pole is required. This would result in a circular tent. Alternatively a longer shape will be achieved by moving the centres further apart.

Sporting events, garden fetes, flower shows, and encampments of one sort and another may also inspire models involving a marquee of the sort described.

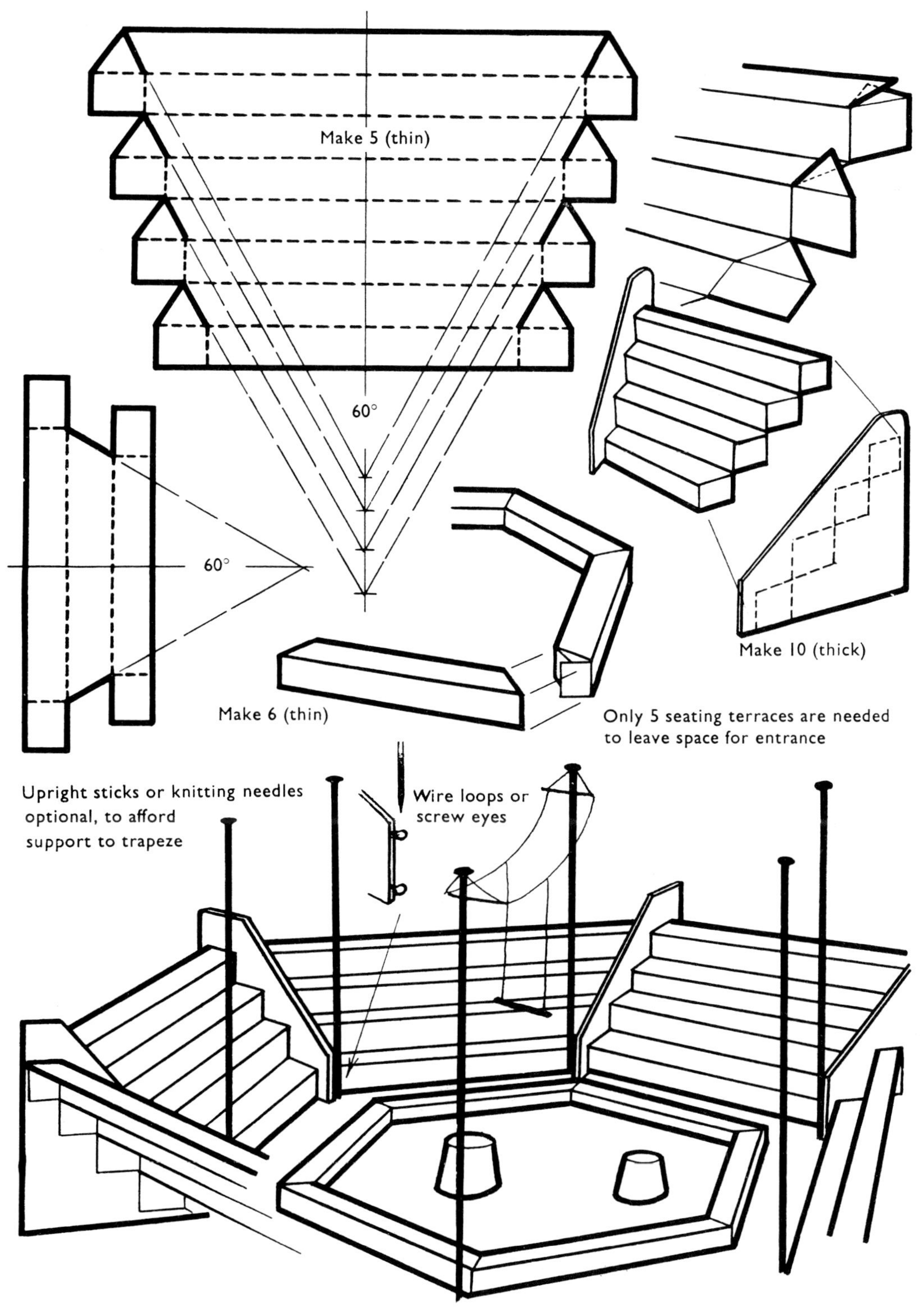
Make 5 (thin)
60°
60°
Make 10 (thick)
Make 6 (thin)
Only 5 seating terraces are needed
to leave space for entrance
Upright sticks or knitting needles
optional, to afford
support to trapeze
Wire loops or
screw eyes

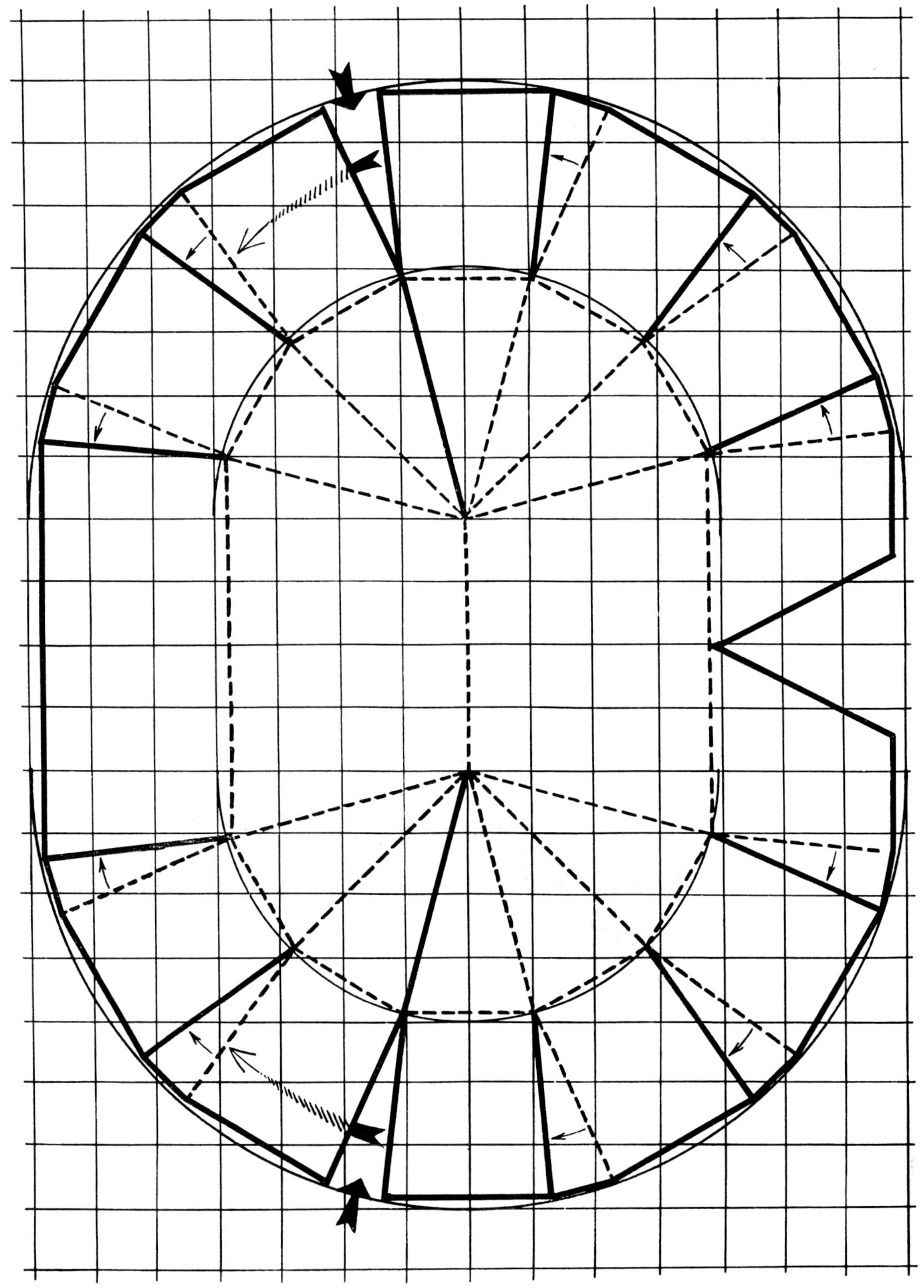

For caravans lorries, trailers etc. see pages 60-71. For side shows, etc. see pages 74-89 and page 121. Also see Fairground 122 and 123.

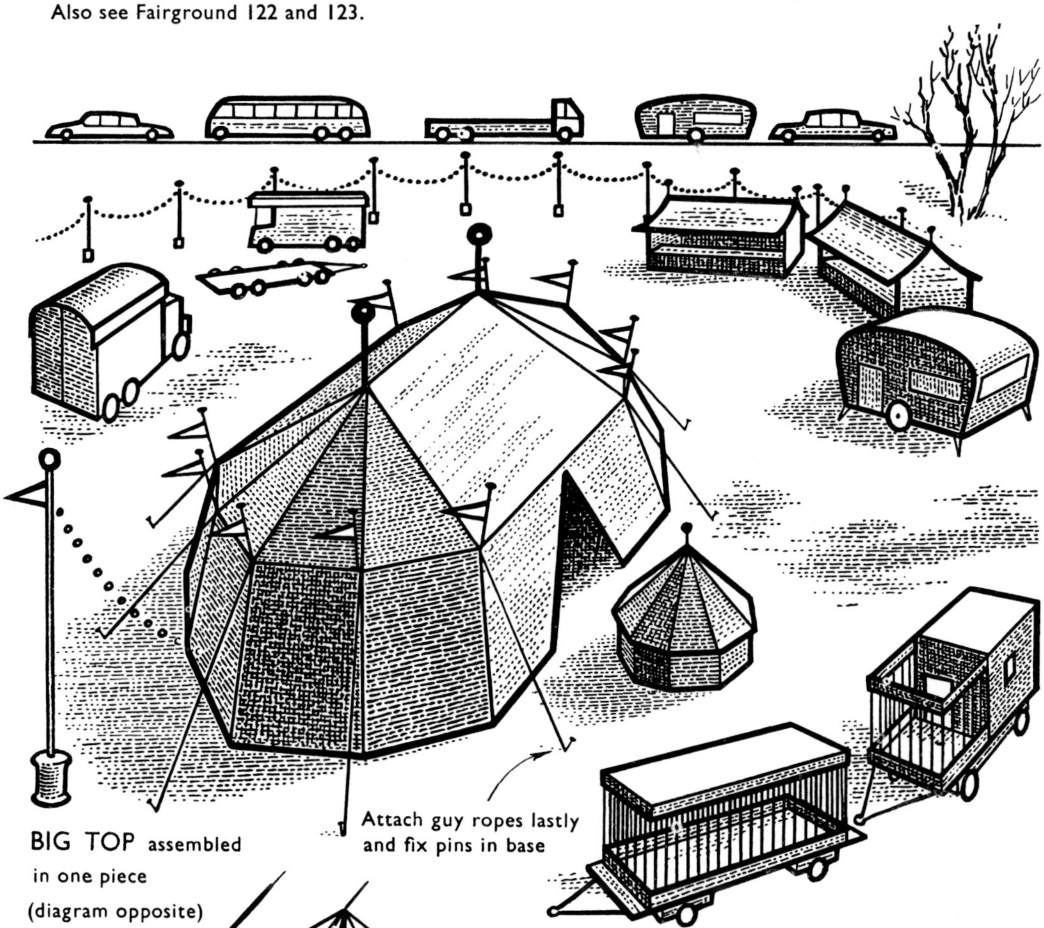

BIG TOP assembled in one piece (diagram opposite)

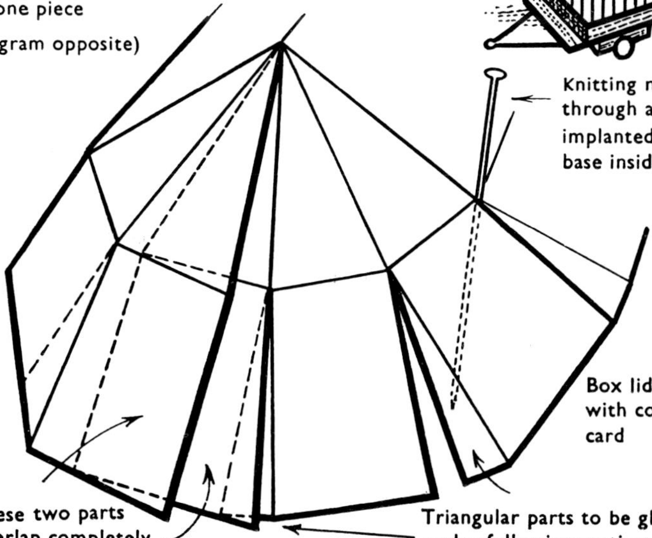

Attach guy ropes lastly and fix pins in base

Knitting needles or garden sticks pushed through after assembly. The ends may be implanted in cotton reels glued to the base inside

CAGES

Box lid lined with corrugated card

Cane or wire bars

These two parts overlap completely

Triangular parts to be glued under following sections

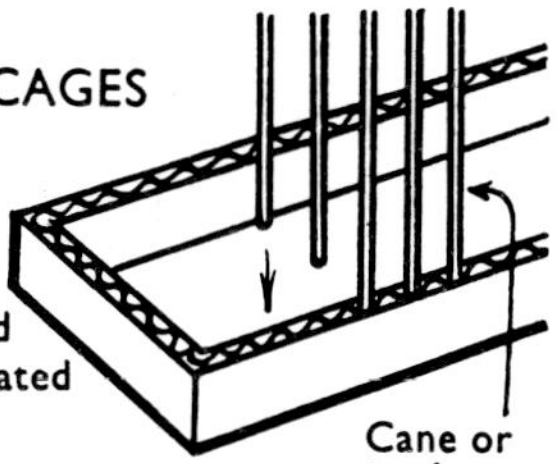

City development. The most ambitious of models is, no doubt, a town or city because it could be developed to include within its boundaries almost every other form of composite model. Models, like real cities, tend to expand indefinitely.

Few school rooms are large enough to house models on such a scale, and even fewer children are capable of this sort of sustained interest. nevertheless, while breakfast cereals continue to be packed in rectangular boxes, and modern architects continue to pursue the trend towards uncomplicated shapes, then there is much to be gained from urban models using simple cartons as their basis.

Working with easy block units, it is possible to reproduce in miniature some of the more elementary problems of the town planner. Considerations of this sort usually promote fruitful discussion among children, and it is helpful if they can translate their ideas at least into cardboard if not exactly concrete terms.

The simple blocks may be interspersed with buildings of a more detailed character and several of the models on pages 74-89 can be brought into play. Considerable variety may be imparted by the free use of coloured and textured surfacing materials–Perspex, veneers, sandpaper (coloured), glossy papers (gummed), wallpapers, etc. Clear acetate sheet (or Perspex), introduced for occasional walls, will give a more spacious appearance, and if the base is constructed on different levels with steps and terraces then the relationship between the various buildings becomes more interesting.

These features are illustrated in a general way on page 131. Also included is the Concert Hall from page 77 and the church from page 84. On page 130 an office block, or block of flats serves to clarify some additional methods of construction. It is intended that these structures be used quite flexibly, and their parts interchanged between one building and another.

Abstract sculptures, mounted on corks or cotton reels, provide an amusing diversion from the structural discipline of the buildings. One or two children in the class will probably like to specialise in making original three-dimensional patterns from cardboard and coloured, plastic covered, wire. Coloured foil, beads, and map pins may be incorporated. A miniature open air sculpture exhibition is not without its possibilities.

Any scheme of civic development will probably take into account the parks and recreation grounds. The diagrams opposite may be used in this connection. It is more likely, however, for reasons of scale, that they should be taken as the subject of an independent model.

Except for the slide, all these amusements are capable of movement. As working models, they should therefore be made large enough to allow the fact to be demonstrated. The component parts are all similar in construction to pieces already explained earlier (particularly under 'Basic shapes' page 26).

RECREATION GROUND AMUSEMENTS

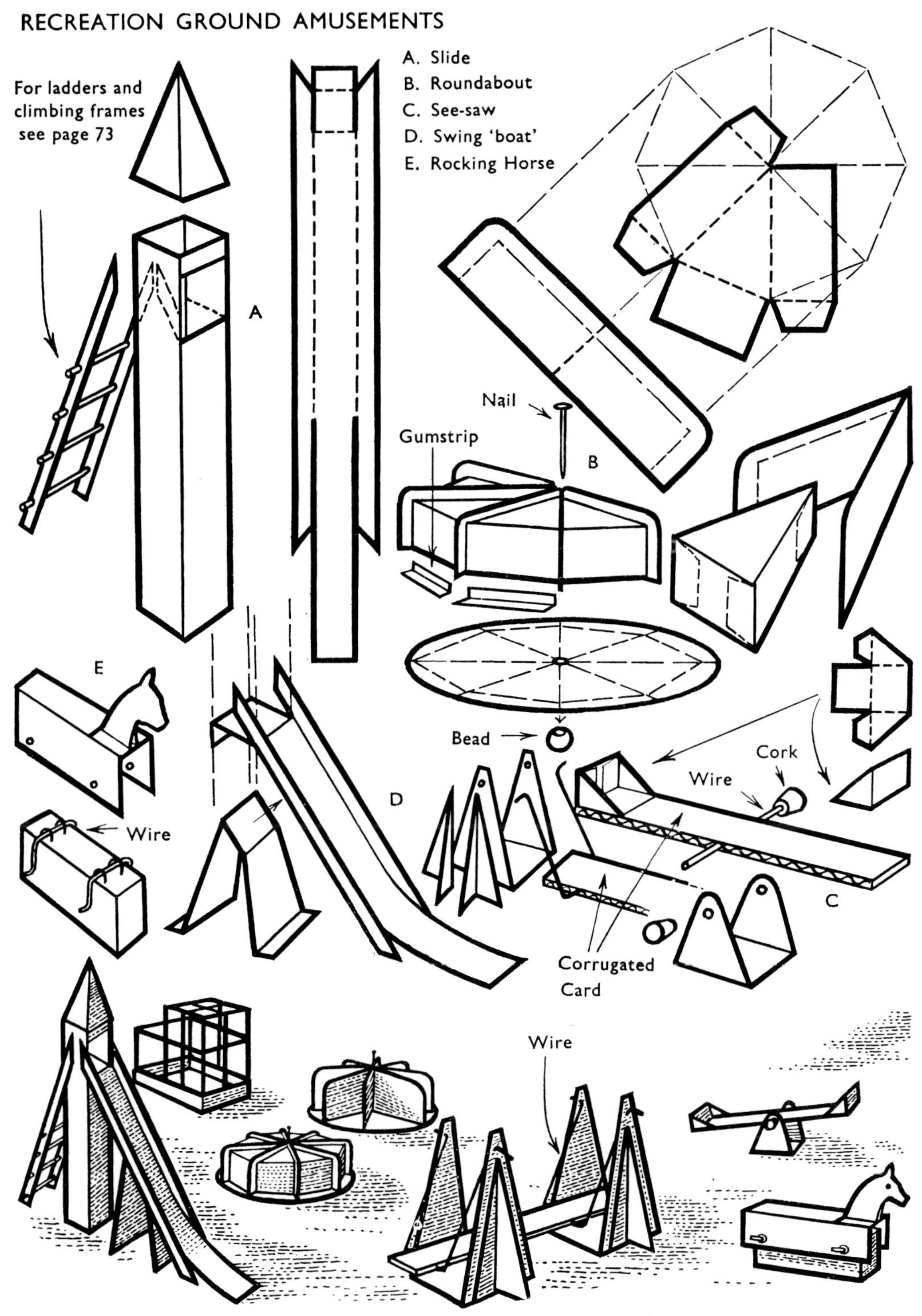

See also pages 77 and 84

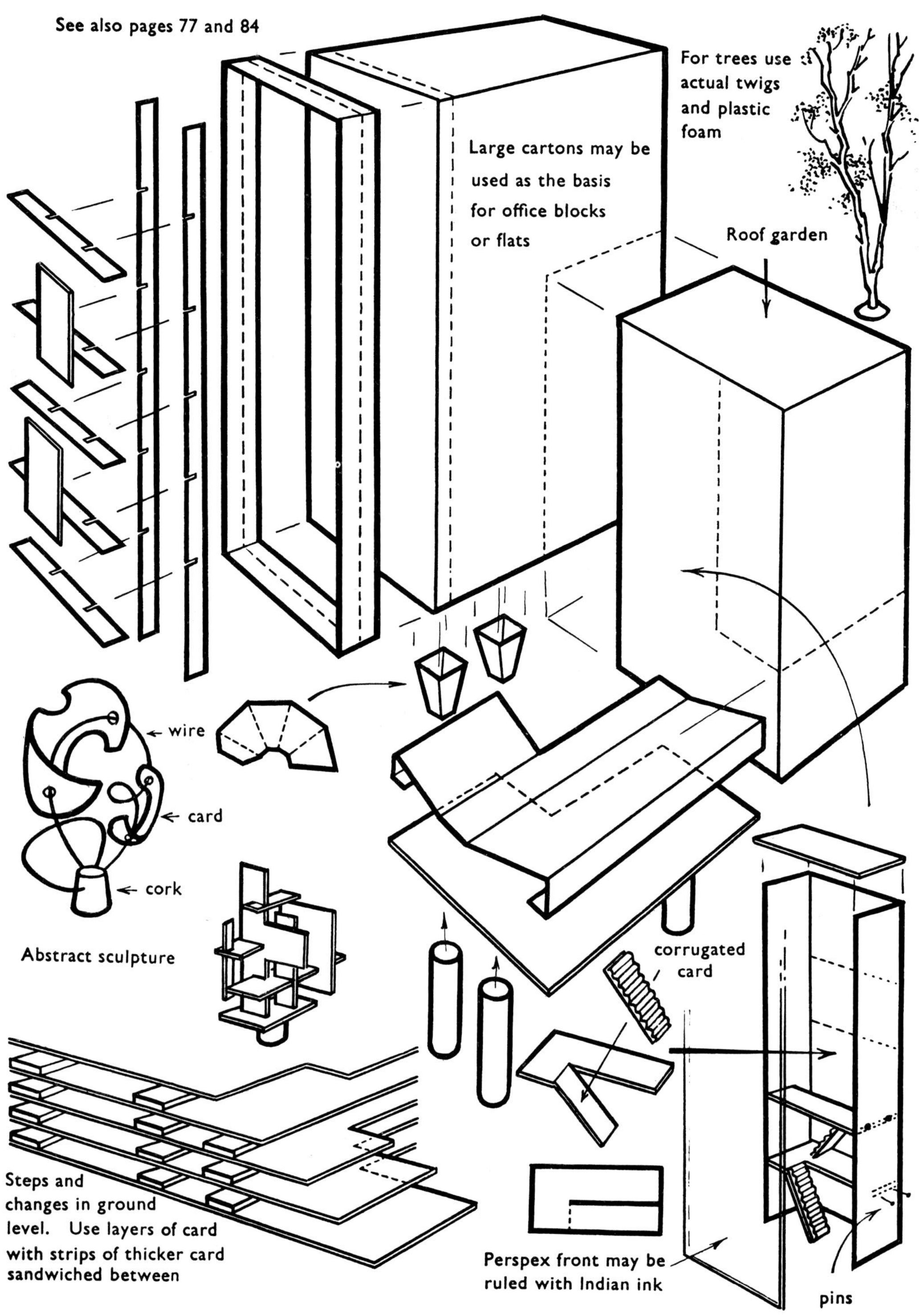

Appendix

These brief sketches are included solely by way of suggestion. While they do not provide any specific instruction, it is hoped that they might evoke some original ideas.

The possibilities are limitless, and as an educational device there are few crafts which may be so readily adapted to the interests of the children, and to the needs of the curriculum.

Index